Cistercian Studies Series: Number Sixty-four

CISTERCIANS IN THE LATE MIDDLE AGES

CISTERCIAN STUDIES SERIES: NUMBER SIXTY-FOUR

CISTERCIANS IN THE LATE MIDDLE AGES

Studies in Medieval Cistercian History VI

Edited by E. Rozanne Elder

Cistercian Publications
Kalamazoo, Michigan
1981

Available in Britain and Europe through

A. R. Mowbray & Co Ltd
St Thomas House   Becket Street
Oxford   OX 1 1SJ

Library of Congress Cataloging in Publication Data
Main entry under title:

Cistercians in the late Middle Ages.

   (Cistercian studies series ; no. 64) (Studies in
medieval Cistercian history ; 6)
   1. Cistercians--History--Addresses, essays,
lectures. I. Elder, Ellen Rozanne. II. Series.
II. Series: Studies in medieval Cistercian
history ; 6.
BX3406.2.C58   271'.12   80-25601
ISBN 0-87907-865-0

TABLE OF CONTENTS

INTRODUCTION

Cistercians in the Late Middle Ages is something of an exception in the Studies in Medieval Cistercian History sub-series,
both in its chronology and in its content. Previous volumes have
been composed, with few exceptions, of papers presented at the
Cistercian Studies Conferences which are held each year at Western
Michigan University in conjunction with the International Medieval
Studies Congress. Previous volumes, too, have tended to concen-
trate, because of the interest of participating scholars, on
twelfth-century Cistercianism.

The present volume, by contrast, begins with the thirteenth
century and spans five hundred years of subsequent cistercian experience. It also draws not on one, but on five, Conferences.
While the first interval is intentional, the second was not. Circumstances delayed the publication of several years' Conference
papers until an embarassing accumulation allowed the editors to
create three specialized volumes. Studies on Bernard of Clairvaux were issued earlier this year as *The Chimaera of His Age*.
Articles on the first Cistercians and their environment will appear early in 1981, bringing the sub-series once more up to date.

To the authors, as well as the auditors, of the papers—the
earliest in this volume was read in 1975—the editors of Cistercian Publications offer their apology and express their gratitude
for the patience these scholars have shown in awaiting publication
and in updating their contributions.

This volume is also anomalous in including two papers which
were never read at Kalamazoo at all. Both of them, quite by chance,
come from Cistercians of the Abbey of Our Lady of Dallas. When the
decision to divide papers into periods had been made, the editors
appealed to Louis J. Lekai to round out late medieval studies by
sharing his current research on Nicholas Cotheret. With characteristic generosity and efficiency, he wrote this preview of his edition and study of Nicholas' *History*.

Several lucky members of the Association of Cistercian Scholars became acquainted with the work of Odo Egres when, during a
meeting in the autumn of 1972, he entertained and enlightened them
with a lively account of the works of the Sibyl of Magdeburg and
her 'editor'. Pressures of teaching and ill health conspired to
prevent Father Odo from completing the book-length study his en-
raptured listeners urged him to write, but discovered among his
papers, after his death in August 1979, was the draft of the paper
published here. His confrère, Bede K. Lackner has kindly taken
time from his own work to edit it for Cistercian Publications. It

communicates much of the flavor of the delightful informal presentation Father Odo made eight years ago, and we present it,
and the other studies in this volume, as a memorial to him.

                                        E. Rozanne Elder

THE RECEPTION OF WILLIAM OF SAINT-THIERRY'S
EPISTOLA AD FRATRES DE MONTE DEI DURING THE MIDDLE AGES

Volker Honemann

In about 1144, William, former abbot of the Benedictine abbey of Saint-Thierry near Reims and now a simple monk in the Cistercian monastery of Signy (east of Reims) visited his friends in the newly founded (1134) Charterhouse of Mont-Dieu, situated in a still very remote valley of the Ardennes, some fifteen miles south-east of Signy. William's visit, which probably lasted several months, had an important literary consequence: shortly afterwards, he wrote his *Epistola ad fratres de Monte Dei*, or *Letter to the Brethren of Mont-Dieu*, later called *De vita solitaria* (*On the Solitary Life*-- which indicates its contents) or *Epistola Aurea* (*The Golden Letter* --because of its renown).

The work consists of two parts: first, an introductory letter which explains the purpose of the work and gives a valuable catalogue of William's other writings; and secondly, the treatise itself. William's aim was, in his own words, to offer some support to the younger brethren and the novices 'ad solatium solitudinis... et sancti propositi incitamentum' ('to console them in their solitude and to provide some support to their holy endeavours').[1] The *Letter* could therefore be said to fall into the genre of treatises for novices.

But this *Letter* is a very specific one: it was addressed to Carthusians. The Carthusian order, founded about fifty years earlier, had tried to retain the merits of the eremitic life without exposing the hermit to complete material insecurity and--more important--to the dangers of scandal, hypocrisy, and religious disorder many of the hermits of the eleventh century had been unable to avoid.

The aim of the Carthusians--an organic union of anchoretic and cenobitic life--was to be achieved by constructing a new type of monastery, the Charterhouse, with a complete house for each monk. There he could pray, meditate, work, and sleep. He left it only to attend services in the church. Manual work was done mainly by lay brothers. This new type of monastic life, leaving far more time for solitary meditation and prayer than any other, was much admired by William when he visited Mont-Dieu. Nevertheless, he felt that some of the younger brothers--a *frater Stephanus* is mentioned--were not quite sure about the practical and spiritual demands and, above all, the spiritual aims of this new way of life. His *guide spirituel*, the *Letter*, gave advice about the right 'order' in eating, drinking, and sleeping and also on various types of prayer and meditation. Most importantly, it gave a detailed

description of the spiritual development of the novice: starting
as *animalis homo incipiens,* one progressed to the state of *ration-
alis* (that is, modest) *homo proficiens,* and ended up as a *spiritu-
alis homo perfectus* (Ep frat 24, p. 81, 11.14-17), who has attained
union with God.

Since the subject of this paper is the reception of William's
Letter during the Middle Ages, these few remarks about the origin
and the contents of the work must suffice.

The influence William's *Letter* exercised from the middle of
the twelfth to the end of the fifteenth century can be shown in
different ways. First, we shall determine the number of manuscripts
of the work, that is, its textual transmission. Secondly, one should
consider whether William's treatise was used by other medieval writers in their own works, whether his thoughts about the spiritual life
influenced other writings about the same or a similar subject. Since
the answer to the second question remains to some extent *terra incog-
nita,* I shall concern myself mainly with the first aspect, namely the
manuscript tradition of the work.

About 280 manuscripts of the *Letter* are known today. These include complete texts and fragments (214 manuscripts); abbreviations
and *florilegia* (twenty-two manuscripts), translations into Old French,
Middle High German, Middle Dutch and Tuscan (eleven manuscripts);
and thirty-four lost (but well attested) manuscripts--bringing the
total to 281 manuscripts. This very considerable number--to which
must be added a great number of manuscripts lost without trace--
shows that William's *Letter* was a very successful work. But why was
it so successful?

First of all, we could answer, it was a work of considerable
literary quality, couched in a very fluent and sometimes even impas-
sioned language. Secondly, we must state that, during the second
half of the twelfth century, something very curious happened to the
Letter which clearly made a very significant contribution to its success: William's name as author disappeared and was gradually replaced by that of his friend, Bernard of Clairvaux. Even today there is
no satisfactory theory to explain this change: all we can say is
that--with a few exceptions--the false attribution prevailed throughout the Middle Ages and was not finally demolished until 1923, when
it was contested by André Adam and Dom Wilmart.[2]

On the whole, these two explanations are inadequate. To explain
the enormous success of the *Letter* satisfactorily, we must go into detail, that is, we must ask: who were the people who wrote the manuscripts, ordered new copies, and transferred them to new places,
where they could be used as models for future copies; and, above all,
who were the people who read the *Letter,* studied it thoroughly (many
manuscripts show marginal notes), or quoted it in their own works?
To produce a literary history of the *Letter* from the readers' point
of view (which is the meaning of the term 'reception' used in the

title of this paper), we must try to find out as much as we can about every single one of the manuscripts if we are to be able to answer the question: why was it written? As it is quite impossible to answer this question 281 times within the confines of this paper, I shall try to give a summary of the historical geography of the text in question, and provide some examples.

One of the manuscripts containing the *Letter* is the Codex AE XIII 17, f. 106ra-118vb, of the National Library in Milan. On the last page, folio 144rb, there is an entry which reads: 'Istud opus est magistri Johannis Matthei ex ferrarijs de gradi mediolanensis quem scribi fecit in papia tempore sui senii ad consolationem spiritus et animae.' Besides the *Letter*, the book contains various mystical tracts. Johannes de Gradi, who died in 1472, had been personal physician of the Visconti dukes and lecturer in medicine at the University of Pavia for a long time. Now, in his old age, he felt the need to concern himself with his soul and did so by reading the collection of spiritual writings he had ordered. It is possible that Johannes de Gradi had already known William's *Letter* from a fourteenth-century manuscript of the work preserved in the library of the Visconti in Pavia (Paris, Bibliothèque Nationale MS. lat. 1727, f. 72ra-82vb). Two other copies (Milan, Biblioteca Nazionale Braidense MS. AD. X. 4, written in 1409, ff. 1r-39r and AD. XII. 11, fifteenth century, ff. 130r-149r) formed part of the library of the Certosa near Pavia, the Certosa whose primary duty was to care for the graves of the Visconti family. In his last will and testament Johannes ordered this and some other books to be sold for the benefit of the poor.[3]

Another manuscript containing the *Letter* is the Codex Kopenhagen Ny Kgl. 119. At the end of the text (f. 229r) we read:

> Anno dominice incarnacionis 1482 in die divisionis apostolorum per me Johannem Nesen de Plone, presbiterum professum in Bordesholm ordinis canonicorum regularium, finitus in monasterio Montis Sancte Marie eiusdem ordinis Carthusiensium prope Stettin tunc temporis ibidem stans in eadem domo cum duobus fratribus pro reformacione.

Bordesholm had become a member of the Windesheim reform movement some years before and had been ordered to send monks to reform the run-down monastery of Marienberg. Apparently Johann Nesen, who was one of these monks, spent his spare time searching out interesting texts in the libraries of the Stettin area. The manuscript of the *Letter* he used as a model is today the Cod. theol. quart 53 of Berlin, Staatsbibliothek Preussischer Kulturbesitz.

But why did Nesen copy this particular text? He does not say. Nevertheless, I think we can suggest a reason: apart from the

Kopenhagen text, there are several fifteenth-century manuscripts
from monasteries of the Augustinian Canons, such as Windesheim
(Deventer, Stads- of Athenaeumbibliotheek MS. 78 ff. 18r-46r), St.
Martin/Louvain (Brussels, Bibliotheque Royale MS. 1373-1381, ff.
109vb-138va), Rookloster (Brussels, Bibliothèque Royale MS. 2037-
2048, ff. 47v-72r and MS. 480-485, ff. 115vb-117va, shortened version), Marienhage (Utrecht, University Library MS. 184, ff. 201r-
215v), Eberhardsklausen near Trier (Trier, Stadtbibliothek MS. 201,
ff. 1r-170rb, shortened version), Cologne (Abbey of Gethsemani MS.
7, ff. 1r-32v), Leipzig (Leipzig Universitätsbibliothek MS. F. p.
139 nr. 15, ff. 33v-46r), Wittenborg/Schöningen (Wolfenbüttel, Herzog-August-Bibliothek MS. 20.14 Aug. 4°, ff. 1r-43v).

Nearly all of these monasteries were members of the Windesheim
reform group which had been very successful in re-establishing spiritual life, that is, contemplation and meditation, in the houses of
canons regular. One of their spiritual guidebooks was William's
Letter.[4]

A few examples may serve to prove this statement. 'Bernard's'
Letter was quoted several times by Florent Radevijns.[5] Jan van
Schoonhoven mentioned it in a letter to his nephew Simon of the
monastery of Emstein.[6] Several reading lists of spiritual writings
included the *Letter*. John Gerson recommended the work in his *Apolo-
getica sive Responsiva...qui Libri essent fructuosius frequentandi:*

> Sunt Libri plures beati Bernardi viri devotissimi,
> et praesertim Epistola ejus ad Fratres Carthusienses
> de Monte Dei.[7]

A reading list produced by one of Gert Groote's disciples, perhaps
Radevijns himself, recommended the *Letter*.[8] At the end of the Middle Ages, Johannes Mauburnus (Jean Mombaer) of Brussels listed the
work in the *Tabula librorum praecipue legendorum* of his *Rosetum*
(Paris, 1510).[9]

Without daring, we can therefore conclude that a whole spiritual movement, the whole 'milieu' of the Windesheim Canons, were
very interested in William's *Letter*. Johann Nesen was only a member
of this 'milieu.'

By my first example I have tried to demonstrate why an individual, as Johannes de Gradi, became interested in William's *Letter*.
The second was aimed at explaining why the *Letter* became one of the
favourite books of a whole 'milieu,' as the fifteenth-century Windesheim Canons. In a third and final step I shall try to give an
idea why, on the whole, the *Letter* became such a successful work
in the course of the Later Middle Ages. As guidelines, I shall use
three different coordinates: first, time; secondly, space; and
thirdly, the 'milieux,' representing different groups of readers/
manuscript owners.

During the twelfth century, William's *Letter* was copied only a few times: only 4.5 percent of all manuscripts came into being before the year 1200. This may be explained partly by the fact that the attribution to Saint Bernard took place rather late. Nevertheless, the number is a very small one; by way of contrast, of all the existing manuscripts of the writings of Aelred of Rievaulx, who died in 1167, not less than 22 percent were written before 1200.[10] Another noteworthy point is that only one of the twelfth-century *Letter* manuscripts can be traced to a Charterhouse, and that is a manuscript of Mont-Dieu, a copy of the original (Charleville, Bibliotèque Muncipale MS. 114, ff. 1v-37r), written in Signy and sent to Mont-Dieu by William himself. Furthermore, for the thirteenth century, there is also only one Carthusian MS. (Paris, Bibliotèque Nationale MS. lat. 2883, ff. 50ra-82vb), written in Mont-Dieu itself. This is **very** surprising since the *Letter* was directed to the Carthusians--even if we remember that the order was a tiny one compared with the Benedictines or the Cistercians, and that--as a result of later historical events such as the French Revolution or the dissolution of the houses of contemplative religious orders in Josephite Austria--many more Carthusian libraries were destroyed than libraries of any other order.

Almost all the twelfth-century manuscripts were written in Cistercian monasteries such as Clairvaux (Bruges, Bibliothèque de la Ville MS. 131, ff. 55v-83v--this MS. was soon transferred to Ter Duinen), Pontigny (Brussels, Bibliothèque royale MS. IV 187, ff. 43va-80vb), Longpont (Paris, B. N. MS. lat. 9574, pp. 250-324), or Himmerod (Berlin, Staatsbibliothek MS. lat. fol. 752, ff. 62r-82v). The existence of twelfth-century Cistercian manuscripts in Austrian houses such as Reun (Reun, Stiftsbibliothek MS. 21, ff. 61r-116r), and Heiligenkreuz (Heiligenkreuz, Stiftsbibliothek MS. 222, ff. 1r-31r) can be explained by the system of filiations (branches) to which each Cistercian monastery belonged, which meant close contacts (including literary ones) between the houses of each filiation.

Apart from that, the Cistercians produced the first abridged form of the *Letter* (London, British Museum MS. Add. 15218, ff. 103r-104v, from Cambron) which adapted the text to cenobitic life by leaving out all the anchoritic parts. During the thirteenth century, this abridged version was copied in other Cistercian monasteries such as Aulne(Brussels, B. R. MS. II 1064, ff. 141rb-143va) and Villers (Brussels, B. R. MS. II 2556, ff. 178rb-181ra).

All the other milieux produced only one manuscript, which came into being in a benedictine monastery (St Germer de Flay; Paris, B. N. MS. lat. 2944, ff. 1r-31r). The final twelfth-century manuscript to which I shall refer is remarkable in that it is the first translation of the text. It was probably made for the lay-brothers of the Premontratensian **monastery** of Saint Paul in Verdun (Verdun, Bibliothèque municipale MS. 72, ff. 1r-140r). Although we know of a

few copies of this translation--all of which are lost today--it
was, on the whole, an unsuccessful one.

At the end of the twelfth century, the fate of the *Letter*
clearly depended on the Cistercians. They apparently regarded
William's--or, later on, 'Bernard's' *Letter*--as an important work
written by a famous member of their Order. Although this was already valid for William, the *Letter* gained momentum once the work
had been attributed to Bernard. On the other hand, the Cistercians
seem to have been the only Order of the time who really cared for
the propagation of literary works. Already during the first half
of the twelfth-century (perhaps in 1134) their Chapter General had
stated that all new books written by members of the Order had to be
presented to the Chapter, which would decide whether they should be
propagated or not.[11] In 1200, for example, the abbots of Ourscamp
and Cercamp in northern France were ordered by the Chapter General
to check an Old French translation of the Song of Songs in the library of Chaalis, north of Paris, which some had claimed to be obscene
and demanded be burned if it came to light.[12]

The Carthusians, during the twelfth and thirteenth centuries,
on the other hand, were too weak in numbers and too isolated from
one another to propagate the *Letter* and, as far as I can see, even
the Charterhouse of Mont-Dieu failed to circulate it in its own
area: The Old French translation produced in Verdun--which is only
some twenty miles from Mont-Dieu--used as its model a Cistercian
manuscript and not the manuscripts preserved in Mont-Dieu.

The thirteenth century saw a considerable increase in the number of manuscripts: 17.4 percent of them were written between 1200
and 1200; a noticeable percentage but not very great compared with
the 39.4 percent of the thirteenth-century Aelred manuscripts. Most
manuscripts still come from the Burgundian--Northern French--Belgian
region and from such Cistercian monasteries as Cîteaux (Berlin [East],
Deutsche Staatsbibliothek MS Phillipps 1772, ff. 40r-55v; Dijon, Bibliothèque municipale MS 183, ff. 122r-162v), Clairvaux (Troyes, Bibliothèque municipale MS 433, ff. 107r-118v, fragment), Saint Urban
(Lucern, Zentralbibliothek P. MS 31/4, first item), Foucarmont (Paris,
B. N. MS lat. 2945, ff. 1r-46v), Clairmarais (St Omer, Bibliothèque
municipale MS 261, ff. 112r-144v), Ter Duinen (Bruges, Bibliothèque
de la Ville MS 126, ff. 43r-63r). The twelfth-century Austrian manuscripts now became models for a number of thirteenth-century Cistercian
manuscripts in Austria, Bohemia, and Bavaria: Lilienfeld (Lilienfeld,
Stiftsbibliothek MS 96, ff. 98r-126r), Zwettl (Zwettl, Stiftsbiblio-
thek MS 144, ff. 108rb-125va and 132ra-132rb), Königssaal (Leipzig,
Universitätsbibliothek MS F. p. 94 nr. 15, f. 1r-49v), Aldersbach
(Munich, Bayerische Staatsbibliothek Clm 2610, f. 74v-89v). The important Cistercian monasteries of Heilsbronn near Nuremberg (Erlangen,
Universitätsbibliothek MS 284, ff. 176r-194v) and Buch near Leipzig
(Leipzig, Universitätsbibliothek MS F. P. 144 nr. 10, f. 21v-46r)

probably copied French or West German texts.

Apart from the Cistercians, a certain number of Benedictine monasteries produced copies of the work: Metz (Metz, Bibliothèque de la Ville MS 305, 5th item, a manuscript destroyed in 1944), Liège (Darmstadt, Hessische Landesbibliothek MS 815, ff. 2v-23v), Marchiennes (Douai, Bibliothèque municipale MS 374, ff. 31r-54v), St Amand-les-Eaux (Valenciennes, Bibliothèque municipale MS 183, ff. A-B, fragment) and Lyre (Evreux, Bibliothèque municipale MS 14, ff. 70r-71v, florilegium)--all of them situated in or near the region where the *Letter* originated. Outside this area, only important Benedictine centers with lively literary traditions and activities such as Ripoll in Catalonia (Barcelona, Archivo de la Corona de Aragon MS Ripoll 56, ff. 120rb-133ra) or Oberaltaich in Bavaria (Munich, Bayerische Staatsbibliothek Clm 9517, ff. 81r-107r) provided themselves with copies of the text. Most of these Benedictine manuscripts probably came into being in the course of the Order's normal literary activities. Moreover, the Benedictines did not regard the Cistercians as a completely different order but rather as a species of their own order which distinguished itself by being 'reformed.'

A few thirteenth-century manuscripts were written in houses of Dominicans (Gent: Stuttgart, Württembergische Landesbibliothek MS theol. et phil. qu. 159, ff. 23r-29v), Leipzig: Leipzig, Universitätsbibliothek MS F. p. 139 nr. 15, ff. 33v-46r) and Franciscans (Cortona: Cortona, Biblioteca Comunale MS 30, ff. 119r-141r; Hereford: Cathedral Library MS o. l. IV., ff. 115r-123r and Oxford, Bodleian Library MS Hatton 102, ff. 69r-85v), but by and large, the number of mendicant manuscripts remained very small. From the beginning, they produced their own spiritual writings, and in particular, their own mystical guidebooks: one need only mention the writings of Saint Bonaventure which had a tremendous success throughout the Middle Ages.

The proliferation of manuscripts during the thirteenth-century did not continue at the same rate in the fourteenth century: The Black Death (1348/49), famine, and wars (the Hundred Years War between England and France) were detrimental to book production in general. Nevertheless, 26.3 percent of all manuscripts of the *Letter* were written between 1300 and 1400; the figure for the Aelred manuscripts declined to a mere 10.4 percent.

The real developments in the reception of the *Letter* lie now not so much in numbers as in the variety of milieux and in geographical expansion. Manuscripts of the *Letter* came into being in the whole of central Europe and among all the milieux, with the exception of parish churches/cathedrals and--perhaps--libraries of the aristocracy. Copies were produced in the Stettin charterhouse (Berlin, Staatsbibliothek MS theol. qu. 53, ff. 94r-113v) as well as in the Benedictine monasteries of St Martial, Limoges (Paris, B. N. MS lat. 3640, ff. 60ra-71rb, book I only) or San Severino, Naples

(Naples, Biblioteca Nazionale MS Vind. lat. 35, ff. 1r-21v); the
Augustinian Canons of Klosterneuburg near Vienna got their copy
of the *Letter* (Klosterneuburg, Stiftsbibliothek MS 251, ff. 131r-
166v) as did the library of the Sorbonne in Paris.[13] The Canons
of the Twelve Apostles Monastery in Utrecht had the *Letter* in their
possession (Utrecht, University Library MS 375, ff. 95r-125r), as
did the Franciscans in the remote monastery of Sarnano, Marche (Sarnano, Biblioteca Comunale MS 61, ff. 1ra-28v). For possibly the
first time a manuscript entered a private library: the Dukes of
Savoy now or at the beginning of the fifteenth century bought a
copy of the *Letter* (Torino, Biblioteca Nazionale MS D. V. 27, ff.
84r-90v).

     Among the 'new' milieux (i.e. milieux now gaining a certain
importance for the distribution of the *Letter*) the most prominent
is that of the Carthusians. The considerable number of fourteenth-
century Carthusian manuscripts can be explained easily by the fact
that most Charterhouses then producing copies had only recently been
founded. Among these were Bourg-Fontaine (founded in 1325; Paris,
B. N. MS lat. 2042, ff. 153ra-159rb), Stettin (fd. 1360; Berlin,
Staatsbibliothek MS theol. qu. 53, ff. 94r-113v), Maggiano near Si-
ena (fd. 1314; Toledo, Biblioteca Catecral MS 9-28, ff. 1r-30v) or
Pavia (fd. 1396; Paris, B. N. MS lat. 1727, ff. 72ra-82vb). Thus
the great number of Carthusian manuscripts represents the expansion
of the Order on a larger scale during the fifteenth-century (manuscripts of Basel, Schnals etc.; see below).

     The second 'new' milieu, the Augustinian Canons, do not contri-
bute much to the distribution of the *Letter* in terms of numbers:
only seven of thirty-five Augustinian manuscripts were written before 1400, and most of them must be regarded as 'special cases':
Three of them, for instance, come from the Slovak monastery of Tre-
bon, founded in 1367 by the Rosenberg dukes as a reformed monastery;
it soon developed a lively intellectual atmosphere which resulted in
the production of a great number of books and especially spiritual
handbooks (Prague, University Library MS 201, ff. 60r-72v; ms. 2374,
f. 92v-123v; Rome, Vatican Library MS Reg. Lat. 66, ff. 116r-142r).[14]

     The beginning of the fourteenth century saw the production of
another translation. In or near Augsburg, a relatively free Middle
High German translation was made which remained as unsuccessful as
the earlier French version. Only one manuscript, most probably a
direct copy of the original, is known today: Donaueschingen, Fürstlich Fürstenbergische Bibliothek MS 421, ff. 1r-155r, which during
the fifteenth century became part of the enormous library of the
Dominican convent of St Catherine in Nuremberg.

     The fifteenth century was to become the most important period
for the reception of William's *Letter*: 48.6 percent, nearly half
the manuscripts, were written during this century (by comparison
with Aelred's 18.8 percent). Even if we have to admit that the

fifteenth century experienced a strong increase in literary activities in general, the figure at first glance (especially when compared with the percentage of the Aelred manuscripts) remains surprising-
ly high. Could we explain it by new milieux becoming interested in
the *Letter*? Perhaps manuscripts were being ordered by the nobility,
like the Medici in Florence (Florence, Biblioteca Laurenziana MS
Plut. XVI, cod. I, ff. 302v-333r; Plut. XVI, cod. II, ff. 7r-28v),
the Duke of Urbino, Federigo da Montefeltro (Rome, Vatican Library
MS Urbin. lat. 90, ff. 161r-177r, book I only), the Dukes of Nassau-
Dillenburg north of Frankfurt (The Hague, Koninklijke Bibliotheek
MS 73 E 24, f. 75vb, dutch translation of a part of D 7 - 8), or
came into the possession of parish church or cathedral libraries
such as Danzig (Gdańsk, Biblioteka PAN MS Marienbibliothek F 285,
ff. 167r-190v), Prague (Metropolitní kapitula u sv. víta MS 1564,
ff. 34v-48v) or Schlettstadt in Alsace (Sélestat, Bibliothèque
municipale MS 12, ff. 192ra-200ra). On the other hand, the interest of 'old' milieux continued: fifteenth-century **Cistercian** manuscripts can be found in the libraries of Paradies (Poznan, Miejska
Biblioteka Publiczna im. Edwarda Raczynskiego MS 165, ff. 130r-
152r), Rauden (Wrocław, Biblioteka Uniwersytecka MS I F 297, ff.
27r-55v), or Maulbronn (Solothurn, Zentralbibliothek MS S 231, ff.
236v-266r).

Yet, this explanation still falls short of a satisfactory answer: all the aforementioned copies only account for about one
sixth of all fifteenth-century manuscripts. The rest, more than eighty
percent, came from the Benedictine, Augustinian Canon, and Carthusian
milieux. Why did those orders produce such a wealth of copies at this
time? To start with the Augustinians: The example of Johann Nesen
(Bordesholm-Stettin) I mentioned earlier already demonstrates that the
canons of the Windesheim reform were very interested in the *Letter* and
produced a considerable number of copies. This result can be extended
to the other reform movement of the canons, namely, the Raudnitz-Ind-
ersdorf reform which started in Bohemia (remember the three Třebon manuscripts mentioned above) and soon spread to Austria (manuscripts of
St Florian: St Florian, Stiftsbibliothek MS XI/36, ff. 126vb-144ra,
XI/126, ff. 77ra-92vb) and Bavaria: manuscripts at Indersdorf (Munich,
Bayerische Staatsbibliothek Clm 7745, ff. 108ra-140ra), Polling (same
library, Clm 11924, ff. 46v-92v) and Diessen (same library, Clm 5606,
ff. 139ra-153rb). It also applies to the northwest German-Dutch Brethren of the Common Life: manuscripts at Herford (which was soon transferred to Lübeck: Lübeck, Stadtbibliothek MS theol. lat. 188/65, ff.
201ff., lost during World War II), Butzbach (Giessen, Universitätsbibliothek manuscript Acad. DCLXXXIII, ff. 331r-350r) and Königstein
near Frankfurt (Aschaffenburg, Hof- und Stiftsbibliothek MS Pap. 34 4°,
6th item). The importance of the *Letter* in this milieu has already
been demonstrated; most probably the fifteenth-century Dutch translation[15] also originated here.

Among the Benedictines, the reason for the great number of manuscripts is almost the same: All the Benedictine reform movements of the late fourteenth and fifteenth centuries frequently used and busily copied the *Letter*: The Kastl (east of Nuremberg in the Upper Palatinate) reform is represented by manuscripts from Reichenbach (Munich, Bayerische Staatsbibliothek Clm 2991, ff. 13r-99r), St Emmeram in Regensburg (same library, Clm 14161, ff. 100va-126ra), St Aegidien (Giles)/Nuremberg[16] and St Mang/Füssen (Harburg, Fürstlich Oettingen-Wallersteinsche Bibliothek cod. II, 1 2° 171, ff. 276vb-268rb--an abridged version), whereas the interest of the Melk-Tegernsee reform resulted in at least fourteen Bavarian and Austrian manuscripts and the production of a 'Benedictine' abridgement (from St Mang: Lambach, Stiftsbibliothek MS Ccl 452, ff. 190v-192r; Melk, Stiftsbibliothek MS 1101, ff. 29v-30r; MS 1562, ff. 105r-106v; Salzburg, St Peter MS B X 22, ff. 163v-166r) which stressed the points of *stabilitas loci* and 'solitary life in the cell,' both dealt with by William. No wonder, therefore, that Johannes of Kastl quoted the *Letter* several times in his writings,[17] and that Ulrich von Landau, *magister* of Vienna University and from 1465 onwards prior of Tegernsee, mentioned the *Letter* as one of the few books which should be given to the monks during Lent.[18]

Finally, lesser contributions to the number of fifteenth-century Benedictine manuscripts were made by the reforms of Bursfelde in Northern Germany and S. Giustinal, Padua.[19] Manuscripts were written in Paderborn (Paderborn, Erzbischöfliche Bibliothek MS Ba 35, contains only the *Letter*), Bosau (Zeitz, Domherrenbibliothek and Stiftsbibliothek MS LXXII, ff. 73r-91r) and Brunswick (Wolfenbüttel, Herzog-August-Bibliothek MS 17.20. Aug. 4°, ff. 144v-146r, fragment) and from the reform of S. Giustina/Padua came manuscripts from Padua itself (Naples, Biblioteca Nazionale MS Vind. Lat. 35, ff. 1r-21v), Polirone (Mantua, Biblioteca Comunale MS 380, ff. 1r-56v) and Bobbio (Torino, Biblioteca Nazionale MS D. V. 27, ff. 84r-90v).

The many fifteenth-century Carthusian manuscripts can be explained by the significant number of newly founded Charterhouses (during what was for them *saeculum aureum*), and by the special circumstance that in many Charterhouses, apart from the 'central' library of the monastery, the monks had private libraries in their cells. This is the reason for the seven and five copies of the *Letter* from the Charterhouses of Basel (Basel, Offentliche Bibliothek der Universität MS A VIII 35, ff. 82v-102v; B X 26, ff. 17ra-37ra; B XI 12, ff. 72bis r, fragment; A VI 14, ff. 100r-103r; A VII 20, ff. 176v-182v; A IX 14, ff. 216r-219v [three copies of an abridgement]; A XI 74, ff. 199v-200r, a paraphrase) and Schnals (Innsbruck, Universitätsbibliothek MS 98, ff. 152r-173r; 373, ff. 1r-50r; 523, ff. 192r-267v; Padua, Biblioteca Universitaria MS 1517, ff. 166v-174v; 2028, ff. 14r-48v). How important the *Letter* was to the Carthusians can be shown by the existence of a special shortened version produced in Basel.

This abridgement (mss. A VI 14, A VII 20, A IX 14) forms part of a
volume (which has been copied out twice) given to people outside
the Charterhouse who were interested in the Carthusian way of life.
    The fifteenth-century also saw the only relatively successful
translation of the *Letter*. Of the Tuscan 'Pistola di S. Bernardo
a' frati del Monte di Dio,'[20] at least five manuscripts are known
today: Fanfani's manuscript, now lost; Florence, Biblioteca Laurenziana ms. Acq. e doni 54, ff. 199ra-219vb; Biblioteca Nazionale Cen-
trale ms. Magl. Cl. XXXIX Cod. 4, ff. 1r-8v, incomplete; Biblioteca
Riccardiana ms. 1413, f. 1r-78v; Padua, Biblioteca Universitaria ms.
1381, ff. 100v-161r).[21]
    In concluding this survey,[22] I must admit that the method appli-
ed here is not able to answer all the questions concerning the reception of the *Letter* during the Middle Ages. Let me ask two of the
questions myself.
    First: Why do we have almost no manuscripts from central and
southern France, Spain, or southern Italy? Why no manuscripts in
Scandinavia, why relatively so few in Great Britain?
    Second: Why were the medieval translations of the *Letter*--
apart from the Tuscan one--unsuccessful?
    Tentative answers could be given. (1) The countries mentioned
did not experience the monastic reforms which proved so important
for the propagation of the *Letter*. (2) Could it be that in general
the *Letter* was judged to be too difficult for the simple lay brethren who knew not Latin?
    These are suppositions. There is only one way in which the
thesis may be proven: more studies of the reception of widely
spread medieval writings, which would make further comparisons
possible. Fortunately, there are more reception-studies in progress: but these could provide subjects for future lectures.

Freie Universität, Berlin

NOTES

1. M.-M. Davy (ed.), *Un traité de la vie solitaire. Epistola ad fratres de Monte Dei par Guillaume de Saint-Thierry*, Etudes de Philosophie Médiévale, (Paris, 1940) § 1, p. 66 (hereafter cited as D + §, page, and, if necessary, line).

2. A. Adam, *Guillaume de Saint-Thierry. Sa vie et ses oeuvres* (Bourg, 1923); A. Wilmart, *'La préface de la Lettre* aux frères du Mont-Dieu,' *Revue Bénédictine* 36 (1924) 229-247; Idem, 'Les écrits spirituels des deux Guigues,' *Revue d'Ascétique et de Mystique* 5 (1924) 127-158.

3. H.-M. Ferrari, *Une chaire de médecine au XVe siècle* (Paris, 1889) 91.

4. J. van Mierlo, 'Hadewijch en Wilhelm van St. Thierry,' *Ons Geestelijk Erf* 3 (1929) 45-59; Paul Verdeyen, 'La théologie mystique de Guillaume de Saint-Thierry' *Ons Geestelijk Erf* 51-53 (1977-79).

5. M. Viller, 'Le *speculum monachorum* et la dévotion moderne,' *Revue d'Ascetique et de Mystique* 3 (1922) 46.

6. H. Gleumes,'Gerhard Groot und die Windesheimer als Verehrer des hl. Bernhard von Clairvaux,' *Zeitschrift für Askese und Mystik* 10 (1935) 108.

7. Johannes Gerson, *OEuvres*, ed. E. du Pin, vol. II, (Antwerp, 1706) c. 709; the *Letter* is also quoted in other writings of Gerson, who was on very good terms with the Carthusians. See P. Glorieux, 'Gerson et les chartreux,' *Recherches de théologie ancienne et médiévale* 28 (1961) 115-153.

8. P. Debongnie, article 'Dévotion moderne,' *Dictionnaire de Spiritualite*, vol. III (Paris, 1957) 741f.; see also E. Mikkers, 'Sint Bernardus en de Moderne Devotie,' *Citeaux in de Nederlanden* 10 (1953) 149-183, in particular pp. 155, 157, 159, 161f., 167-169.

9. P. Debongnie, *Jean Mombaer de Bruxelles* (Louvain, 1927) 322.

10. A. Hoste, *Bibliotheca Aelrediana...*, Instrumenta Patristica II, (Steenbrugge, 1962) 19.

11. J.-M. Canivez, *Statuta Capitulorum Generalium ordinis Cisterciensis* vol. I (Louvain, 1933) p. 26; see also *Analecta S. O. Cist.* 6 (1950) 34.

12. Canivez, Statuta I: 255; see also H. Suchier, *Zeitschrift fur romanische Philologie* 8 (1884) 415.

13. L. Delisle, *Le cabinet des manuscrits*....vol. III (Répertoire méthodique des ouvrages contenus dans les volumes de la grande librairie) (Paris, 1881); the 'Répertoire' dates from 1338.

14. I. Hlaváček, *Studie k dějinám knihoven v Českém státe v době Před-husitské*, I: *Knihovna kláštera Třebonského, Sbornik historicky* 12 (1964) 5-52.

15. Ms. Leiden, University Library 2423, edited by J. M. Willeumier-Schalij, *Willem van St.'Thierry's Epistel totten Brueren vanden Berghe Godes, ingeleid en van een modern nederlandse vertaling voorzien...*, (Leiden, 1950).

16. Library Catalogue from the end of the fifteenth century, mss. A 40, 0 45, F 46, now lost, see P. Ruf (ed.), *Mittelalterliche Bibliothekskataloge Deutschlands und der Schweiz*, vol. III, 3 (Munich, 1939) pp. 438, 471, 479, 508.

17. J. Sudbrack, *Die geistliche Theologie des Johannes von Kastl*, Beiträge zur Geschichte des alten Mönchtums und des Benediktinerordens, Heft 27, 1-2 (Münster, 1966) vol. 1: pp. 144, 149, 327 n. 348, 334, 335, 378; vol. 2: pp. 70, 72-74, 108; Cl. Stroick, *Unpublished theological writings of Johannes Castellensis* (Ottawa, 1964) p. 26 n. 4, and 160 n. 49.

18. V. Redlich, *Tegernsee und die deutsche Geistesgeschichte im 15. Jahrhundert* (Munich, 1931) 54.

19. The famous *Liber ordinarius* of the monastery of St Jacob/Liège at the end of thirteenth century (ed. by P. Volk, *Der Liber ordinarius des Luetticher Jakobsklosters*, Beiträge zur Geschichte des alten Mönchtums und des Benediktinerordens, 10 [Münster, 1923]) mentions the *Letter* among the books 'qui utiliores sunt ad informationem ipsorum' (i.e. noviciorum), see Volk p. 35. The *Liber ordinarius* was used by Abbot Johannes Rode of St Mathias/Trier (died 1439) for the compilation of the statutes of the Bursfelde congregation (ed. P. Becker, *Consuetudines et observantiae monasteriorum sancti Mathiae et Sancti Maximini Treverensium ab Johanne Rode abbate Conscriptae*, Corpus consuetudinum monasticarum 5 [Siegburg, 1968]), where the *Letter* is recommended in the chapter 'Quid studere debeant Novitii' (p. 192, l. 1-7; see also p. 199, l. 7-9).

20. *Pistola di S. Bernardo a' frati del Monte di Dio. Volgarizzamento del secolo XIV, dato fuori pel la prima volta da P. Fanfani,*

Scelta di **Curiosità** letterarie inedite o rare...dispensa LXXXIV
(Bologna, 1867). It is doubtful whether the translation was
made during the later fourteenth (as Fanfani assumed in his preface) or the early fifteenth century; all manuscripts--Fanfani's
included--were written during the fifteenth or the early sixteenth century.

21. Some of these manuscripts were discovered only last year, so I
    am unable to give **many** details about the milieu(x?) which brought
    them into being.

22. The history of the reception of the *Letter* was by no means fi-
    nished at the end of the fifteenth century. In about 1480, the
    work was printed for the first time (in Cologne); further early
    editions appeared at Modena, 1491; Brescia, 1495; Paris 1519, 1521:
    see Davy, (*Un traité...*) p. 29 and J.-M. Déchanet, *OEuvres chois-
    ies de Guillaume de Saint-Thierry* (Paris, 1944) 41-43. A full
    description of all the manuscripts mentioned above and a map may
    be found in my *Die* Epistola ad fratres de Monte Dei *des Wilhelm
    von Saint-Thierry*. Lateinische Ueberlieferung und mittelalter-
    liche Uebersetzungen, Münchner Texte und Untersuchungen zur deut-
    schen Literatur des Mittelalters, Bd. 61 (Zurich-Munich, 1978).

MECHTHILD VON MAGDEBURG
THE FLOWING LIGHT OF GOD

Odo Egres, O. Cist.

Books have a history of their own; if they are of medieval vin-
tage, quite frequently their historicity is better attested and they
claim a greater interest than the hunble anonymity of their authors.
Books of value are keys to man's rational and irrational aspirations.
They unlock thoughts and emotions in subsequent generations and de-
liver a time-enclosed cultural heritage which has a life of its own.
The author, left behind in time, loses control over the impact of
his work; it runs its own course and enjoys its own independence.

When Carl Greith, later Bishop of Sankt Gallen, in 1860, discovered a two-hundred twenty page leather-bound manuscript adorned with
gothis miniatures, Mechthild von Magdeburg was a forgotten name. The
benedictine library of Einsiedeln (Switzerland) rewarded the bishop's
fondness for poking in the cultural caves of the past by containing
the book whose interesting story began to unfold. Philologists set
out to reconstruct the circumstances of its origin, the place of its
birth, and to determine its literary importance in the stormy development of religious thought in Germany. As it turned out, the manu-
script--Cod. 277 in the library of Einsiedeln Abbey--was well-preserv-
ed, written in the gothic minuscule of the thirteenth century. Its
pages are 7 1/2 by 4 1/2 inches. Originally bound in white leather,
the manuscript has now, with the grace of the years upon it, a soft
golden tint. The body of the writing was done in black ink, and the
capital letters in red are as clear and vivid as when they were written. The first part of the manuscript, 166 pages, contains the only
complete German text of Mechthild's masterpiece, *The Flowing Light of
God*. The next few pages were written by a 'Friend of God' and the
rest contains several sermons by Meister Eckhart. Soon after his dis-
covery Bishop Greith published selections of Mechthild's poetry in an
anthology of medieval mystical writings[1] and commissioned the librarian of the Abbey, Father Gall Morel, to transcribe the manuscript for
publication, with a modern German rendering.[2]

Mechthild had no literary ambitions when she began to write down
her spiritual experiences. As she told her readers, 'God himself is
my witness that I never asked him knowingly to tell me the things
which I have written' (IV, 2). It was Henirich von Halle who collected the loose sheets of 'underground' poetry, written in Middle Low German, tainted by theological terms and poetic phrases in Middle High
German. The scholar from Halle arranged them into six books subdivid-
ed into chapters, according to his own judgments. He disregarded the
chronological sequence which would certainly have told us something
about the history of the Beguine movement. In his introduction to

Mechthild's writings, Heinrich wrote:

> In the year of Our Lord 1250, and for fifteen years there-
> after, this book was revealed by God in German to a sister
> who was holy both in body and soul. She served God de-
> voutly in humble simplicity, abject poverty, and heavenly
> contemplation, suffering maltreatment and scorn for more
> than forty years. She steadfastly followed the light and
> teaching of the Order of Preachers, advancing steadily
> and growing holier from day to day. This book was copied
> and put together by a brother of the same Order. There
> is much good in this book about many things, as can be
> seen from the table of its contents. Read it nine times,
> faithfully, humbly, and devoutly.

The First Book of the work begins with a dialogue between God
and the Soul. God announces that 'this Book I send forth as a mes-
senger to all the religious, the good as well as the bad.' To the
Soul's question, 'What shall this book of your glory be called?,'
he answers, 'it shall be called *das vliessende liht der gotheit*
[*The Flowing Light of God*], which enters all hearts that dwell in
it without falseness.' The following dialogue between *minne* and
sele, that is, Love and the Soul, intones the ever-recurring theme
and the poetic mood of all mechthildian writings. The atmosphere
is medieval; the language is that of the *minnesänger* and reflects
courtly life. Love is a lady of high rank in the Court of Heaven
who solicits the Soul's affections for her Lord:

Soul:	Lady, your name is known to me:
	it is Love!
Love:	God reward you, my Queen!
Soul:	Lady Love, I am happy to meet you!
Love:	And I am greatly honored by your greeting.
Soul:	Lady Love, you have wrestled long years
	with the Holy Trinity
	till the overflow fell once for all
	in Mary's humble lap!
Love:	But, my Queen, these things were done
	for your honor and delight.
Soul:	But Lady, you have taken from me
	all I had won on earth!
Love:	A blessed exchange, my Queen!
Soul:	To deprive me of my childhood?
Love:	In exchange for heavenly freedom.
Soul:	You have taken away my youth.
Love:	In exchange for many virtues.
Soul:	You have taken my friends and my family!

```
Love:    My Queen, that is a false charge!
Soul:    And you have taken from me
         the world, honor and all my possessions!
Love:    All these goods, my Queen, I shall restore
         in one hour, if you wish,
         by the power of the Holy Spirit.
Soul:    Lady Love, you have troubled me
         through suffering. Now my body
         can barely carry its weight.
Love:    In return, my Queen,
         you have gained great understanding.
Soul:    Dear Lady, you have consumed
         my very flesh and blood.
Love:    And you are enlightened
         and raised up to God.
Soul:    But, Love, you are a robber:
         return my goods to me!
Love:    That I will do, my Queen,
         I beg you--take myself!
```

The forty-six chapters of the First Book are variations or repetitions of the same theme. The Soul is reluctant to let Love 'steal her body.' In spite of the Heavenly Knight's endearing song, 'I come to my love as a dove descends on flowers,'

> Ich kum zuo miner lieben
> als ein touwe uf den bluomen (I, 13),

she refuses to dance with him, unless he seduces her: 'If you want me to leap with joy, You must first dance and sing; then I leap for love,'

> ich mag niht tanzen, herre,
> du enleitest mich,
> wilt du, das is sere springe,
> so muost du selber voran singen,
> so springe ich in die minne (I, 44).

Being asked to dance with the Lord of the Heavenly Palace puts the Soul in the state of grace which leads to a certain *ebrietas spirituale*. In the tradition of the Song of Songs, the Bridegroom invites his chosen one to ecstatic feasting: 'eat and drink, friends! Drink freely of love' (5:1). Mechthild's soul, 'the unwilling dancer,'[3] could not refuse the invitation; 'the bride has become inebriated, drunk by looking at his noble face,'

                    die brut is trunken worden
                    von der angesihte des edeln antlutes (I, 44).

    The Second Book, consisting of twenty-six chapters, is an account of Mechthild's experiences with the Lord of Heaven. The Soul finds fulfillment in love only after humility subdues the senses; only then will 'God free the simple soul and make her wise in love' (II, 17). For 'bitterness of heart comes from human frailty, weakness of body from the flesh alone' (II, 14). The allegorical figure of Understanding admires the soul-bride's loyalty to her heavenly Lover:

> Loving Soul, I have been watching you,
> wondrously dressed in your love.
> A light was given me
> that I might see you...
> You are striving like a man,
> though you are a maiden richly adorned
> in the Palace of your Lord,
> a happy bride in the bed of love.
> God-loving Soul, in your struggles
> you are armed with measureless might.
> So great is the power of your soul
> that all the peoples of the world,
> all the charms of your own body,
> all the legions of the devil,
> all the powers of Hell—
> cannot separate you from God.
> You arm yourself as with flowers,
> your sword is the glorious rose, Jesus Christ,
> therewith you protect yourself.
> Your shield is that white lily, the Virgin Mary,
> not only standing at your side,
> but also adorning and increasing in you
> the immeasurable glory of God.
> All who engage in this warfare
> will be richly rewarded by his Majesty (II, 19).

    In the last chapter of the Second Book, in a dialogue between God and the Soul, we learn that the real author of *The Flowing Light* is God himself.

Soul: Ah! my Lord, if I were a learned priest,
           and you had worked this wonder in him
           then you would receive praise for it.
           But how can anyone believe

that on this unworthy soil of my soul
You could build a golden house
and live therein with your Mother
and all creatures
and all the heavenly host?
Lord, no earthly wisdom will find you there.

God: My daughter, many a wise man loses his precious gold
carelessly on the great highway
on which he wished to reach the school on high;
but someone must find it!
It is my way: I always give my special grace
to the lowest and smallest and most hidden.
The highest mountains may not receive
the revelations of my grace,
for the flood of my Holy Spirit
flows by nature down into the valleys.
One finds many a wise writer of books
who, in my eyes, is a fool.
And I tell you further: It honors me greatly
and strengthens my Church
that unlearned lips should teach
the learned tongues of my Holy Spirit (II, 26).

The last words **are** a prayer on behalf of Heinrich von Halle, who
collected Mechthild's 'revelations' and attested to their authenti-
city with his signature, thus making them reputable reading for God-
seeking souls:

My Lord, with sighs I **pray** for your scribe
who has copied this book for me,
that you would reward him also
with grace never granted to a man;
for your grace, O Lord, is a thousandfold more
than your creatures can ever receive! (II, 26).

The Third Book has twenty-four chapters. It begins with a
vision of heaven: 'Great Lord! Open, and let me in!' Two angels
appear to Mechthild and say:

Lady, what do you want here above? For you are still
clothed in the darkness of earth. - 'Sirs,' she answered,
'do not say that, but greet me with words of warmer kindness! I want to go to my Love. The nearer *you* sink to
earth, the more you lose your angelic glow; while the
higher *I* rise, the **brighter** I shine!' Then they **took her**
between them and led her in with joy.

> When the Soul beheld the land of the angels,
> where she was known without illusion,
> Heaven was opened to her.
> And she stood there with melting heart
> and looked on her Love and said:
> 'Lord, when I look at you,
> I must praise you in your wondrous wisdom!
> Where am I now?
> I have lost myself in you.
> I can no longer think of the earth
> nor of my heart's sorrow--
> I had thought that when I saw you here above,
> I would lament to you of many things on earth--
> But no, my Lord, the sight of you
> has in one moment raised me above my best self....

In Mechthild's symbolic vision, heaven seems to be funnel-shaped, with the throne of God at the top. It is surrounded by choirs of angels in ever-widening circles. Between them is a yawning void to which human beings are assigned according to their merits.

> Above the throne of God is nothing but God, God, God--
> immense, great God. Above the throne is seen the mirror
> of the Godhead, the image of the humanity, the light of
> the Holy Spirit. And it is known that the three Persons
> are one God and that they are joined in One. On this in-
> effable matter it is not proper for me to say more (III, 1).

Mechthild's description of hell begins with a vision that inspires the same awful dread as Dante's inscription over the gate of *Inferno* in *Canto* III; the two texts show a striking similarity in poetic perception. Dante's warning,

> Through me is the way into the doleful city;
> through me the way into eternal pain;
> through me the way among the people lost

is similar to Mechthild's opening lines:

> I have seen a place whose name is Eternal Hatred.
> It is built in the deepest abyss out of stones
> laid there by mortal sin.
> Pride was the first stone laid by Lucifer...
> Anger, falseness and murder were
> the three stones brought by Cain.

> Lying, betrayal, despair, were the stones used
> by Judas to kill himself.
> The sins of Sodom and false piety are the
> corner stones of this work.
> It took many years to build:
> Woe to all who helped in it! (III, 21).

In Mechthild's vision, heaven was funnel-shaped, with the throne of God at the top. In Hell

> the whole place is upside down, the highest [Hell] being
> in the lowest and most unworthy places. Lucifer sits in
> the depths bound by his sin and out of his burning mouth
> there pour ceaselessly all the sin, torment, and infamy
> by which hell...[is] so piteously surrounded (III, 21).

'Think of this, sister,' Mechthild writes in the last chapter, 'and let no one drive you from your good habits.'

> True love praises God constantly;
> longing love gives the pure heart sweet sorrow.
> Seeking love belongs to itself alone.
> Understanding love loves all things equally.
> Enlightened love is mingled with sadness.
> Selfless love bears fruit without effort,
> it functions so quietly that the body
> has no knowledge of it.
> Pure love is still; in God alone
> seeing that both have one will
> and there is no creature so noble
> that it could separate them. This
> is written by knowledge out of the
> everlasting book. God is often
> flecked by copper, just as perfidy and vainglory
> blot out virtue from the human soul.
> The ignoble soul to whom passing things are so dear
> that it never trembles before Love, never heard
> God speak lovingly in it.--
> Alas! to such [a soul] this life is all darkness! (III, 24).

The twenty-eight chapters of the Fourth Book tell us almost everything we know about Mechthild. She was twelve years old when the Holy Spirit greeted her so overwhelmingly that she 'could no longer yield to serious sin. The loving greeting came every day...the sweetness and glory increased daily; and all this continued for thirty-one years' (IV, 2). Thus we may assume that she was forty-three years old when she wrote this passage. In this Book she also informs us about the

hard battles she had fought in her soul. In a truly overpowering
image she bewails that her sins tower like a dark mountain above
everything else: 'Lord, my guilt...is before me like a high mountain and has for a long time brought darkness and distance between
you and me.'[4] Yet this 'mountain of guilt' is the object of divine
love, and in the twelfth chapter she states without blushing, with
words exceeding the limits of poetic license, 'God has enough of
all the good things. The only exception is his intercourse with
the soul; of this he can never have enough.' Mechthild uses the
word *triuten*, the Middle German expression for sexual intercourse,
which in her realistic way of thinking was the only term that could
express the intensity of God's love for the soul. Hence she added
in wonderment: *wie du truiten kanst die reiniu sele in dinem schos*,
'how greatly you love a poor soul in your embrace...dear Lord, let
me sink further down, to your glory! Then soul and body came into
such mysterious darkness that I lost light and consciousness and
knew no more of God's intimacy. Love ever-blessed also went its
way' (IV, 12).

In a terse statement in the last chapter of Book Four, Mechthild deplores the inadequacy of words to describe her mystical experience. Words vanish into silence, but there remains the experience of ineffable spiritual joy. 'This Book was begun in love and
shall also end in love. For there is nothing so wise or so holy,
nor so beautiful, nor so strong, nor so perfect as love....I will
now be silent just as you were silent in the mouth of your Son when
he burned for love for ailing mankind' (IV, 28).

The thirty-five chapters of the Fifth Book, the most learned
part of *The Flowing Light*, have penance as their dominant theme.
Repentance makes love grow to such a degree that it

> melts through the soul into the senses, that the body
> may also have its share, for it is drawn into all things.
> When the soul walks with Love, with eager desire for God
> in its heart, and when it has come to the mount of power-
> ful Love and blissful knowledge, then it does as pil-
> grims do who have eagerly climbed the summit: they des-
> cend with care....So it is with the soul. Irradiated
> by the fire of its long love, overpowered by the embrace
> of the Holy Trinity, it begins to sink and to cool--

> as the sun from its highest zenith
> sinks down into the night,
> thus also, God knows, is it with the soul
> and with the body (V, 4).

The Sixth Book, consisting of forty-three chapters, is the last part of *The Flowing Light* to have been circulated during Mechthild's lifetime and collected by Heinrich von Halle. Her life as a Beguine has come to an end; her life in the cistercian monastery of Helfta was about to begin. In a poetic address to all monastic superiors Mechthild voices her thoughts on how a superior should deal with subordinates:

> Beloved, I, unworthy of merit,
> I am your servant.
> I am not your master.
> Power is made for service.
> Go forth in God's true love!
> Do you suffer? I too suffer....
> Now I send you forth
> In God's name, as Jesus
> went out seeking lost sheep
> till he died of loving.
> May God's love teach you too
> to be kind and useful.
> Take with you my prayers,
> take with you my soul's desire,
> take my sinful tears!
> May God's mercy lead you home....
> Thus comfort your brethren
> when they leave, and rejoice with them
> when they return.
> Go daily to the guest-house
> and act according to the loving-kindness of God!
> Give the young novices
> all the help in your power!
> Yes, you yourself should wash their feet!
> Only then will you be a true superior
> when serving in humility.
> Do not stay too long with the guests!
> You must diligently order the convent.
> The guests shall not keep long vigils,
> for that is a sacred thing.
> Visit the infirmary every day
> and heal the sick with comforting words of God!
> Cheer them gently with earthly joys
> for God is rich above all price!
> It is good to wash the sick,
> to be merry and laugh with them
> in a godly manner.
> Carry their secret needs in the confidence of your heart
> and truly and lovingly discover their secret sorrow!

> If you thus stand truly by them,
> then the love of God will flow sweetly
> into your own soul.
> Also go to the kitchen:
> to make sure that the needful provision is good;
> that neither your own meanness nor the cook's laziness
> may rob the Lord of sweet music in choir!
> For no hungry priest sings sweetly,
> or studies deeply.
> Thus our Lord may not get the service
> which is his due (VI, 1).

Then with a narrowing range of images and less glowing poetry, she looks back on her own life. Displeased, she exclaims:

> Alas, dear God! I am now worse than I was thirty years
> ago. For those who then helped me bear my homeless life,
> did not help me much--if only my body was to recover!
> Therefore I must always set two guardians between my
> soul and all earthly things that they may not tempt my
> body more than my poor condition can take....One guard
> is Prudence who orders all my needs according to the
> will of God, so that the human heart sits lightly on
> all human things; so much so that if it looses them...
> the soul becomes free and the senses untroubled, then
> all is well with it in God, as if its dearest friend
> had taken away its heaviest burden....My other guard is
> Holy Fear which, inspired by the wisdom of God, prevents
> my soul from smiling on earthly gifts....for those darken
> the soul of many laudable persons in the spiritual life;
> they so completely lose the light of discretion, the fire
> of love, and the touch of God's sweetness, peace and com-
> passion, that they hardly recognize them' (VI, 4).

At the beginning of the Sixth Book, Mechthild began in a marginal note to refer to her death. When she wrote it, she was probably not more than fifty-three years old and had over thirty more years to live; but she was ailing and in a momentary indulgence over the success of her writings she told her admirers: 'Any honest woman or good man who would want to speak with me but cannot after my death, should read this little book' (VI, 1).

The Seventh Book, consisting of sixty-five chapters, was written down, or rather dictated to the nuns of Helfta, for by that time Mechthild had lost her eyesight. *Du mir nu dienest mit froemden ougen*, 'now You serve me with the eyes of others,' she says in the 'Prayer of the Beggaress.' It is a remarkable prayer; from the yellow pages of an old manuscript it leaps into a living human

experience which is in touch with eternity; it is a prayer of someone who had already found security beyond the limits of man's earthly needs. Firmly and absolutely immersed in the infinite Source of
all things the Beggaress prays to God:

> Lord, I thank you that in your love you have taken from me
> all earthly riches, that you clothe and feed me through the
> goodness of others, so that everything which might clothe my
> heart in pride of possession, is no more known to me.
> Lord, I thank you that you have taken from me the sight of
> my eyes, that you now serve me through the eyes of others.
> Lord, I thank you that you have taken from me the power of
> my hands...and the power of my heart, that you now serve me
> with the hands and hearts of others.
> Lord, I pray for them: Reward them here on earth with your
> divine Love that they may faithfully serve and please you with
> all virtues till they come to a happy end.
> I pray for all those with pure hearts,
> who gave up all for love of God.
> They are all true beggars
> and on the Last Day
> Jesus our Redeemer will judge them (VII, 64).

Poetic elements of Mechthild's earlier bridal mysticism and
her metaphors of conjugal love also crept into the late-life lyrics
of the Seventh Book, but its ever-recurring theme is a welcoming of
death. She still invites her Bridegroom to take possession of her
'as noble bridegrooms are wont to do by showering their brides with
gifts on the day after marriage,' and she still longs for his loving
embrace

> Come, dear Spouse of mine: take possession of me,
> as a noble husband does
> who lavishes rich morning gifts on his Bride--
> Come, take me in your loving arms,[5]

but the longing, and life itself, seemed to have lost its fascina-
tion. The *hoverise* had been a journey long enough and Mechthild's
fervent wish to enter the Court of God returns in almost every line:

> Lord, close now your precious treasure
> by a holy end!
> Then open it up that it may be an instrument of your praise
> in heaven and on earth (VII, 42).

Heinrich von Halle, the dominican theologian who edited the
first six books of Mechthild's writings, also made of them a Latin

translation so that the revelations *in lingua barbara* sould be available to a wider circle of readers. His Latin version of *The Flowing
Light*, entitled *Lux divinitatis fluens in corda veritatis*, is one of
the most valuable possessions of the University Library of Basel in
Switzerland (manuscript B IX 11). Heinrich, used to precise scholastic terms, was at first appalled by the 'bold and uninhibited' language of Mechthild's poetry. The loose sheets lacked coherence and
all logical connection. His main objection was to Mechthild's robust style and worldly metaphors, which had unmistakably been sensual
figures of speech and, as Middle German did not as yet differentiate
between 'clean' and 'dirty' words, they were distasteful to Heinrich.
Their overtone, the *minnesang* phrases, was an outright offense against
the polished vocabulary of his scholastic background. The glow of
Mechthild's poetry was, in Nietzsche's words, conceived by 'red-hot
moments of inspiration.' Heinrich had no idea that poetic charism
is an earthly sister of divine grace, that the splendor of unspoiled
speech can be as revealing as a theologian's reasoning within the
framework of careful syllogisms. Heinrich struggled with his conscience, but then he came to admire 'the sayings and writings of Sister Mechthild' and made his Latin translation. A comparison of even
a few of the original phrases with his Latin version will clearly
illustrate the conflict between Mechthild's lusty vocabulary and
Heinrich's polished Latin in which down-to-earth emotions appear in
the sublimated technical terms of professional theologians. Here
are some examples:

     In I, 2, the original text says: *er gruesset sie mit der hove-
sprache, die man in dirre kuchin nit vernimet*--'He [God] welcomes
her [the Soul] in the language of the Court [Heaven] which is not
understood in this kitchen [earthly life],' a most expressive image
in which she compares the noble word of God with the inarticulate
and senseless chatter of kitchen servants. Heinrich's translation
dilutes this striking contrast by saying simply: *quodamque modo in-
scrutabili eam salutando alloquens*,--'He addresses her with inscru-
table salutations.' In I, 20, the ecstatic outcry: *du bist ein sturm
mines hertzen*--'You (God),are a storm in my heart'--sounded too "storm-
y" to the self-disciplined theologian; his translation is: *status
cordis mei es*--'You are the form of my heart.' Then in I, 22, in a description of God's union with the Soul which implies erotic borrow-
ings from the secular imagery of the *minnesang*, the Soul makes her
point by referring to an old proverb: *Je das minne bet enger wirt,
je di unbehalsunge naher gat*. The translator found the expression
too strong for pious readers and left it out completely; the popular
saying, 'the narrower the bed of love, the tighter the embrace' is
missing from his text. He likewise did not know what to do with the
phrase *sie will tanzen*--'she is anxious to dance' (I, 44)--and omit-
ted it completely. And when the soul complained about the protracted dancing, *nu bin ich ein wile dez tanzens muede*--'now I am tired
of dancing for a while' (I, 44)--Heinrich took it as a repudiation
of worldly pleasures and had the Soul say: *cogitationum circuitu*

lassata sum--'the running around of my thoughts made me weary.'
    In the same chapter I, 44, an unusual phrase with an unmis-
takable ring of heresy, *ir sint so sere genaturt in mich*--'You [God]
are so physically drawn to me [we have become one flesh]'--must have
shocked the sensitive ear of the theologian; he wrestled with the hy-
brid *genaturt* till he came up with the acceptable *per unionem natura-
rum* [sic!] *ineffabilis gratia nos coniunxit*--'grace binds us together in an unutterable union of natures.' In II, 19, the Soul assumes
the whims of a noble lady who demands that every one of her wishes
be obeyed by the knight dedicated to her service. In a startling
metaphor, Mechthild takes from the three divine Persons their absolute transcendence and lowers them to the rank of enamoured knights.
Die helige drifaltekeit muos mir eweklich untertenig sin--'the Holy
Trinity must submit to me for all eternity'--she wrote with matter-
of-fact certainty. This seemingly blasphemous statement loses much
of its arrogance if one keeps in mind that the God-fearing Beguine
poetess often sublimates the secular motives of courtly love into
the bridal emotions of a *connubium spirituale* in which God never
ceases to serve his chosen lady. Heinrich seems to have been aware
of this metaphorical reversal of intrinsic values, because his translation changed this actually absurd statement only slightly into a
less offensive form of admiration: *amando tantummodo Deum meum digne
efficior amari, complecti et honorari a summa Trinitate*--'having loved
God so much I was made worthy to be loved, embraced, and honored by
the Most Holy Trinity.'
    One more passage, from II, 23, will illustrate how difficult it
was for Heinrich von Halle, distinguished theologian, to render poetic
immediacy into respectable scholastic Latin. This passage of full-
blown eroticism describes the mystical union of God and the Soul in
a straightforward reference to the marital act: *contingit virginem
tactu mundissimo in florido castitatis lectulo*--'He touches the virgin with the purest touches in the flowerbed of chastity'--wherein
the words *mundissimo* and *castitatis* are artificial additions to Mechthild's blunt image of a perfect union.
    From these few examples one can see that the Middle German text
of *The Flowing Light* has deep roots in life; it is unreflective, the
experience of pleasure and pain is personal and, therefore, in every
respect more poetic than the Latin. It is also interesting to note
that the Solesme edition of Heinrich's Latin version (in *Revelationes
Gertrudianae ac Mechtildianae*, Paris, 1877-78) found it necessary to
explain even the pruned and polished language of the numerous metaphors referring to the connubial aspects of a spiritual love affair:
in the introduction to Mechthild's poetry the editors vindicated the
propriety of their action by a statement of St Paul, *omnia munda mun-
dis*. The Sibyl of Magdeburg had no inhibitions; she did not restrain
her language when an inner voice urged her 'to write out of God's
heart and mouth' (IV, 2). Her talent refused to remain what Milton

called 'a fugitive and cloistered virtue.' The central theme of her
life was *minne*--a steady holding-on to one's love--about which she
had learned so much from the songs of the *minnesänger*. The phenomenon of *minne* must be understood in the light of medieval psychology.
It was an emotional state of mind created by real or imagined attrac-
tions, by a refreshing **directness** or concealed passion between *ritter*
and *vrowe,* a knight and his lady, whereby a heightened consciousness
of love was attained, a love so intense that the question of a physi-
cal union was beside the point. Sexual abstinence actually facilitat-
ed the attainment and continuation of mutual devotion in the practice
of courtly love.[6] As a young girl, Mechthild had been under the
spell of the *minne* lyrics; their passionate celibate eroticism per-
suaded her to become a noble lady cultivating an intimate relationship with God, her *adeler ritter,* her noble Knight. Fully aware of
her womanhood, she declared herself willing to be his chosen bride:

> I am now a full-grown bride,
> I must go to my Lover's side![7]

She did not need to borrow the courage to write about what Petrarch
called 'the beautiful yearning' of a woman's heart. To her the word
'chastity' ceased to be a hidden treasure; she had surrendered it to
God in an irrevocable vow of love. A beautiful passage in I, 28,
speaks of this total surrender which characterized Mechthild's life.
It also shows a growth in poetic intensity: the beginning is calm,
written in prose, but then a growing force of metaphoric expressions
escalates into the rhythm and rhyme of inner convictions:

> I rejoice that I must love him who loves me; indeed, I
> want to love him till my death, without measure and with-
> out end. Rejoice, O my soul, for he gave his life for
> love of you; now love him so greatly that you would glad-
> ly die for love of him. Thus you will burn inextinguish-
> ably as a living spark in the great fire of his living
> Majesty.
>
> Thus you will be filled with the fire of Love
> that gives you even here on earth such great and full pleasure.
> You need not teach me any longer,
> for I can never turn away from Love.
> I must be its prisoner,
> else I would not live.
> Where Love is, there will I dwell
> in death as in life.
> Life without sorrow
> would be a fool's folly.

In another poem (II, 3), the absence of emotional rewards is portrayed in the noble lady's lament about the inattention of her lover, who is irresponsive to the desires of her heart; life is a meaningless void:

> O soaring Eagle! Darling Lamb!
> O glowing Spark, set me on fire!
> How long must I endure this thirst?
> One hour is already too long,
> one day is as a thousand years
> when you are absent!
> Should you be absent for eight days,
> I would rather go down to hell
> --where, indeed, I am already--
> than that God should hid himself
> from a loving soul.
> For that were greater anguish than human death
> and pain beyond all pain,
> believe me. The nightingale
> must ever sing, because its nature is love,
> and whoever takes that from it
> would bring it death.
> Ah! mighty Lord! Look on my need![8]

The nightingale must sing and the soul must be loved. God is Love Itself. With ever-recurring endearments he assures the Soul of his enduring love, if the Soul responds in kind; for God too wants to be ardently loved; he says:

> To love you continuously is my nature,
> for I Myself am Love.
> To love you fervently is my desire,
> for I long to be greatly loved.
> To love you everlastingly comes from my eternity,
> for I am everlasting and without end (I, 24).[9]

St Bernard defined love as an ardent longing for God. The earthly pilgrim's progress is no progress at all, if his search for happiness does not find its way from the narrow den of self-love to its divine source. Mechthild understood this teaching; in a poem reminiscent of medieval folk songs, she gives us her version of the anonymous poet's *du bist mîn, ich bin dîn:*

> I am in you and you are in me,
> we could not be closer.
> For we two are fused in one,
> poured into one mould,
> and shall be thus forever.[10]

The original **writings** of Mechthild of Magdeburg, arranged by
Heinrich von Halle into books and chapters, were done in the Middle
Low German dialect. This original shared the common fate of so many
other medieval manuscripts: *The Flowing Light of God* written in Mechthild's Middle Low German dialect is no longer extant. The only complete Middle German manuscript, Cod. 277 of Einsiedeln, Switzerland,
is written in the Middle Alemanic dialect spoken in the Upper Rhine
region which included the city of Basel in the thirteenth and fourteenth centuries. It is another **Heinrich**, the priest Heinrich von
Nördlingen who understood Mechthild's Saxon dialect, to whom we owe
this Alemanic version of *The Flowing Light* and its circulation among
the religious houses of the area. He corresponded with the best-
known mystics of his time, among them Johannes Tauler, Margarete and
Christine Ebner, and Heinrich Suso. Their approval of Mechthild's
bridal poetry made *The Flowing Light* one of the most popular spiritual readings in religious houses.

Heinrich von Nördlingen resided in Basel during the 'forties of
the fourteenth century. Since all his letters were written before
1351, we may assume that he died in or shortly after that year. In
1345, he wrote to Margarete and Christine Ebner, two nuns in the
dominican convent of Maria Medingen near Nuremberg known as The Valley of Angels: 'I am sending you a book called *The Flowing Light
of God*. I am impelled to do so by the living light of the radiant
love of Christ; for to me this book, **written** in delightful and powerful German, is the most impressive love-poem I have ever read in
our language. Read it eagerly with the perception of your heart,
but please pray the *Veni Creator* seven times before the altar. Do
not open this sealed book till you have said this prayer. Then take
with **you** all those who are anxious for such knowledge and start to
read it modestly and sparingly. Mark any word you do not understand
and I will put them in an easier form for you, for the book was given
to us in such an unusual language that it has taken us two years of
hard work to translate it....'

A copy of **Heinrich's** labors was sent to Hochtal, in the neigh-
borhood of Einsiedeln, where *Einsiedlerinnen*, anchoresses, had lived
from time immemorial, first in separate huts, then in small communities called by the people of the mountains *Waldschwestern*, Sisters
of the Forest. One of their houses was known as *die vordere Au*,
the Front Meadow. Heinrich von Rumerschein, a priest of St Peter's,
Basel, donated a copy of Heinrich von Nördlingen's Alemanic version
of *The Flowing Light* to this community living in an Alpine valley of
pine trees and snow fields. He acted on behalf of Margaret zum Goldenen Ring, whose confessor he was. The Einsiedeln **Codex** also contains
his letter, which gave instructions regarding the use of this book:
'To the Sisters in the Front Meadow: Know that this book, a gift of
Margarete zum Goldenen Ring, is called *The Flowing Light of God*. Han-
dle it with care so that it may be used by all the houses of the

Forest. Keep it no longer than one month in a house so that it may be circulated from one house to another as may be needed. Be careful with it! She [Margarete zum Goldenen Ring] is greatly devoted to you. It has a special message for you!'

No one knows when or how this manuscript of *The Flowing Light* came into the possession of Einsiedeln. That is its own secret. A handwritten note from the fifteenth century says: 'This book belongs to the four houses in the forest;' another marginal remark from the sixteenth century adds: 'Property of the Church of St Peter's at the Brook in Schwyz.' In 1860, Dr Carl Greith, the future Bishop of St Gallen, working on his *History of German Mysticism (Die Deutsche Mystik im Predigerorden*, Freiburg, 1861), visited the Library of Einsiedeln to see whether he could find any useful material for his subject; he discovered the only complete manuscript of Mechthild's writings. At the urging of Dr Greith, Father Gall Morel, the librarian of the monastery, transcribed the Middle Alemanic text into modern German and published it in Regensburg in 1869. In spite of frequent misreadings of the original text, G. Morel deserves our gratitude for discovering a great work of German mysticism. Through the kindness of the cistercian Sisters of Wurmsbach a copy has been made of this first edition and extensively used in this research.

A study of mystical poetry involves difficulties that go beyond the usual problems and explorations in literary values. Mystical poetry is more than a branch in the art of literature; it enters new dimensions, the domains of philosophical and theological implications which to its author are more important than mere aesthetic considerations. As Goethe pointed out in a conversation with Eckermann, while poetry interprets the secrets of nature by employing images and philosophy explores the secrets of reason by means of concepts, the mystic's concern embraces both the secrets of nature *and* reason by shedding light on them through words and images.

Mechthild von Magdeburg, anxious to convey her personal experience with the Ineffable, made extensive use of the most striking images, and of the regimentation of these tools of mystical self-expression. An analysis and exploration of their poetic nature from the platform of literary values will be the chief objective of our ongoing study. It must be emphasized before all else that words and images, when used as metaphors, will never completely express a mystical experience in all its dimensions. Even a mental and emotional comprehension of linguistic metaphors is still a far cry from a comprehension of the experience itself. Yet there is no other, more reliable, way to the mystical experience of an individual or to the mystical heritage of a certain time period than the linguistic study of those images which were used by the mystic touched by grace and intended to make the spiritually attuned reader understand or at least surmise what a blissfully **overburdened** soul wants to say. For, in Goethe's words, mysticism wants to shed light through images on the secrets of an intimate relationship with God.

Mechthild's writings open many doors to these secrets; her metaphors, allegories, and synecdoches are relevant clues to the medieval soul's encounter with God. An extensive reading of the mystics can, however, become a disappointing experience to someone who expects each individual experience to be expressed in unique, never-heard, linguistic vehicles of communication because, no matter how personal the experience is, it is still, basically, a universal experience. Thus, in spite of the poetic wealth one may find in the writings of the mystics, the same words and images recur in them. As Abbot Willibrord Verkade observed, 'mystics, like hunters, have a language of their own; anyone who wants to understand them must learn it.'

To acquaint oneself with the language of Mechthild's poetry is a rewarding experience; her natural talent so often departs from stereotypes, from conventions, from the traditional reservoir of mystical parlance. In *The Flowing Light of God* we inherit a collection of poems which predates the powerful prose of **Meister** Eckhart, the striking analogies of Johann Tauler's sermons, and the 'sweet' ascetical writings of Heinrich Suso by **several** decades. Revealing her sibyllic visions in a splendid robe of poetry, this woman was not afraid to depart from the common lore of mystical motives, nor did she disdain to use the shuttle of secular songsters. The *minnesänger* were her contemporaries and their themes of sensual love have found a valid expression in the testimonials of her consuming love of God.

The University of Dallas

Edited after the author's death by Bede K. Lackner, O. Cist.

NOTES

1. Carl Greith, *Die deutsche Mystik im Predigerorden* (Freiburg, 1861).

2. Gall Morel, *Die Offenbarungen Mechthilds v. Magdeburg* (Regensburg, 1869).

3. The symbol of the 'dancer' re-occurs in Dante's *Paradiso* XXIV, where the saints reveal their ecstasy in groups of a dancing light.

4. IV, 5.

5. VII, 35.

6. See H. Kolb, *Der Begriff der Minne und das Erstehen der höfischen Lyrik* (Tübingen, 1958).

7. I, 44.

8. II, 3.

9. I, 24.

10. III, 5.

THE CISTERCIAN ABBEY IN FIFTEENTH CENTURY FRANCE:
A VICTIM OF COMPETING JURISDICTIONS OF SOVEREIGNTY
SUZERAINTY AND PRIMACY

William J. Telesca

Fontaine-Daniel of the affiliation of Clairvaux is situated
in the Department of Mayenne, in the diocese of Le Mans. Jean
Goulu, its regular abbot after 1447, had been deposed by the General Chapter and replaced by François Cherot. In a determined act of
vengeance Goulu contrived a plot which produced scandal and brought
the authroities into a peculiar rivalry of jurisdictions. He conspired with the ambitious bishop of Angers, Jean de Beauveau, a royal counsellor of Charles VII who received his See from Pope Nicholas V in 1447 at the King's request. A pluralist, Beauveau also
held the abbey of Montmajour of Arles and was the administrator of
the archbishopric of Arles.[1] Goulu was persuaded to resign Fontaine-Daniel before the Holy See for a pension; because of the papal reservation Beauveau intended to obtain its provision by means
of royal intercession. In fact, with Louis XI's solicitation, Beauveau obtained the abbey in commend in 1461. By the papal bull and
royal letters, he had the legal means to strip Cherot of his office,
but the monks denied his proctors, officers of the Count of Maine,
entrance to the abbey. In the meantime Cherot appealed directly to
the bishop, condemning Goulu's deceit and submitting his case to the
Count's judges. The commend was upheld, and Cherot initiated an appeal. Undeterred by being **arrested** and confined by the bishop for
four months, he renewed his claims only to suffer imprisonment a
second time.
    At this point, Jean Balue, friend of Beauveau and royal courti-
er, canon and Grand Vicar of Angers, interceded on behalf of poor
Cherot and presented the case before Louis XI. Reports of Beauveau's excesses had even reached Rome, and the pope had written a
menacing letter seeking redress against his inhumanities. Cherot
was released and proceeded to Rome to obtain justice. Condemning
Beauveau, Louis XI obtained from Pope Paul II a bull of deposition
which excommunicated, interdicted, and deprived Beauveau of Angers
and his other benefices (24 June 1467). Balue, now in the good gra-
ces of both pope and king, received Angers. But when Balue, political activist that he was, fell from favor in 1469 and was himself
arrested, Louis directly intervened to restore Beauveau to all his
honors. Although Rome refused, the Cathedral Chapter acquiesced;
from 1471 Beauveau was in possession of the spiritual and temporal
regimen of the See, and he resisted papal censures until Sixtus IV
complied with Louis' demands and issued absolution. Beauveau also
renewed his claims to Fontaine-Daniel, which Cherot had administered

through a proctor and now resigned in the hands of the Order. Beauveau appointed a monk-vicar and a monk-proctor and began the despoliation of the abbey's treasure.

The monks persisted in their obstinate defence of their liberties. They received the appointment of their own designate, Jean Courtin, as abbot in 1477 from Cîteaux. Determined to occupy the abbey, Courtin petitioned the king to order the judges of Maine to assist him. Royal letters even provided him with twenty *gens d'armes* to gain entrance, and before the end of summer he had succeeded in gaining possession.

Beauveau, however, was able to convince King Louis XI that Courtin's papal bull of confirmation infringed upon the royal Ordinances. Courtin now protested and initiated his appeal before the vacillating king. Impatient, Beauveau recruited one hundred and fifty men at arms and employed cannon in a siege of the abbey.

This was the last straw. The king ordered the case to be heard before the officials of Maine. Both the commendatory and the regular abbot produced their arguments and supporters. Local sympathies inclined to the monks, and Courtin was awarded the abbey. An end? Not quite. Beauveau appealed to Rome, denying all the charges against himself. Preposterous as his case was, he received a papal bull ordering his restoration and Courtin's excommunication. With Louis XI deciding again to support his bishop, the pope acquiesced obsequiously. There is a happy ending! Beauveau died on 23 April 1479, and Courtin was thereupon encouraged to travel to Rome to present his case once more. He obtained a bull of confirmation from Sixtus IV, dated June 1479, and he presided until 1499. But the abbey had been impoverished by the protracted struggle in the courts and the outbreaks of hostilities, and monastic observance was never fully restored.[2]

Royaumont is in the Seine et Oise region of the Ile de France, in the diocese of Beauvais. Its plight is typical of the problems that challenged the abbeys of France in the fifteenth century. With the resumption of the Hundred Years War by Henry V of England, and the confirmation of his successes in 1420 in the Treaty of Troyes, the abbot of Royaumont, Gilles de Cupé (1419-1440), made his homage to Henry, 'roi de France.'[3] His formal adherence to the Lancastrian brought benefits to his abbey: the restitution of property, confirmation of its possession, and a guaranty of free governance under himself as abbot. Situated in the path of the English armies, the abbey had been compelled to pursue a course amenable to the conquerors. Before the Council of Constance had convened to terminate the Great Schism, English influence had already been menacing enough to exact Royaumont's obedience to the Roman popes.[4] Sporadic victories by the French took the abbey back into the Avignon line, but after 1420, it was again subject to the will of the English under the firm and capable administration of the Duke of Bedford.[5]

Cupé's death coincided with the French victories in the final phase
of the war, and Royaumont experienced a restoration under Gilles II
de Roye (1453-58), abetted by the policies of Louis XI, who reunit-
ed all of the major provinces under his centralized government. Until the Concordat of Bologna between Francis I of France and Pope
Leo X in 1516, Royaumont, safely in French royal territory, enjoyed
a steady growth in spiritual and temporal affairs.[6]
     The Hundred Years War meant the *de facto* independence of Aqui-
taine until 1453, and the area exemplified the crises of competing
jurisdictions.[7] The Cistercian abbeys affected were Fontfroide in
the district of Aude, in the diocese of Narbonne, in Languedoc;
Bonnefont in the region of the Haute-Garonne in Gascony, in the diocese of Comminges (today Toulouse); Bonnecombe and Bonneval in the
region of Aveyron, of the diocese of Rodez; Grandselve in the region of the Tarn and Garonne in Gascony, in the diocese of Toulouse.
The abbots of Bonnefont, Bonnecombe, and Bonneval were all promoted
by provision of Benedict XIII.[8] In 1419 Martin V censured Pierre
d'Aunhac of Bonnecombe for his continued loyalty to the now deposed
Benedict. In 1420, Gerald Brie, Martin's papal legate, excommunicated the abbots of Bonnecombe and Bonneval. In 1422, Aunhac of
Bonnecombe submitted and received papal absolution. While none of
the sources offers details, they reveal that the abbeys in Aquitaine
were more subject to direct papal encroachment in their provision
and more removed from royal jurisdiction than the king and perhaps
the Order desired.
     During the pontificate of Eugenius IV, Pierre de Comba and As-
torgius de Sanareto contended for the abbacy of Bonnecombe. The
Pope excommunicated the former in defense of Astorgius, but in
1439, the Council of Basel intervened and sent the abbot of Bonneval to absolve Pierre de Comba from the sentence imposed by the
cardinal legate, Anthony of Ostia.[9] During the period of the Pragmatic Sanction, 1438-1461, the popes could still exercise their
jurisdiction in these abbeys, and to the end of the century, most
of the abbots of Bonnecombe and Bonneval were commendatories.[10]
     Fontfroide also suffered from the rivalries of princes and
prelates, and its relations with the authority of the Chapter and
Cîteaux were marked by stress. Fontfroide remained loyal to the
archbishop of Narbonne during the Schism and supported the Avignon
line of popes. After France's withdrawal of obedience from Peter
de Luna (Benedict XIII), the Duke of Berry ordered seizure of the
abbey's temporalities, and the abbot subsequently participated at
the Council of Pisa in 1409 in the repudiation of both Roman and
Avignon popes and in the election of Alexander V. The abbot, Jean,
was duly rewarded with the cardinal's hat in 1414 by the Pisan John
XXIII.
     Benedict XIII, a diehard, defied the French king and the Coun-
cil of Constance, and he moved against the abbey to confiscate all

its properties. From 1409 to 1423 he could still number some among his obedience who continued the harassment of Fontfroide. At his death support dissipated and Abbot Jean recovered his losses and presided over the abbey till 1440. Pierre Ferrer succeeded as abbot, but he was deposed by his father-immediate, the abbot of Grandselve, for scandalous conduct in 1442. He defied the Order, however, and wreaked havoc on the abbey until 1448. *Gallia Christiana* states cryptically that Marie of Aragon, queen of the Two Sicilies and Jerusalem, and Countess of Barcelona, seized the abbey in the King's name in 1443. But, as in so many of these protracted contests, the records are silent regarding the outcome. In 1441, the General Chapter overturned the father-immediate's excommunication of Ferrer.[11] The next year another Chapter attacked the abbot of Grandselve for his continued oppression of abbot Ferrer, but in 1445 the Chapter commissioned the abbots of Candeil and Cadouin to investigate the charges against Ferrer and, if necessary, suspend him.[12] By 1448, the General Chapter was compelled to seek assistance outside the Order, and the abbot of Ste-Croix was commissioned to undertake the case against Ferrer and to hold a conventual election.[13]

The records indicate that Martial de la Rue was regular abbot from 1448 to 1472. The royal proctor, Charles d'Oms of Rousillon, defending the deposed Pierre Ferrer, however, prevented abbot Martial from taking possession.[14] Ferrer contested his title until his death in 1454.[15] Even more intriguing is the appearance of Jean Magdale, who competed for the abbey for the next eight years. Magdale is mentioned as proctor general of the Order in 1445, when Pope Eugenius IV provided him with the Spanish house of Ovila, in the diocese of Siguenza.[16] Cauvet, in his history, said that he had been elected by the monks of Fonfroide in 1448, before Martial de la Rue, but had refused the office.[17]

Then in 1453, the Chapter gave the abbot of Clairvaux plenary power to investigate the controversy between Magdale and Rue for the abbacy of Fontfroide. The Chapter revealed its sympathy for Magdale, now usually referred to as the abbot of Fossanova, and summoned Rue to appear before the abbot of Clairvaux to answer the charges brought by Magdale.[18] Rue was threatened with all the usual penalties for his failure to appear. But in 1454, the Chapter reversed itself completely. It ordered Magdale to terminate his action against Rue, emphasizing his own provision in the Order, an obvious reference to his abbacy at Fossanova. He was, however, ordered to compel Ferrer to submit, offering him the opportunity to make his profession in another monastery, or to imprison him as a fugitive. Were Ferrer and Magdale acting in collusion against Martial de la Rue? Magdale does appear suspect. Apparently he was the beneficiary of papal favor for his promotion in the Order, and he abused his office. It is not clear with what authority he adjusted the tax rates of the Order upon the Spanish houses, but the Chapter revoked his assessments in 1454.[19] At last, in 1456, the Chapter achieved a settlement at Fontfroide. The cryptic language of the statute only whets our curiosity to know more. The Chapter maintained that Jean Magdale had been canonically elected to Fontfroide; that he had also presented bulls of his provision from the Holy See; and that therefore he had the right to the abbatial dignity. Nevertheless, out of pure generosity, the Chapter noted, he has resigned his office into the hands of the abbot of Cîteaux who has examined the qualifications of Martial de la Rue and, duly satisfied, has promoted him to the abbacy of Fontfroide--all of which the Chapter ratified and confirmed.[20]

Val-Richer is in the region of Calvados, diocese of Bayeux, in Normandy. Vulnerable to the armies of the Hundred Years War, it was compelled to transfer its loyalty from France to England and back to France. It exemplifies the specific challenges to which a monastery might be subjected. The cooperation of the French king and the Avignon pope produced a rival to the abbot-elect in 1385, and the contest erupted in a year of violence. The ducal court of Rouen finally awarded the abbey to the regular abbot.[21] With the renewal of hostilities under Henry V, and his successes down to the Treaty of Troyes (1420), monastic life was disturbed again. Henry V ordered the seizure of all ecclesiastical and monastic properties which he then restored in return for an oath of loyalty to his rule. Val-Richer lost its possessions, but enjoyed restoration and beneficent patronage under the Duke of Bedford after 1422. With the English withdrawal in 1449, King Charles VII extended his rule over the reconquered areas and introduced institutions for centralization that were often harsh. His policies toward the church were motivated by the Pragmatic Sanction, and his government intended to preclude competing English, feudal, and ecclesiastical jurisdictions in newly acquired territories.

In 1452, the abbot of Val-Richer swore homage and fealty to Charles VII, who regarded the abbey as a royal house to which he accorded his protection. His authority superseded episcopal and papal, and he reserved obedience to himself alone. His order for and inventory of the abbey's wealth was in fact completed by Louis XI in 1465.[22] *Gallia Christiana* does not offer much information on the history of the abbey under Louis XI. After the abrogation of the Pragmatic Sanction (1461), the abbey did not join the protest of the Gallican clergy and the Parlement of Paris against the king. For his part, Louis XI did ratify the abbey's exemption from his feudal impositions in 1465, and he permitted free elections against papal provision and offered letters of protection, but in 1476, he prevented the monks of Normandy from attending the General Chapter 'outside the Kingdom.'[23] The struggle between pope and king had repercussions upon monastic life and created tensions that could not have been anticipated by an earlier age.

One more example can suffice to show how the administrative system of Cîteaux could not defend itself against the political interests of the fifteenth century. Tamié, in the diocese of Tarentaise, was in the Duchy of Savoy, today the Department of the same name. The abbot, Peter VI de Burigniaco, was promoted by the Roman pope in 1400 and governed twenty years. In 1431, the Chapter designated Claude Pareti of Tamié (d. 1454) as one of its representatives to the Council of Basel, at which he was conspicuous for his activity. He was also one of the electors of the antipope Felix V in 1439. When he offered homage to the antipope, he was given a special privilege of exemption from the commend for his abbey. Burnier, the historian of Tamié, said that the solemn papal promise was observed scrupulously. In fact, it was not,[24] but it did bring honor to the abbey during Pareti's governance. The abbot's prestige increased over the other Savoyard houses, and he became a vicar of the abbot of Cîteaux in the Duchy. He obtained the rights of visitation to all houses there, of monks and nuns, and received special responsibility for the preparation of the novices of all Savoyard houses.[25]

Claude Pareti was succeeded by Georges Jocerand (1454-72). Elected unanimously, he was confirmed by his father immediate, the abbot of Bonnevaux of Vienne. Yet he did not take possession of the abbey. Neither Burnier nor I can determine why. The Duke of Savoy, Louis, had supported his election in Rome and everything seemed canonical and regular, yet Jocerand wrote to pope Nicholas V expressing doubts over his election. Pope Nicholas appointed the Benedictine prior of Tallories to investigate Jocerand's qualifications, and he ordered the prior to take an inventory of the abbey's temporalities and to examine the abbot's management of revenues. Although prepared to confirm the election of Jocerand, the pope authorized the prior to take whatever action was necessary and to determine whether Claude Pareti had resigned freely *extra curiam* or even before a notary public and witnesses and if the abbey might belong to the general or special disposition of the Holy See. Nicholas concluded by enjoining the abbot to obtain proper obedience and reverence from the monks and vassals of the abbey.[26] Jocerand was in fact installed as abbot and held the position till 1472.

The General Chapters of the third quarter of the century indicate yet other problems in the houses within the Duchy of Savoy. There is again the hint that competing jurisdictions produced a confusion that undermined the Order's central administration. In 1451, the Chapter admitted that Savoyard Cistercian houses had received a special favor predating the Council of Basel and the resultant schism (after the election of the antipope in 1439) regarding their contributions, but decreed that now they were obliged to pay their contributions to the Order again as well as the special

subsidy imposed on the abbeys to send the Cistercian delegation to
the Council.[27] In 1472, the problem still confronted the Chapter.
The abbot of St Sulpice was commissioned with plenary power to take
action against the abbots of ducal Savoy to compel them to pay their
contributions.[28] As a result of non-compliance with the Chapter's
order, Tamié had lost its favored position in the Order. What happened? We can only guess. Urbain de Chevron became abbot in 1472.
He was an apostolic protonotary, a Benedictine prior, and a canon
of Geneva; his family were founders of the abbey. Ambitious, a
pluralist, and a political activist, he renounced the abbey when he
received the See of Tarentaise in 1483. Burnier maintains that Chevron made his monastic profession at Tamié and was a good abbot.[29]
Yet the Chapter of 1473 ordered the nuns of Les Hayes, in the diocese of Grenoble, not to obey Urbain, the commendatory of Tamié, and
to receive a confessor duly appointed by the Order.[30] Chevron's successor, Augustin de Charnée was counsellor of Duke Charles of Burgundy and spent his abbatial tenure at the ducal court (1483-92).
Urbain de Chevron's nephews held the abbey from 1492 to 1506, and
their delinquency and absenteeism contributed to Tamié's decline.[31]

Confusion reigned throughout the century. Even with the paucity
of evidence, there are still many examples showing how the Order
yielded again and again to pressures that eroded its jurisdiction.
The whole period of the Pragmatic Sanction (1438-61) and of the Hundred Years War (1339-1453) not only disrupted regular monastic observance but challenged the Order's ability to decide on a policy
consistent with its own best interests, spiritual or temporal. In
fact, inconsistency prevailed. There were accommodations with the
papacy, with the conciliarists at Basel, with the Gallicans, and
with the monarchy in a France that had as yet no boundaries. There
were, besides, relationships with the powerful feudal houses that
defied every jurisdiction and exploited every opportunity to increase
their own independence.

Charles VII followed up his victories over the English with the
imposition of royal controls over territories that had enjoyed *de
facto* independence from the Kingdom of France for too long. He introduced the Pragmatic Sanction throughout the South and the West,
from Provence to Guienne, to advance notable men and natives of the
Kingdom to benefices once in the popes' provision, and to ensure
their administration and possession by men loyal to the crown.[32]
But royal centralization always met some resistance. The Order of
Cîteaux might be the issue in the rivalry. In the monastery of Les
Châteliers in the diocese of Poitiers, the Department of Deux-Sèvres,
Guillaume Furgant occupied the abbatial office by force in 1450,
claiming that his 'papers' from the king recognized his rights in
accord with the principles of the Pragmatic Sanction. But Jehan du
Jeu, protonotary of the Holy See, also claimed the abbey in commend
from the pope. The Order commissioned the abbot of Clairvaux to

investigate the latter's provision, and on 8 November 1453, he em-
powered the abbots of Valence and Grace-Dieu to oversee the election of an abbot. The abbey's history did not report the outcome,
except to note that Furgant died around 1456.[33] Igny, in the diocese of Reims, was seized by Charles VI in 1419; then suffered English occupation. In 1448, Thibault de Luxembourg, a great lord and
manager of the estates of Charles VII, was elected abbot with the
king's approval. Apparently deserving, he enjoyed both royal and
papal patronage, and participated in Louis XI's coronation. He was
elected in succession to Morimond (1462) and to Ourscamp (1466).
He was also made bishop of LeMans in the latter year, and by papal
dispensation he was permitted to keep Ourscamp in commend. Igny,
however, was again placed under royal control in 1466, though the
reasons are not clear.[34] Thibault of Ourscamp was made a cardinal
by Sixtus IV in 1474 at Louis XI's request.[35] If the papal and
royal candidates contested for Cistercian abbeys under Charles VII,
the Order might find it an opportunity to derive some advantage in
taking sides. After 1461, the revocation of the Pragmatic Sanction,
the monks were powerless against the combined efforts of pope and
king in the provision of their abbeys.

　　Anglo-Burgundian France preferred, in one scholar's description,
a 'quasi-concordat' with Martin V in 1418.[36] The Pragmatic Sanction
had little effect on benefices in the Duchy of Burgundy and the duke
was not adverse to cooperating with the papacy against the king even
after the end of the war. Down to his death in 1477, Charles the
Rash oppressed ecclesiastical institutions indiscriminately in his
battles with Louis XI.[37] Brittany concluded its own concordat with
the papacy after the Pragmatic Sanction of 1438. The Duchy avoided
union with the Kingdom before the 1480s and in 1441 the Concordat of
Redon gave Jean V the same control in Brittany that the Dukes of Burgundy had over the church in their lands.[38]

　　Gascony was even more difficult for royal power to penetrate.
It had been a fief of the English since 1259, and it provided the
papacy opportunities to exercise provision of abbeys throughout the
first half of the century. Charles VII moved in swiftly after the
English defeat in 1453, and his commissioners protested that the ecclesiastical authorities were encroaching on the Pragmatic Sanction.
This induced the king to set up the *Grand Jours* (the royal court
which held sessions in 1456 and 1459) to judge on appeals emanating
from the collation of benefices, the application of the Sanction,
and the defense of Gallican liberties. In fact, the ecclesiastical
courts were greatly restricted by the *Grand Jours,* and by its more
permanent successor, the king's Parlement of Bordeaux.[39]

　　In the Bourbonnais, the duke and the pope also found it con-
venient to maintain ties of friendship in their common resistance
to monarchic authority. I have shown elsewhere how Pope Eugenius
IV and Duke Charles V cooperated in the provision of Monpeyroux to

a Franciscan commendatory abbot, one of the earliest examples of
the commendatory grant in the Order.[40] In short, P.S. Lewis' comments on the independence of the dukes of Brittany and Burgundy
and the English have valid general application:

> All rulers had the same problem: concerning the poli-
> tical control of the greater benefices, concerning the
> supply of the lesser ones, concerning ecclesiastical
> taxation, concerning ecclesiastical jurisdiction.[41]

The Order of Cîteaux tried desperately to cope with this menacing situation. It had recourse only to the authorities who were
often the offenders. It sought papal protection but resisted papal
provision. It appealed to the king for cooperation but complained
of royal encroachments. It condemned the use of secular courts for
litigation but appointed proctors in the major courts to protect
its interests. It decried the poor attendance at General Chapters
and authorized abbots to hold national congregations; then it cri-
ticized the congregations for acting too independently, to the dis-
regard of the Order. It promulgated the common plea that the religious should not obey non-regular superiors, and entrusted abbatial
responsibility to priors in the absence of regular abbots; then it
rebuked the priors for abusing their authority to the detriment of
their abbots-immediate.

In 1433, the Chapter adopted the decrees of the Council of
Basel on elections.[42] In 1442 the influence of the Pragmatic Sanction was also felt when the Chapter distinguished between elections
more gallicano and *more romano*.[43] However, as we saw above, too
much emphasis on Basel as an authority could create problems: the
Savoyard houses defended their privileges from Basel against the
Chapters even after the Council had been dissolved by Pope Nicholas V. In fact, the General Chapter protested that there were abbots who were flaunting privileges obtained at Basel to the detriment of the Order, adding that no privileges had validity unless
the Chapter had inspected and approved them.[44]

The pope remained the major enigma to the Order in the fifteenth century. The papacy in general and several popes in particular battled the pretensions of the Valois kings and the implications of the Pragmatic Sanction relentlessly. Pope Eugenius IV,
paranoic over threats to his primacy, in using every opportunity to
combat the monarchy brought disaster to the Order of Cîteaux. A man
conventionally religious, with some reputation for reform,[45] Eugenius introduced practices that challenged and perplexed the abbots at
the Chapters. Not only is he identified with the earliest commendatory provision of Cistercian abbeys, but he exercized his prerogatives of reservations even in the nomination of regulars.[46]

The General Chapter was not pleased at the concessions Pope

Eugenius made to the abbots of England and Wales. He permitted them to hold their own triennial chapters because of the state of war prevailing between England and France, and he absolved them from any excommunications imposed by the General Chapters of the Order.[47] A year later the fathers of the Order were even more chagrined at the privilege which the Spaniard Martin de Vargas obtained from the pope. A monk of B. M. of Mont Sion in the diocese of Toledo, he received a bull which designated him reformer of all abbeys in Castille and Leon, with authority to hold triennial provincial chapters.[48] A letter of the proctor general of the Order to the pope accused Martin de Vargas of deceiving the pope and keeping the truth from him. The proctor general's attempt to inform the Holy See of the facts did not alter the decision. It is ironic that in 1438, the Chapter included this bull of Pope Eugenius, *Ad universalis ecclesiae*, among its own papal privileges. Abbot Jean Picart of Cîteaux had petitioned the Holy See regarding the independence of those abbots whom it had promoted and who consequently exempted themselves from the Chapters and scorned the Order's visitors and reformers. The papal bull responded almost apologetically that it was never intended to exempt apostolic promotions from regular superiors, and more emphatically threatened with excommunication those who continued to reject the regular jurisdiction.[49]

A study of the period reveals the futility which the hierarchy of the Order experienced in these years. The line of direct petitioners to the Holy See continued to grow, to the infringement of the Order's liberties. The Chapter complained of the abuse by a number of abbots who were approaching the Curia in violation of the statutes, and it ordered the proctor general to seize and arrest the offenders.[50] Four years later, in 1445, the Chapter condemned those demoted and banished by the visitors of the Order who defiantly appealed to the Holy See for absolution.[51]

Yet for all the protests, the peculiar relationship of the Order to the Holy See persisted throughout the century. The papacy supported the pleas of the Order and issued privileges *ad petitionem* while it simultaneously granted favors to individuals in violation of Cistercian exemption. The General Chapters had more frequent recourse to the papacy to combat infringement of its liberties as the fifteenth century wound down. Yet, paradoxically, the statutes emphasize that the conflicts occurred between regular and papal nominees for the possession of the abbatial office. In 1442, the Chapter called upon the Holy See's support in its condemnation of the intruder Hervé to the abbatial office of le Loroux; the record implies that Hervé had papal approbation against the regular abbot-elect.[52] In 1450, the Chapter annulled the promotion of a Friar Minor to the abbot's stall of Val-croissant in the diocese of Die and called for a new election.[53] Again the claimant presented an apostolic rescript in

his defense. In 1454, the Chapter requested the abbot of Boulbonne
to present to it the bulls which authorized the union of Calers to
Boulbonne.[54] Six years later, the Chapter annulled a 'union of this
kind made by the Supreme Pontiff.'[55] In 1460, the Chapter examined
the dispensations granted by Pius II to a Minor who had been promoted to the abbacy of la Benissons-Dieu, diocese of Lyon, and then
acquiesced.[56] Likewise, the 'official' papal provision of the abbot of la Charite in 1461 was confirmed after capitular review.[57]
A year later, the Chapter created a commission to judge the pretensions of a monk of Châtillon to the abbacy of Bullion, in the
diocese of Besançon, by virtue of apostolic letters.[58] In 1464,
another capitular commission challenged the validity of the apostolic bulls and letters of the pretender to Foigny.[59]
      Occasionally a show of strength worked. When the commendatory
abbot of Bonnevaux of Vienne attempted to exercize his jurisdiction
over his filiation by virtue of his apostolic letters, the Chapter
rebuked him and ordered all abbots and abbesses to resist his attempted intrusions under pain of excommunication; and it urged them
to issue a summons to him to appear before the next Chapter or before the Apostolic See.[60] On the other hand, the papal provision
to Maizières in the diocese of Chalons was accepted by the Chapter.[61]
In 1470, the Chapter commissioned the abbot of Calers to move against
the abbot of Loc Dieu, in the diocese of Rodez, who refused to support a student at the Cistercian College of Toulouse according to
the constitutions of the Order. Although he defended his derelic-
tion on the basis of an apostolic indult, the Chapter retorted that
possessing an indult was contrary to the Order's statutes.[62] And so
it went. The Order had to depend on papal protection but could no
longer escape the awkward intrusion of papal prerogatives.
      It is especially ironic that Pope Eugenius IV showed a fondness
for the Observantist movement, and for the Franciscans in particular.
The Cistercian Order, on the other hand, seemed to be bothered by
the Friars Minor in mid-century. After the Chapter of 1450 had re-
jected the promotion of a Friar to the abbacy of Val-croissant, it
designated the abbot of Aiguebelle as visitor and reformer of the
monasteries of Senanque, Val-croissant, Tironneau, Val-saintes, and
charged him to implement and derogate, and to expel, the Mendicants
and others of a dishonorable life, if necessary, by employing the
secular arm.[63] In 1453, the Chapter threatened to initiate action
in the Curia against the commendatory abbot of Monpeyroux if he failed to desist in his oppression of the abbey's affiliations.[64] He too
was a Franciscan, though now professed in the Cistercian Order and
elevated to the titular bishopric of Birsheba. The Franciscan problem became very irksome to the regular abbots and in the following
year, after the recovery of Gascony from the English, the Chapter
designated the abbot of Valence, in the diocese of Poitiers, visitor and reformer of all the houses in the diocese of Bordeaux,

'which were recently held in obedience to the English, and in several
of which some Mendicants are said to be installed and promoted sur-
reptitiously and clandestinely as abbots and presidents, to the great
prejudice of the Order itself.' The Chapter added the command that
the abbot of Valence 'should expel and remove from those places those
Mendicants by every method and means and with the support of law and
justice, and with the gratuitous expenses of those places, and with
plenary power of the General Chapter itself.'[65] The Chapter was prepared to inflict harsh punishment on violators of its statutes. The
threat of excommunication was always included as a matter of course,
but often there was added the penalty of arrest and imprisonment,
with the help of the secular arm if necessary.[66]

The statutes unfortunately present only the Order's responses
to its problems. They do not mention the political situation in the
Kingdom of France and royal encroachment upon provincial government.
The Chapters often reveal no awareness at all in the profound inter-
action of the various parties--royal, papal, Gallican, episcopal.
But I am convinced that more often than not the implicit competition
of these had disastrous consequences for the Order. Furthermore, the
Order was unable to resist the political implications of the emerging
monarchies with the remedies of another age. All kinds of expedients
were resorted to to maintain control of the houses, but non-regular abbots interrupted the pyramidal structure of jurisdiction erected in
the twelfth century and disrupted communications between the Chapters
and the monastic communities. The regulation of abbatial elections
became a major preoccupation of the Cistercian fathers in these years.
The Order was in fact losing its jurisdiction over individual houses,
and could do nothing about it. The Chapter passed a statute in 1449
which ordered those promoted to abbacies to appear before the Chapter
within the year to swear before the definitors that they would not
obtain any privileges or exemptions from the payment of contributions,
from the Supreme Pontiff or from any other princes.[67] The subsequent
repetition of this kind of enactment attests to its futility. Even
earlier the Chapters showed concern over the increasing number of abbatial resignations and tried to regulate the practice. Those abbots
and abbesses who had no embarrassment in resigning their monasteries
into hands of seculars were threatened with the usual penalties.[68]
The Order recognized no resignations submitted outside the General
Chapter or outside the secret consistory of the Apostolic See.[69] On
the other hand, the Chapters eventually adopted a very liberal policy
which encouraged resignations made into the hands of fathers-immediate,[70] or to the abbot of Cîteaux and the four proto-abbots.[71] In
fact, the Chapter permitted the abbots of Gimont, Nizors, and Escal-
adieu to resign their houses without penalties to the abbots of Grandselve and Berdoues, to one or both, for their own good and without
the stigma of simony. Apparently, here, in its desperation, the Order was willing to encourage resignation to gain control of the

houses without complications.[72]
    There is no doubt that free elections were a thing of the past.
Everybody had a stake in promotions. Fathers-immediate were warned
about promotions procured by means of secular intervention.[73] The
Chapter complained that there were elections and postulations of
abbots who had not been professed for a year in the Order.[74] Furthermore, there were religious who were obtaining from the *potentes*,
secular and ecclesiastical, favors that permitted them to ignore
their superiors and their vows of obedience.[75] There were abbots
and monks who defied and resisted visitors and reformers, and called
upon the same *potentes* to support their rebellion, or who obtained
from the *potentes* letters, imprecations, and even threats to sustain their insolence.[76] Again, those corrupted by ambition and av-
arice were denounced by the Order and those who solicited the intervention of the powerful by means of such letters, imprecations, and
threats to obtain promotion were declared ineligible for any office
in the Order.[77]
    Neither prelates nor princes respected Cistercian exemption.
The Privilege of Paschal II, confirmed again and again by his successors, offered no protection. The Chapters decried the infringement of their liberties and demanded to resolve their disputes before the Order's own properly designated judges. Yet the statutes
indicate that the Order was dragged into the secular courts time
and time again. Apparently the regular monks were also guilty of
introducing litigation in non-regular courts, for the Chapter ordered contestants for office expelled from their monasteries, and ordered monks not to bring suit against co-religionists in a secular
court.[78] The repetition of the warning betrays its futility. The
Chapter also decreed that if any persons, ecclesiastical or secular,
who had been designated conservers of the Order's privileges should
summon any religious before them, the religious should avoid the
summons and invoke the exemption of the Order.[79] Finally, the abbots, abbesses, and members of the Order were instructed to resist
the jurisdiction of anybody, of whatever province, be he king, duke,
or bishop, under pain of deposition from their dignities.[80] Although the statutes were addressed to all abbots, the following examples emphasize their special application to France. The Chapter created a commission to seize the temporalities of the abbey of Lanvaux
while its abbatial office was being contested in secular courts.[81]
The Chapter declared null and void the summons of the abbot of Bar-
beaux to the city of Tours by the abbot of Bellebranche.[82] It called upon the abbot of Balerne to judge a case between a monk and the
curate of St Theodolus before it fell into the hands of the bishop
of Besançon.[83] The abbot of Chaalis was asked to bring the abbess
of St Anthony of Paris before the Order's judges.[84] Interestingly,
this matter was not resolved after five years, and the abbot received more severe threats in the Chapter's exhortation to submit to the

Order's justice.[85] In 1466, the Chapter created another commission
to bring the abbot of Chaalis before the abbot of Longpont to adju-
dicate and terminate the controversies, processes, and litigation
set in motion by the abbot of Chaalis.[86] When a monk of Beaubec
not only invoked the secular power against the convent of Penthé-
mont for justice but for the seizure of the monastery's temporalities as well, the Chapter sent the abbots of Royaumont and le Val
to hear the case.[87]

By the end of the 1460s the breakdown in the centralization of
the Order and the irreparable damage to Cistercian government were
evident everywhere, and always acutely so in France. The deterior-
ation must be read against the chaos of fifteenth century France and
the emerging power of the French monarchy. Royal administration
moved into the political vacuum created by the withdrawal of the
English and the submission of the great magnates to the officials
of the Valois. In the confusion the papacy often exerted its influence and invoked its primacy in the sphere of benefices, but the atmosphere of the fifteenth century was not as amenable to papal pretensions as earlier centuries had been. The Order sought and obtained bulls of protection even under the Pragmatic Sanction down
to the Concordat of Amboise in 1472, but it also established proctors to defend its privileges and liberties against ecclesiastics
and seculars.[88] Against local aggressors, papal sanctions were in-
effective. Expedient remedies had to be found. The abbots were ad-
vised to band together for mutual assistance in defending their liberties in the Duchy of Brittany.[89] The abbots of Troisfontaines,
Igny, Signy, Vauclair, Val-roy, Elan, and Bonnefont were enjoined
to cooperate in a vigorous prosecution against exactions made by the
city of Reims.[90] The abbots of the province of Sens were encouraged
to refuse payment of the impositions of bishops or laymen.[91] The
Chapter commissioned the abbots of Lorroy, in the diocese of Bourges,
Aubepierre, in the diocese of Limoges, and Le Bouchet, in the diocese
of Clermont, to unite all abbots of their province (it did not speci-
fy which) for the defense of the Order's privileges.[92] And so it
went.

Nothing worked. Abbeys continued to fall into the hands of non-
regular abbots. By the Concordat of 1472 between Louis XI and Sixtus
IV, no protection existed against the commendatory provision of Cistercian houses. Charles VII had more often than not been a rival of
the papacy in maintaining Gallican liberties under the Pragmatic Sanction. Louis XI felt that the rivalry often benefited the clergy and
the princes at the expense of the monarchy. Perhaps he was right.
Writing of the peculiar political conditions of fifteenth century
France, Lewis commented:

> The confusion thus apparent throughout the fifteenth
> century in France at every level of the church, from

the king at its head to the merest clerk after a benefice
at its base, thus sprang from a confusion about the best
means, at any particular moment, to achieve for each particular person his own particular ends.[93]

Elsewhere he added that as far as the ' "recovery of France" is
concerned, the essential aspect of this relationship was the asser-
tion of the king's authority over the Church in the Kingdom.'[94]
During the period of the Pragmatic Sanction, local magnates still
harassed Cistercian abbeys and the popes continued to exercize
their rights of provision against capitular election. Under Louis
XI the establishment of royal authority more firmly throughout the
kingdom brought little relief to the Order of Cîteaux. Louis exerted himself vigorously in the nomination to benefices and Cistercian
commendatory abbeys increased in numbers after 1461.
     The Order could not turn back the clock. Not only did the
privileges emanating from Rome have little or no effect on the
Christian society of fifteenth century France, but the popes preferred to interpret primacy more politically than spiritually and
sought to control benefices rather than protect exemptions. The
conflict of the century had not been seen before, a conflict 'between the old medieval idea of unity, and the new demands for re-
cognition of ideas which had grown out of the institutions of national states now passing out of the stage of infancy and becoming
dimly conscious of their "national" rights and powers.'[95] The Cistercians experienced the conflict. McIlwain's judgment of fifteenth
century society is certainly applicable to them, though they could
not comprehend it. They could not stem the tide of decline, and the
regular authority of the Chapters and the father-abbots could not
preserve the structural unity with traditional means. In fact, when
reform did come, it was not imposed by the leadership, but it was a
grass roots movement, a return to the pristine spirituality, redis-
covered in the lonely monasteries and spreading anew from below.

Le Moyne College
Syracuse, New York

NOTES

1. Canon law did not permit the pluralist to hold more than one 'care of souls' and Beauveau retained the see of Arles *in administrationem*, as administrator. He received Fontaine-Daniel *in commendam*, as a commendatory abbot. As the system of reservations and provisions of benefices was expanded and exercized among papal prerogatives after the thirteenth century, it became a usual practice to appoint pluralists to their non-pastoral benefices as administrators of sees and commendatories of abbeys. The latter provision was an abbey *in commendam*. There is no English translation, and it is customary to describe the grant as a *commendam* or *commende* (French). However, for convenience in this study, I intend to use the English expression *in commend* and *commend* to describe the grant. For the commend and the canonical references, see R. Laprat, 'Commende' in the *Dictionnaire de droit canonique*, III (Paris: Librairie Letouzey et Ane, 1942) 1029-85.

2. This startling tale is recorded in A. Gross-Duperon and E. Gouvrion, *L'Abbaye de Fontaine-Daniel*, 2 vols., (Mayenne, 1896) I: 98ff.

3. The last Capetian king of France died in 1328, and Edward III, son-in-law of Philip IV, laid claim to the Kingdom of France against Philip IV's nephew, Philip of the House of Valois. With Edward's arrival on the continent in 1339, the Hundred Years War began. No more than a state of hostility that lasted until 1453, it was interrupted by campaigns and truces, and fortunes shifted dramatically from time to time. After Henry IV, the first Lancastrian, became king in 1399, he resumed preparations for war against France; his son and successor Henry V (1413-22) brought his plans to fruition with remarkable successes culminating in the defeat and capitulation of Charles VI, the 'Mad,' who accepted the humiliating Treaty of Troyes which through marriage conferred the succession upon Henry V. Charles VII (1422-61) withdrew to Bourges and ultimately led the French to victories over the English and the end of the War in 1453. For a good survey, E. Perroy, *The Hundred Years War*, trans. W. B. Wells (New York: Capricorn Books, 1965).

4. After the papal residence at Avignon (1307-1378), Gregory XI returned to Italy in 1378. With his death, the cardinals elected the imperious and ascetic Urban VI, who intimidated the French party by his threats and insults, and the French cardinals withdrew into friendly Naples to repudiate his election and elect Robert of Geneva as Clement VII. Thus began the Great Schism with two popes and Christian Europe divided into two obediences. Political self-interest was not an unusual condition of obedience. The French often supported the line of popes at Avignon; the English the Roman popes. Attempts to resolve the Schism in 1409 in the

Council of Pisa only led to a third line, the Pisan popes.
Finally, the emperor Sigismund of Germany used political coer-
cion to bring termporal and spiritual leaders together at the
Council of Constance in 1414. Its primary task was to restore
the unity of Christendom and to decree important reform measures.
With the election of Martin V in 1417, the Council completed its
work and adjourned in 1418. There is a good examination and analysis of the relevant sources and documents in W. Ullmann, *The
Origins of the Great Schism* (London: Burns Oates and Washbourne
Ltd., 1948); still useful too is L. Salembier, *The Great Schism
of the West* (London: Kegan Paul, Trench, Trubner and Co., Ltd.,
1907).

5. G. Duclos, *Histoire de Royaumont*, 2 vols., (Paris, 1867) I: 516,
    542-547. Curiously, the author criticizes Cupé for sacrificing
    France's national interests to a particular and ephemeral one;
    II: 15. The Duke of Bedford, John of Monmouth, was Henry V's
    brother and the Regent of France.

6. Duclos, II: 58.

7. J. Patourel, 'The King and Princes in 14th Century France,' in
    Europe in the Late Middle Ages, ed., by Hale, Highfield, Smalley,
    (Northwestern U. P., 1965) 163; also G. Hubrecht, 'Jurisdiction
    and Competence in Guyenne after its recovery by France,' in *The
    Recovery of France in the Fifteenth Century*, ed. by P. S. Lewis,
    New York, 1972) 85.

8. Peter de Luna was elected by the **cardinals** at Avignon in 1394 to
    succeed Clement VII. As Benedict XIII, he resisted all efforts
    to depose him or to persuade him to resign, and he exercized his
    prerogatives boldly, indifferent to the extent of his support,
    down to his death in 1422; G. **Pillemont**, *Pedro de Luna, le der-
    nier pape d'Avignon*, (Paris: Librairie Hachette, 1955); Salem-
    bier, *The Great Schism*, 258-356.

9. Eugenius IV requested Pierre de Comborn to come to Rome to re-
    solve the matter with Astorgius in a bull dated 18 January 1441;
    P. A. Verlaguet (ed.), *Cartulaire de l'Abbaye de Bonnecombe*, (Ro-
    dez, 1918), 196-201, *Gallia Christiana in provincias ecclesias-
    ticas distributa qua series et historia archiepiscoporum, epis-
    coporum et abbatum Franciae vicinarumque ditionum ab origine ec-
    clesiarum ad nostra tempora*, 16 vols. (Paris: Victor Palmé, 1856-
    99) I: 253-55; 1117. Hereafter cited *Gallia*.

10. Conciliarism was a movement in fourteenth and fifteenth century
    Christianity which called for regular councils to assist the pope
    in the reform of the Church. The Council of Constance called for
    frequent councils, at ten year intervals (the decree *Frequens*),
    and in *Haec sancta* maintained that even the pope must obey such
    authorized councils. Although the Council of **Basel** (1431-49) was
    convoked by Martin V in 1431, his successor Eugenius IV engaged
    in a protracted struggle to assert his primacy over it. In the

meantime, Charles VII of France summoned his clergy to Bourges
in 1438, and he adopted the major principles of conciliarism
upheld at Basel and promulgated them in the Pragmatic Sanction
of Bourges. Essentially they were aimed at restricting papal
prerogatives in the Gallican Church in the provision of benefices, taxation, appeals, and in the administrative jurisdiction of the popes over the French clergy, asserting the primary
responsibility of the king in the **temporal** affairs of the Church.
In short, the liberties of the Gallican Church were contained in
the Pragmatic Sanction and it became an issue between popes and
kings down to 1516, when the Concordat of Bologna superseded it.
The relevant historical developments of the fourteenth and fifteenth century conciliar movement are presented against the back-
drop of Vatican Council II by F. Oakley, *Council Over Pope?* (New
York: Herder and Herder, 1969) 33-101. For the Pragmatic Sanction, N. Valois, *Histoire de la Pragmatique Sanction de Bourges
sous Charles VII,* (Paris: Alphonse Picard et Fils, éditeurs,
1906).

11. J.-M. Canivez (ed.), *Statuta capitulorum generalium ordinis Cisterciensis,* 8 vols. (Louvain: Bureau de la Revue, 1934-41), 1441,
50. Hereafter I shall refer to this work as *Statuta* with specific
reference to statute by year and number.

12. *Statuta,* 1442, 93; 1445, 57.

13. The abbot of Ste Croix appears to be an ecclesiastical official
requested to exercize his jurisdiction in this monastic dispute
on behalf of the Order. There are several Benedictine abbeys in
the Pyrenean region of Aquitaine, and the records do not identify
'the abbot of Ste Croix' precisely; V. Chevalier, *Répertoire des
sources historiques du moyen age-topo-bibliographie,* 2 vols.
(Montbéliard: Société anonyme d'imprimerie Montbéliardaise)
2791-92.

14. *Gallia,* VI: 213; and E. Cauvet, *Etude historique sur Fonfroide*
[sic] *abbaye de l'Ordre de Citeaux,* (Montpellier, 1875) 555.

15. He is in the statutes of that year; 1454, 64.

16. The Chapter tried to avoid an embarrassing situation and appointed
a commission of three abbots to obtain the renunciation of the abbey by a monk duly elected under the supervision of the abbot of
Morimond; *Statuta,* 1445, 40.

17. Cauvet, 554.

18. *Statuta,* 1453, 34 and 73.

19. *Ibid.,* 1454, 76.

20. *Ibid.,* 1456, 77.

21. G. Dupont, *L'Abbaye du Val-Richer* (Caen, 1866) 138-9.

22. *Ibid.,* 157-8.

23. *Ibid.,* 162-4.

24. E. Burnier, *Histoire de l'abbaye de Tamie en Savoie,* (Chambèry,
1865) 58.

25. Anon., *L'Abbaye cistercienne de Tamié*, (Abbaye de Tamié, 1943)
     17.
26. Burnier, 58-9; the author has included relative documents among
     the *pièces justificatives* in the Appendix. For Pope Nicholas
     V's letter, see pièce 18, 258-60.
27. *Statuta*, 1451, 89.
28. *Ibid.*, 1472, 49.
29. Burnier, 60.
30. *Statuta*, 1473, 57.
31. Burnier, 61-62.
32. E. Laurière et al. (eds.) *Ordonnances des roys de France de la
     troisième race*, 21 vols. et Table (Paris, 1723-1849) XIII: 177.
     Also P. S. Lewis, *Later Medieval France--the Polity*,(New York,
     1968) 327.
33. L. Duval, *Cartulaire de l'abbaye royale de Nôtre-Dame des Châtel-
     liers* (Niort, 1972) lxxxviii-lxxxix, Introduction.
34. J.-B.-E. Carré, *Histoire du monastère de Nôtre-Dame d'Igny* (Reims,
     1884) 308.
35. He died on the journey to Rome in 1477; *Carré*, 290.
36. For the settlement between the French and the papacy and the Bur-
     gundian 'quasi-concordat,' see Lewis, *Polity*, 316.
37. On the devastation, A. Vandekerckhove, *Histoire de l'abbaye Cis-
     tercienne de Val-Dieu* (Bruges, 1939) 117.
38. Lewis, *Polity*, 327.
39. There is an excellent discussion of this technical question in
     G. Hubrecht (n. 7).
40. W. Telesca, 'The Cistercian Dilemma,' Ch. 9 in *Studies in Medi-
     eval Cistercian History* I, (Spencer, Mass., 1971) 174-5.
41. Lewis, *Polity*, 327.
42. *Statuta*, 1433, 39.
43. *Ibid.*, 1442, 15.
44. *Ibid.*, 1451, 60.
45. Vespasiano da Bisticci credits Pope Eugenius with using reform
     Observantists in his provisions; Vespasiano, *Renaissance Princes,
     Popes, and Prelates*, translated by W. George and E. Waters, (New
     York: Harper and Row, 1963) 20-22.
46. A. de Chalvet de Rochemonteix, *Histoire de l'abbaye de Feniers
     ou de Val-Honnète en Auvergne* (Clermont-Ferrand, 1882) 101-2;
     on his provision of same abbey, also J. Regne, *Abbaye de Mazan
     et des Chambons* (Ligugé, 1925) 29, n. 1; on the provision of
     Chambons.
47. Statuta, 1437: *Eugenii IV Concessio Angliae et Walliae Abbatibus*.
     The Order of Cîteaux exercized the privilege of 'excommunication'
     over its own members. It deposed and banished the victim and de-
     barred him from any functions or offices until he received abso-
     lution from the commissioned reformer or visitor, or from the
     father-immediate, or from the Chapters. Because the superior of

the exempt Order was the pope, it was not unusual at this time
for the excommunicates to have recourse directly to the Holy
See to receive absolution countermanding the Order's censure.
48. *Statuta,* 1438, 58.
49. C. Henriquez, (ed.), *Regula, constitutiones et privilegia Ordinis Cisterciensis: item congregationum monasticarum et mili-
tarium quae Cisterciense institutum observant,* (Antwerp, 1630),
LXXVIII, 120-1.
50. *Statuta,* 1441, 56.
51. *Ibid.,* 1445, 20.
52. *Ibid.,* 1442, 68.
53. *Ibid.,* 1450, 76.
54. *Ibid.,* 1454, 69.
55. *Ibid.,* 1460, 49.
56. *Ibid.,* 1460, 3.
57. *Ibid.,* 1461, 7.
58. *Ibid.,* 1462, 53.
59. *Ibid.,* 1464, 26.
60. *Ibid.,* 1466, 82.
61. *Ibid.,* 1469, 18.
62. *Ibid.,* 1470, 49.
63. *Ibid.,* 1450, 85.
64. *Ibid.,* 1453, 30.
65. *Ibid.,* 1454, 39.
66. *Ibid.,* 1461, 148. The Chapter attacked an unusual problem in
this statute. There were monks who claimed to be honorary chap-
lains of the pope, and in violation of stability traveled about
and avoided the Order's jurisdiction. Calling them dissolute
and vagabonds, the Chapter ordered all abbots to apprehend these
offenders and confine them.
67. *Ibid.,* 1449, 25. In 1443 the Chapter had also demanded of those
to be promoted to any rank an oath that they would not leave
their monasteries without permission, or seek dispensation from
the oath; 1443, 69. The intent, though a little different here,
still betrays the Order's inability to regulate the lives of the
monks in the historical atmosphere of the fifteenth century.
68. *Ibid.,* 1437, 49.
69. *Ibid.,* 1442, 72.
70. *Ibid.,* 1450, 51; 1452, 100; 1453, 91; 1454, 93.
71. *Ibid.,* 1451, 73.
72. *Ibid.,* 1469, 71.
73. *Ibid.,* 1448, 16.
74. *Ibid.,* 1453, 93.
75. *Ibid.,* 1460, 15. As early as 1445 the Chapter rebuked those
who attempted to place themselves above their co-abbots either
through secular intervention or because of their affluence, and
defined the rank of the abbots from the abbot of Cîteaux and the
four proto-abbots to abbots of Preuilly and Savigny and then

according to antiquity of their foundations; 1445, 23.

76. *Ibid.*, 1460, 20. In 1437 the Chapter rebuked those who 'trusted more the power of armed laymen'; 1437, 57.
77. *Ibid.*, 1460, 21.
78. *Ibid.*, 1437, 51; also 1445, 21; 1460, 24; 1461, 32 and 150.
79. *Ibid.*, 1445, 26.
80. *Ibid.*, 1458, 60.
81. *Ibid.*, 1439, 22.
82. *Ibid.*, 1443, 12.
83. *Ibid.*, 1446, 67.
84. *Ibid.*, 1452, 78.
85. *Ibid.*, 1457, 58; and still in 1458, 29. In 1466 the Chapter was still attempting to terminate the litigation set in motion by Cherlieu; 1466, 71.
86. *Ibid.*, 1466, 71. The statutes do not provide sufficient information to determine if the case of 1452 was still unresolved, or if the abbot himself was a litigious person.
87. *Ibid.*, 1462, 108.
88. *Ibid.*, 1449, 7; also 22 and 23.
89. *Ibid.*, 1438, 33.
90. *Ibid.*, 1466, 11.
91. *Ibid.*, 1446, 81.
92. *Ibid.*, 1452, 53.
93. Lewis, *Polity*, 325.
94. Lewis (ed.), *The Recovery of France in the Fifteenth Century*, (New York, 1972) p. 15 of Introduction.
95. McIlwain, *The Growth of Political Thought in the West* (New York, 1932) 346.

THE EXTENT OF CISTERCIAN LANDS
IN MEDIEVAL IRELAND

Colmcille S. O Combhui, OCSO

At the end of the middle ages there were in Ireland thirty-three houses of Cistercian monks. These houses were distributed over the four provinces, the great majority being in Leinster and Munster. On the eve of the dissolution of the monastic houses under Henry VIII there were Cistercian monasteries in twenty out of thirty-two counties and in twenty-two out of twenty-six dioceses. Many of these abbeys had lands in more than one county so that the landed possessions of the Order in Ireland were more extensive than the distribution of the abbeys would suggest. They extended, in fact, into twenty-eight of the thirty-two counties and comprised, at a moderate estimate, almost half a million acres of land.

Considerations of time and space make it impossible to give in this paper a detailed account of the process by which the lands held by each monastery on the eve of the dissolution have been not only identified but equated with specific lands on the modern ordnance map. In many cases these lands have changed their names more than once, while lands which formed single units in the sixteenth century have, by a process of subdivision, become groups of separate townlands all bearing distinct names. Hence it seems desirable that I should give here a more detailed explanation of the sources listed already. This will serve to illustrate the process by which it has been possible to show on the modern map the bulk of the lands held by the Cistercian Order in Ireland at the dissolution of the religious houses in the sixteenth century.

Although the great mass of Irish **Cistercian** documents, including monastic archives, cartularies, registers, liturgical books, account books, rentals, and others, has long since perished, a small number of manuscripts survive. These include two chartularies of St Mary's Abbey, Dublin, the Register of Dunbrody Abbey, Co. Wexford, and an *Ordinarium* from Monasterevan containing *inter alia* a copy of a charter granted to that abbey in 1289. A number of deeds and charters pertaining to the abbeys of Duiske, Jerpoint, Killenny, Holy Cross, Inishlounaght, and Owney are preserved among the Ormond Deeds in the National Library, Dublin, which also houses the Drogheda Papers containing original **charters** and deeds from Mellifont Abbey. A few **original** charters from other dissolved abbeys have survived, as well as copies of others, the originals of which have disappeared. The more important of the monastic deeds in the Ormond collection have been printed *in extenso* by Dr Newport White in his compact **volume** *Irish Monastic and Episcopal Deeds* while the chartularies of St Mary's Abbey, Dublin, with the annals of that house and the **register** of

Dunbrody, together with additional material which included the surveys made in 1540-1541 of the possessions of these two abbeys, have
been edited by John T. Gilbert (*The Chartularies of St Mary's Abbey,
Dublin*) in two volumes.[1]
    Some Irish Cistercian charters had been enrolled in the great
Charter Rolls of the kings of England. These are now preserved in
the Public Record Office, London, and abstracts or translations of
the more important ones have been published in the *Calendar of Charter Rolls* (five volumes) and the *Calendar of Patent Rolls* (England).
Others again have been preserved in whole or in part in copies transcribed into two great compilations known as *King's Collectanea* and
the *Harris Collectanea* which are lodged in the Library of Trinity
College, Dublin, (T.C.D.) and in the National Library of Ireland,
respectively. The T.C.D. *Collectanea* dates from the last quarter
of the seventeenth century while the Harris *Collectanea* dates from
the middle of the eighteenth century and incorporates in volume
thirteen of its nineteen folio volumes practically the whole of
the T.C.D. *Collectanea*. Other volumes, particularly volume fourteen also contain some scattered Cistercian material. It should
be noted that references to individual abbeys and to abbey lands
are met with in various medieval sources such as the *Patent and
Close Rolls* (English as well as Irish), the *Pipe Rolls*, the *Justi-
ciary Rolls*, the *Statute Rolls of Ireland*, and various other compilations.
    Our most important source for the landed property of the Irish
Cistercians at the time of the dissolution of the monasteries is,
of course, the series of surveys made in the period following the
dissolution, 1540-1541. These surveys were made by a commission
issued to Sir Anthony St Leger and others in 1540. Of the thirty-
three houses of men then in existence only twenty-one are mentioned in the published 'extents'. Even for those so listed all the
details are not given. For four of them (Abbeyshrule, Kilbeggan,
Monasteranenagh, and Monasterevin) no particulars at all are given,
while the figures for Abbeyleix are incomplete. This last abbey
did not, in fact, surrender until 1550, and we obtain a more correct estimate of its possessions from later grants of its properties and from four paper copies of inquisitions taken in 1550 and
1551, comprising in all eighteen sheets, part of the Ormond Deeds
now lodged in the National Library of Ireland. A note of the rents
of this abbey preserved in the same collection and dated May, 1636
gives additional information. For Abbeyshrule, too, we must rely
on grants made of the property at a later date as well as on inquisitions taken at various times. The Abbeylara extent published in
White's *Extents of Irish Monastic Possessions* is also very meagre,
and not until we consult the grant made by Queen Elizabeth I to
Sir Richard Nugent of the monastic possessions of this house do we
get any real details of their extent.

For all the foregoing abbeys as well as for others not dissolved until a later period, Mervyn Archdall supplies details in his
Monasticon Hibernicum. Archdall, who wrote in the eighteenth century, seems to have copied from the originals then extant in the office of the Auditor-General and Chief Remembrancer. The details
supplied by him are of great assistance in filling the gaps in Dr
White's volume on the monastic extents. The Public Record Office,
Dublin, contains a number of transcripts and calendars of Chancery
and Exchequer Inquisitions made by the Record Commissioners (1810-
1830). These inquisitions, particularly the exchequer ones, afford
quite an amount of information concerning monastic land, and cover
every county in Ireland. The transcripts of the Exchequer Inquisitions have never been published but they may be consulted at the
Public Record Office, and are far more informative and helpful concerning the extent of the monastic possessions at the time of the
dissolution of the monasteries than are the Chancery Inquisitions.
Two volumes of the latter have been published: those for Ulster and
Leinster. Those for Munster and Connacht were never printed and
all the originals perished in the destruction of the Four Courts
during the Civil War of 1922. However, two sets of manuscript Calendars are in existence, one in the P.R.O. Dublin and the other in
the Royal Irish Academy, and may be consulted by the student. There
is, therefore, no dearth of material for the study of the possessions
of the Irish Cistercians at the period of the dissolution of the monasteries in Ireland. The Patent Rolls have already been mentioned.
I should point out here that although the printed Calendars of Patent Rolls of Henry VIII, Edward VI, Philip and Mary, Elizabeth I,
and Charles I are more notable for what they omit than for what they
contain, nevertheless, in view of the fact that the originals have
for the most part utterly perished, they do provide us with a certain amount of information otherwise unobtainable. One set of Patent Rolls deserves special mention: those of James I contained a
mass of information relating to the dissolved abbeys, and included
abbeys which had not actually been dissolved until the conquest and
the plantation of Ulster in the early seventeenth century. They em-
body numerous inquisitions of monastic property and the grants themselves include detailed lists of lands under a variety of names and
spellings with an *alias* in cases where a particular parcel of land
had more than one name at any one time or at various times. Although
the originals have perished in the flames of Civil War, a *Calendar
of the Patent Rolls of James I* had been published before their destruction, and this calendar, though not at all perfect, is a veritable mine of information for the purpose of our study.
   Substitutes of various kinds for original records destroyed in
1922 or earlier may be found in abundance and include the *Ferguson
Collection* of transcripts of old exchequer records in the Public
Record Office of Ireland, the *Lodge Collection* of transcripts mainly

from Patent Rolls in the P.R.O. and the *Record Commissioners' Transcripts* which include the inquisitions already mentioned, as well as transcripts and calendars of ancient records from the time of Henry III onwards, especially patent rolls, plea rolls and memoranda rolls, all of which merit serious investigation. A certain number of the original Crown Patents which had been preserved in private hands for centuries, and include grants of monastic lands, has come with other material into the possession of the Irish Land Commission. Many of these patents are now lodged in the P.R.O. while others remain in the Records Branch of the Land Commission. The Records Branch of that Department contains a great mass of material including rentals, mortgages, fee farm and other grants, abstracts of title, leases, and various other deeds and papers relating to estates which originated in grants made by the Crown of the lands of dissolved religious houses. The **patent rolls** in particular give the names of the grantees who acquired possession of these lands together with the conditions on which they received their grants, the term of years for which they held the lands of the Crown, and the rents they paid to the Crown therefore. Most of the grantees continued to hold the lands thus acquired until the middle of the seventeenth century. At that period those of them who were Catholics lost their lands which under the Cromwellian and Restoration 'Settlements' passed into English Protestant hands. The documents connected with the Commonwealth, Restoration and Williamite governments during the period 1641-1703 are therefore of prime importance in tracing the subsequent history of many of the former monastic lands. They are also important--and indeed indispensable--for the satisfactory identification of the medieval lands and their equation with the denominations of the Cromwellian and post-Cromwellian eras as depicted on the Down Survey maps of the seventeenth century and the ordnance survey maps of modern times. Indeed the importance of the Cromwellian and post-Cromwellian material can scarcely be overestimated. Although much has been lost much still remains: what is left of the *Strafford Survey* of 1636, the *Civil Survey* of 1654, the *Down Survey* of 1655, and the fine series of records known as the *Books of Survey and Distribution* which in their original form must have been compiled during the period 1662-1688, and to which were added particulars relating to the forfeited estates of 1688 and the sales of the forfeited lands in 1703. The Books of Survey and Distribution comprise in all twenty volumes, cover every county in Ireland, and are based on the various surveys already mentioned as well as on a great number of official records of various kinds. Every parcel of land set forth therein bears a particular number which corresponds to the number attached to the same denomination on the map of the Down Survey. By a comparison of one with the other we can determine on the map exactly what particular parcel of land belonged to a particular proprietor, the number of acres of land

contained therein, the name of the original 'Irish Papist' proprietor who held the land in 1641 as well as that of the new Cromwellian
or Williamite grantee who supplanted him, and various other details
which need not be mentioned here.

The Civil Survey of 1654, on which the Books of Survey and Distribution as well as the Down Survey are in part based, gives us not
only the names of the proprietors of 1641 with their qualifications
('Irish Papist' or 'English Protestant'), but indicates also the
titles by which they held their lands, whether by descent from their
ancestors, by patent from the Crown, or by purchase. These particulars can often be extremely useful in affording a clue as to whether any particular parcel of land is confiscated monastic land or not.
Let me illustrate this by one example out of many: In volume One of
the Civil Survey we find on page sixty-four particulars relating to
the parish of Holycross in Co. Tipperary. 'The tythes of this parish,'
we are informed, 'are an intire rectory and impropriat conferred many
yeares past upon the Earle of Ormonds Ancestors by pattent from the
Crowne, as we are informed.' In all but one of the denominations named as part of this parish from page sixty-four to page sixty-six the
Earl is said to be the inheritor of the said lands by patent from the
Crown or by patent from the Crown conferred on his ancestors by way
of descent. The one exception to this is the denomination of 'Beakestowne and Ballycormock.' Here, then, is a clear case for investigation. Fortunately, we have not far to go to find the patent, which
is preserved among the Ormond Deeds in the National Library of Ireland. This patent grants to Thomas Butler, Earl of Ormond, the site,
ambit, and precinct of the late monastery of the Holy Cross in Co.
Tipperary, the lands of the said monastery in Holy Cross and else-
there, and the rectories, churches or chapels of Holy Cross, Bally-
cahill and Templebeg, with all tithes, oblations, alterages and ob-
ventions, etc., pertaining to the said rectories, churches or chapels.
On page sixty-six of the same volume of the Civil Survey the proprietor of 'Beakestowne and Ballycormock' is stated to be Theobald Purcell who held the lands in fee 'by descent from his Ancestors As we
are informed.' And rightly were the Commissioners so informed, for
the medieval *Red Book of Ormond* shows that these lands were held by
the Purcell family *in capite* of Edmund Butler as far back as 1308.
This was the Edmund Butler who in 1315 became Earl of Carrick and
whose son, James Butler, became first Earl of Ormond in 1328. The
tithes of the denomination of 'Beakestowne and Ballycormock' were
not, however, held by Theobald Purcell. The Civil Survey is our
evidence for the fact that these tithes, great and small, belonged
in 1640 to the impropriate rectory of Holy Cross, of which the Earl
of Ormond was proprietor 'conferred upon him by his ancestors by
patent from the Crown.' How the said tithes came to belong to Holy
Cross Abbey in the first instance may be read in Dr Newport White's
volume of Irish Monastic and Episcopal Deeds[2] which calendars two

deeds relating to their appropriation to Holy Cross abbey by Richard
(O Hedian), archbishop of **Cashel,** in the year 1430.

For this study use was made of composite maps of Counties Tipperary and Carlow which were the only two composite maps available
at that time. These maps were drawn for the Irish Manuscript Commission by Mr Robert Johnston under the direction of Dr Robert C.
Simington, the learned editor of the Civil Survey and of such of the
Books of Survey and Distribution as have been published. These maps,
representing the superimposition of the Down Survey of 1655-58 on
the original ordnance survey maps of 1839-43, show the respective
boundaries of territorial units, and contrast old and new place names.
Without the help of such composite maps or, failing that, a compre-
hensive study of the Down Survey, the Civil Survey, the Books of
Survey and Distribution, and the Ordnance Survey, this paper could
never have been written. For the purpose of my study all the sources
mentioned above had to be used and, in the case of areas not contained in the counties of Carlow and Tipperary, the boundaries of the
Down Survey maps had to be plotted on the Ordnance Survey maps. For
those two counties, of course, the composite maps already referred to
were available so that the labour involved was much less and the time
saved considerable. The Down Survey, carried out under the direction of Sir William Petty, was so called because the lands were plotted or laid *down* on paper by admeasurement. The Strafford Survey
which preceded both the Civil Survey and the Down Survey was also
based on the actual admeasurement of the lands surveyed but was by
no means as precise as the Down Survey, and only a few fragments now
survive of the maps so plotted. Petty's survey, a very thorough one,
was carried out in what was for those days a very scientific manner
so that Petty has been called with some justice 'the world's first
exact geographer.' The Civil Survey, on the other hand, was based
on estimates and was essentially a descriptive survey. It relied
on the sworn testimony of the native inhabitants of the areas surveyed, mostly the landowners of 1641 who were formed into juries
for that purpose. It recorded not only the **tenures,** Gaelic as well
as Norman, by which the lands were held, but gave detailed descriptions of the lands as well as an account of their amenities, and
it rendered phonetically into English of the period a great wealth
of place names. **Since** it is unlikely that the boundaries of denominations noted in the monastic extents of the sixteenth century had
undergone any significant change before 1641 it is probably safe to
say that in most cases the boundaries **noted** in the Civil Survey and
shown on the Down Survey maps, **which can be plotted on the modern** ordnance map with reasonable accuracy, represent the boundaries of the
same denominations as they existed at the time of the dissolution
of the religious houses. In this way it has been possible to ascer-
tain with reasonable certainty the bounds of many **if** not most of the
monastic lands.

At the end of the middle ages, then, there were in Ireland thirty-three houses of Cistercian monks. There had at one time been other houses in existence which had either died out or had been suppressed by the General Chapter and/or reduced to the status of granges. There had been at least two houses of nuns, neither of which seems to have survived until the dissolution of the monasteries. It would appear from references in the Register of Stephen de Lexinton, abbot of Stanley and later abbot in turn of Savigny and Clairvaux, that there had been numerous houses of nuns —or perhaps houses in which monks and nuns formed a joint community—in the early decades of the thirteenth century. But these houses had given rise to such abuses and scandals that the abbots were absolutely forbidden to receive any more nuns, while the nuns already established in or near houses of monks were banished to more distant locations.

Of the thirty-three abbeys which existed at the end of the middle ages thirteen were located in Leinster, twelve in Munster, six in Ulster and two in Connacht. Every county in Leinster but two had at least one Cistercian abbey. Counties Kilkenny, Longford, and Wexford had two each, while only Counties Carlow and Offaly had none. The lands belonging to those abbeys, on the other hand, were distributed over eleven of the twelve counties of that province, the county of Offaly being the only county in the whole province which had neither abbey nor land belonging to the Order.

In Munster five out of the six counties had Cistercian abbeys. Tipperary and Cork had four each, Limerick had two, and Clare and Kerry had one each. Waterford had no abbey. There had been one there in the early part of the thirteenth century which had been suppressed in the year 1228 by the General Chapter. The lands belonging to the suppressed abbey remained in the possession of the Order, which also held lands in the north of the county adjoining Tipperary. All these lands in Co. Waterford, with the exception of a small parcel containing about forty-eight acres, amounted in 1539 to approximately 5,000 acres and formed part of the possessions of the abbey of Inishlounaght in Co. Tipperary. The forty-eight acres forming the exception were the remnants of a more extensive estate held by Dunbrody Abbey, Co. Wexford, at an earlier period.

In Ulster there were six abbeys, four of which were located in Co. Down and one each in Counties Derry and Donegal. The landed possessions of these six abbeys extended beyond the boundaries of the counties just mentioned and included lands in Armagh, Antrim, and Fermanagh.

Although there were only two Cistercian abbeys in Connacht, their lands were very extensive and were distributed over the whole province. One of the reasons for this would appear to have been the inclusion of many monastic estates belonging to pre-Cistercian Irish communities, some of which had died out before the coming of

the Cistercians to Ireland. There is good reason to believe that
much of the land granted by Cathal Crobhdhearg, king of Connacht,
to the abbey of Knockmoy in Co. Galway was former monastic land;
and indeed there is some evidence that similar grants had been made
by other **provincial** kings or kings of Tuatha in various parts of
Ireland. I may mention in this connection that among the monasteries which received land of this kind were, besides Knockmoy,
those of Baltinglass, Jerpoint, Monasterevin, and Kilbeggan in
Leinster; Holy Cross, Kilcooly, Owney and Inishlounaght in Munster; Comber, Assaroe, Macosquin and Inch in Ulster; and Boyle and
Knockmoy in Connacht. Besides the lands held by the two last-named
abbeys in Connacht, one of the Munster houses (Corcumroe, Co. Clare)
and the important abbey of St Mary's outside Dublin also held lands
there, the combined acreage of the lands held by Dublin and Corcumroe amounting to close on 3,800 **acres**.
    I may sum up the distribution of the **Cistercian** lands in Ire-
land at the time of the dissolution of the monasteries province by
province and county by county as follows:

    In the province of Leinster the total area held by the Cister-
cians amounted to 188,541 statute acres distributed as follows:

Co. Carlow	7,157 acres	Co. Louth	23,360 acres
Co. Dublin	17,079 "	Co. Meath	25,759 "
Co. Kildare	16,284 "	Co. Westmeath	7,902 "
Co. Kilkenny	32,710 "	Co. Wexford	30,758 "
Co. Laois	11,056 "	Co. Wicklow	19,383 "
Co. Longford	8,093 "		

    In the province of Munster the total landed possessions of the
Order amounted to 103,528 statute acres, distributed as follows:

Co. Clare	5,367 acres	Co. Limerick	40,336 acres
Co. Cork	20,524 "	Co. Tipperary	28,438 "
Co. Kerry	3,693 "	Co. Waterford	5,170 "

    In the province of Ulster the total lands held by the Irish
Cistercians amounted to 60,538 statute acres distributed as follows:

Co. Antrim	1,018 acres	Co. Donegal	18,195 acres
Co. Armagh	6,208 "	Co. Down	32,992 "
Co. Derry	1,801 "	Co. Fermanagh	324 "

Scale of Miles

0   10   20   30   40   50

Finally, in the province of Connacht the landed possessions
of the Order amounted to 63,050 statute acres and were distributed
as follows:

Co. Galway	37,727 acres	Co. Leitrim	796 acres
Co. Mayo	790 "	Co. Roscommon	14,003 "
Co. Sligo	10,524 "		

This gives a grand total for the whole of Ireland of 426,665 statute
acres. We have not got full details of some of the possessions and
further research may reveal that the above figure is an underesti-
mation.

I should also mention that in this paper I have not taken into
account certain lands--admittedly not very extensive--held by some
English Cistercian houses in Ireland. I should also point out that
the figures given in this paper relate exclusively to the lands actually held by the Irish Cistercians at the time the monasteries
were dissolved. All the available evidence goes to show that many
of the monastic properties had been reduced by dilapidation and ali-
enation between the thirteenth and the sixteenth centuries, and in
the fifteenth century in particular. That the monastic estates as
a whole underwent a great development in the twelfth and thirteenth
centuries is shown by the available evidence. The ravages of war
and pestilence, however, had their effect on the Order and led in
many cases to the breakdown of discipline and the wasting of temporal possessions. In the course of time much land was alienated and
Mellifont itself was brought to the verge of ruin in the fifteenth
century not only by reason of the great extortions practised by the
nobility, who oppressed the tenants and vassals of the abbot and
convent and did not scruple to invade, unjustly occupy, depopulate,
devastate and lay waste the lands and possessions of the community,
but also by reason of the conduct of some of the abbots themselves,
who made grants of fees, annuities, rent charges, leases, and offices
to various people including their friends and relations for half
their value and sometimes indeed for nothing. Many of the houses
were in straitened circumstances in consequence of such dilapidation
of monastic property. Nevertheless, as the figures I have given
show, the amount of land held by the Order in Ireland on the eve of
the dissolution was still considerable. The dissolution of the
monasteries marked the end of an epoch. The fallen abbeys with their
vast landed possessions eventually found their way into the hands of the
king's favourites. Many of the leading Irish Catholic families--
Gaelic as well as Norman--shared in the monastic spoils; but ill-
gotten gains have a way of disappearing, and most of the families
thus enriched by the plunder of the monasteries lost not only the

abbey lands but, with them, their own hereditary possessions in the great confiscations of the following century.

Mainistir Mhellifont, Co. Lú

NOTES

1. *Chartularies of St Mary's Abbey Dublin with the Register of Its House at Dunbrody and Annals of Ireland.* Edited by John T. Gilbert, 2 vols. Published by the authority of the Lords Commissioners of Her Majesty's Treasury, under the direction of the Master of the Rolls (London, 1884).

2. *Irish Monastic and Episcopal Deeds A.D. 1200-1600.* Edited by Newport White (Dublin: Stationary Office, 1936) 22-23.

NICOLAS COTHERET AND HIS HISTORY
OF THE ABBOTS OF CITEAUX

Louis J. Lekai, O. Cist.

Few of the presently active scholars in the field of Cistercian history are familiar with the name of Nicolas Cotheret and
even fewer have a clear notion of the nature of his voluminous
work, the only monograph on the abbey of Cîteaux in existence. Although two copies of the manuscript had been acquired toward the
end of the nineteenth century by the Municipal Library of Dijon,[1]
they remained unread, gathering dust on the shelves for decades.

It happened only some forty years later that the emergence of
a third copy of the same manuscript drew the attention of a few
Trappist-Cistercian scholars. In 1935, through some intermediar-
ies, a Parisian bookseller offered the untitled bulky folio to Abbot Alexis Presse of Tamié, who promptly purchased it for 1,500.00
francs.[2] Dom Alexis' subsequent break with his Order and his efforts to revive the abbey of Boquen prevented him from the exploi-
tation of his new acquisition, but the volume passed through the
hands of J.-M. Canivez who, for the benefit of the scholarly public, inserted a few lines on Cotheret and his manuscript in the
thirteenth volume of the *Dictionnaire d'histoire et de géographie
ecclésiastiques*, published in 1956.[3] His alert confrère, Anselme
Dimier, did some further research into the matter and discovered
the two other copies in Dijon. He incorporated his new findings
into another short article on Cotheret in the *Dictionnaire de bio-
graphie française*,[4] where he repeated what he learned from Canivez,
including the erroneous date of 1738, for the writing of the book.

I made my first acquaintance with the Tamié manuscript a few
years later, while working on the history of the Cistercian Strict
Observance in the seventeenth century.[5] I found Cotheret's work
fascinating, although his knowledge of the topic of my interest
was restricted to the same pamphlets I had known for some time.
But the fact that Cotheret was the author of the only extant monograph on Cîteaux made me return to him a decade later. The few
pages below attempt to give a brief account of my preliminary research, although I plan to publish a selective edition of the work
itself in the near future.

The manuscript

According to the introduction of the Tamié manuscript, by a
much later hand, the history of Cotheret's work in question is
briefly the following:
The author began his study of the history of the abbey of

Cîteaux some time early in the 1710s, as archivist and librarian of the same monastery. Although on fol. 72^v of the manuscript the author mentions the year 1736, the exact date of its completion is unknown, for it ends only on fol. 582^v, i.e., on page 1165. Cotheret planned to add to the text a selection of documents; in fact, throughout the manuscript he made many references to it, the last being to p. CXXIII. This obviously substantial supplement, however, is missing from the Tamié manuscript, although a probably abbreviated version of it is attached to both Dijon manuscripts. This may indicate that the collection of sources remained incomplete, or was never fully handed over to the individual who became the possessor of the autograph some time shortly after the General Chapter of 1738.

The reason for the transfer of the original manuscript to an outsider was Cotheret's sharply critical attitude, throughout the whole work, toward most abbots of Cîteaux. He assumed, not without foundation, that if the manuscript were to be discovered, it would be immediately seized and destroyed by his abbot, Andoche Pernot (1727-1748). Cotheret therefore passed the autograph for safekeeping until further notice to his close friend, Dom Pothier, prior of the Cluniac abbey of Saint-Vivant. But Cotheret died first, whereupon Pothier donated the manuscript to his nephew, M. Belot le Cadet, a retired businessman, who appreciated and read the gift with great interest. The work was still in Belot's possession when his friend, Jean-Baptiste Faux, procurator of the parlement of Dijon, noticed the curious volume and asked permission to make a copy of it for his own personal use. The request was granted and the work executed by professional scribes. After the death of Belot, the autograph was inherited by his brother, Michel Belot who, unaware of the nature of the volume, wished to oblige the last abbot of Cîteaux before the Revolution, François Trouvé, and donated the manuscript to him. The abbot promptly had it destroyed in the good conscience that thereby he prevented the spread of a highly scandalous and very embarrassing work.

Fortunately, the faithful copy in the possession of M. Faux survived and, still before the Revolution, was inherited by his grandson, M. Lardillon, a member of the legal profession of Dijon. He, just as others, found the intimate disclosures about the once famous abbey irresistible and soon other copies began to circulate. This is how, perhaps among several others, the three extant copies of the manuscript came to being. The correlation of these surviving manuscripts is not entirely clear. It is certain, however, that the Dijon manuscript 2475 was produced on the basis of the other, Dijon manuscript 2474; that the former was completed in 1792, and that its copyist believed manuscript 2474 to be the first copy ordered by M. Faux. This last proposition is most unlikely, however. The Tamié manuscript, which was also in Lardillon's possession until

1812, does not seem to be related directly to either of the two
Dijon manuscripts, although it was produced at about the same time.[6]
    Eventually all three presently known manuscripts wound up in
the collection of the famous antiquarian of Burgundy, Louis-Bénigne
Baudot (1765-1844). His son, an equally famous archaeologist, Claude-
Louis-Henri, held together the great collection of rare books and manuscripts until his death in 1880. After this date the collection was
dispersed and the Cotheret manuscripts went into commercial circulation.
    Cotheret gave no title to his great work, although he referred
to it in the text as *mémoires* or *annales*. The two Dijon manuscripts
bear the title of *Mémoires pour servir à l'histoire de l'abbaye de
Cîteaux;* the Tamié manuscript is entitled simply *Annales de Cîteaux*.
    For purely practical purposes the most useful of the three is
the Tamié manuscript. It is a large leather-bound volume (23 x 35 cm)
with wide margins and easily readable script throughout, although the
quality of the last hundred pages is somewhat inferior.
    Both Dijon manuscripts are works of a number of professional
scribes and since their chosen format was much smaller than that of
the original, the lettering is diminutive, the lines are dense and
extended to the edges of the paper. Because of this, manuscript 2474
is condensed to 397 pages (19 x 26 cm); manuscript 2475 is even smaller (17 x 22 cm), although the text proper covers 675 pages in addition to many extraneous insertions, even illustrations. The reading
of manuscript 2475 is made particularly difficult by innumerable marginal notes and footnotes, often intruding between the lines of the
text itself. But the most vexing problem with both Dijon manuscripts
is that the spine of the bindings often covers the ends of the lines.
This defect in case of microfilm copies cannot be overcome.
    The text, except for punctuation, capitalization, accents and
varieties of spelling--as well as occasional human errors (omission
or duplication of words, lines and in a few cases even of paragraphs)
--is virtually identical in all three manuscripts. The same is true
of the documentary supplements attached to the two Dijon manuscripts.

The author

    Toward the end of the seventeenth century the Cotheret family
of merchants in Dijon was a large one. Among the baptismal records
of Dijon citizens during the period in question, carefully preserved
in the Municipal Archives, one may find several individuals bearing
the same name: Nicolas Cotheret. There is little doubt, however,
that the Cistercian author of our *Annales* is identical with the Nicolas Cotheret who was born on 7 February, 1680, and baptized on the
same evening at the collegiate church of Saint Stephen. He was the
child of the 'honorable Simon Cotheret, merchant of Dijon, and of
the honest Pierrette Pignalet, his wife.'[7] He must have joined the

abbey of Cîteaux at an early age, for a participant of the General Chapter of 1699, in listing all monks of the community, mentioned Nicolas Cotheret as the forty-eighth out of the total of seventy-two names.[8] Several of his early writings which have survived in manuscript[9] add after his name *docteur de Sorbonne*, but the legitimate use of this title is doubtful. Another list of the membership of Cîteaux in 1719, where he was named librarian and archivist, does not mention his academic degree, although other monks on the same list were clearly marked as doctors of theology.[10] Moreover, among the many lists of doctors of the University of Paris, his name cannot be found anywhere.[11] It is very likely, nevertheless, that he spent some years at the Cistercian College of Saint Bernard in Paris. He relates lengthily in his great work an incident which happened in 1702, involving a student of the same College, Jean Bouhier, a monk of La Ferté, his abbot, Claude Petit, and the abbot of Cîteaux, Nicolas Larcher. The question concerned the legitimate nature of the permission granted Bouhier by Larcher to complete his studies in Paris.[12] Cotheret could hardly have been so well informed about the episode of modest significance, had he not been Bouhier's fellow-student in the College.

If this is correct, Cotheret was recalled to Cîteaux, for some reason, before he could finish his studies, although by then he must have been an ordained priest. But his scholarly interest was rewarded by his appointment as librarian and archivist of the abbey, positions which he retained for over twenty years. This opportunity accorded him the time and facilities for research and writing dedicated to enriching the history of Cîteaux. His early works, all of them having remained in manuscript, include a critical analysis of a clandestine publication in 1714 by Richard Montaubon, secretary of the abbot of Clairvaux, who attacked Louis Meschet's collection of Cistercian privileges;[13] a short *Dissertation sur l'origine de la maison & ordre de Cisteaux* (1721);[14] remarks on a description of historical monuments of Cîteaux by Moreau de Mautour (1727);[15] and finally a short work known only by its title: *Abrégé historique et chronologique des révolutions arrivées à l'abbaye de Cîteaux depuis sa fondation*, which seems to have been a preview or summary of his great work on Cîteaux.[16]

Although we know nothing about his correspondence or contacts beyond the confines of his monastery, Cotheret's reputation as an expert in the history of his abbey was widely recognized. When a new edition of the *Gallia Christiana* was initiated in 1710, the Maurist editors turned to him for a reliable list of the abbots of Cîteaux.[17]

It soon became obvious, however, that his sharp criticism directed toward most abbots of Cîteaux rendered his position precarious. The issue came to a head in the early years of the administration of Andoche Pernot (1727-1748), who became the target of Cotheret's

merciless attacks. In anticipation of what was to happen, he smug-
gled his great work out to safety, and calmly faced the inevitable.
The irate abbot general obtained a *lettre de cachet* against his out-
spoken subject, who was taken to the abbey of Bonnevaux south of
Chartres, a place of exile where he ended both his scholarly career
and his life. There are indications that Cotheret had a much younger
brother at Cîteaux, who died soon after Nicolas' departure. His pre-
mature death at twenty-five was attributed by this witness to the de-
liberate neglect of his illness by the vengeful Abbot Pernot.[18]
     The exact date of the death of Nicolas Cotheret remains uncer-
tain. According to a note following the title page of manuscript
699 in the Municipal Library of Troyes, he ended his life in August
1799, aged seventy-three. The year is obviously mistaken, but if
his age is correct, he must have died in 1753.

Cotheret, the historian

     To a superficial reader the manuscript may seem disappointing,
particularly to those who would like to find new revelations concerning the first two centuries of Cîteaux's history. The author
himself apologizes for this shortcoming, which he blames on the
lack of documents resulting from the 'negligence of our predecessors.' What he knows about the circumstances of the beginnings
and the rest of the twelfth century is based mostly on the well-
known narrative sources or works of reference available to him.
His only surprising statement is that the *Privilegium Romanum* of
Paschal II was granted conditionally, i.e., as long as the monks
live up to their original rules and intentions (fols. 5^v-7^v). With
all its moralizing digressions, the history of the first hundred
years fills only twenty folios, while the author seems unsure even
of the number and sequence of the abbots.
     Whether for lack of documentation or his personal inclinations,
the author disclaims any intention of presenting a purely factual
narrative. Rather, as he assures us, 'we limit ourselves in this
short *mémoire* to giving a just and faithful account of the upheav-
als *(révolutions)* that afflicted this famous abbey. We shall make
particular efforts in demonstrating that since its foundation more
than six hundred years ago,...it was totally dedicated to accumulat-
ing wealth, without ever succeeding at it.' Since the basic ideals
of the founders, continues Cotheret, were the love of simplicity
and poverty, 'one should not wonder why has God prevented their
successors from achieving that goal.' Instead, as God's just punishment, the abbey's history is full of 'public calamities, bad administration, foolish undertakings, the luxury and vanity of their
abbots. [They] indulged in a life of comfort and leisure while,
as the most crying abuse, they created a reign of outrageous despotism, oppressive and absolute domination. [Furthermore, they

were guilty of] the inexperience, the daring presumptions and in-
fidelities of their officials; of a multitude of lawsuits of all
kinds, each more costly and embarrassing than the other.... These
are truths which we hope to render understandable by the subsequent recital of the most characteristic features of the history
of the common mother of this ancient and distinguished Order of
the Church throughout the centuries' (fol. 1^v).

The reader may rest assured that the author lives up to his
promises. His biased and limited vision of history cannot be contested, but his sincere piety and edifying intentions deserve re-
cognition. He dwells on the mistakes of the past so that a new
generation of monks, instructed by such lessons, might correct
them. Moreover, as he enters the fourteenth century, an increasing volume of sources facilitate a more and more profuse coverage
of his primary subject, the deeds and misdeeds of the abbots of
Cîteaux. Excepting only three abbots, he incriminates all others,
finding them guilty of some or all of the abuses above listed. The
exceptions are Jean de Cirey (1476-1501), Claude Vaussin (1645-
1670), and Jean Petit (1670-1692). The first, the only one without
blemish, deserves an accolade of over hundred pages (fols. 94^v-
147^v) largely for his courageous and eventually successful fight
against his competitor for power, Abbot Pierre de Virey (1471-
1496) of Clairvaux. Vaussin, covered at similar length, is praised for preventing a schism by subduing the Strict **Observance**, Petit is celebrated for his **tireless** efforts to keep within bounds the
ambitions and plots of his four jealous colleagues, the proto-abbots,
i.e. those of La Ferté, Pontigny, Clairvaux, and Morimond.

The focus of Cotheret's interest throughout his work remains
such external affairs of the abbey as the perennial feuding of the
abbots of Cîteaux with the proto-abbots; this alone may very well
account for half of the book. The author gives always revealing
details on the acquisitions and losses of property and the constant litigations over such matters. In particular, the intermin-
able feuding of Cîteaux with the Parisian Benedictine abbey of
Saint-Germain-des-Prés over the possession of Gilly amounts to a
veritable monograph. Less justifiable is the author's attention
to the chronic bickering between the abbey and the bailiff of Dijon over the latter's preposterous claim to the role of Cîteaux's
'guardian' during abbatial vacancies and during sessions of the
General Chapter.

In vain does the reader search for details of the community's
interior life. Yet isolated insights can often be found on occasions of recent abbatial elections, when at least the exact numbers of professed members are given and when the author sketches
the characters of the abbots and their relations with their monks.

When documents are lacking, the author borrows extensively
from printed sources. This is the case in his presentation of the

background and nature of the bull *Parvus fons (Clementina)* of 1265, taken over entirely from the first edition of the *Nomasticon Cisterciense* (1664) of Julien Paris. Cîteaux's relation with Benedictine abbeys, including Saint-Benigne and Saint-Germain-des-Prés, is related according to the works of Maurist historians available at Cotheret's time. When he finds documents in his own archives, the author likes to quote them at great length verbatim, even though the relevance of many of them to his subject is only marginal. As may be expected, he covers the long feud between the Common and Strict Observances with ardent partisanship in favor of the first, but his sources do not go beyond pamphlets published by the Common Observance. He relates the tours of visitation of Vaussin in German lands, and later his trip to Rome, in great detail on the basis of the travelogue composed by one of his companions. Since this source deals only with external events, Cotheret relates nothing about the nature of the crucial negotiations in Rome in the 1660s.

From the administration of Nicolas Larcher (1692-1712) to the end of his narrative in 1728, Cotheret relies mostly on his personal experiences and recollections. This last section of the manuscript (fols. 472-582) abounds in hitherto unknown details of great interest and it is here that the author exhibits the best and worst traits of his character. His keen observations, obvious piety, and dedication to his community, his sense for right and justice, are often clouded by his choleric temper, pessimistic forebodings and his habitual suspicion and distrust directed against any and all office-holders.

On the last few pages of his manuscript, as a corollary, Cotheret summarizes his final judgment on the past, present, and future of Cîteaux, which he finds on all counts most discouraging. One must admit, however, that much of his criticism bears the marks of honesty and truth.

As he saw it, the administration of Andoche Pernot, who had just been received amidst great pomp and display as 'born' councilor in the parlement of Dijon, heralded the beginning of the end for Cîteaux, although Cotheret added: 'May God in his infinite mercy postpone the final revolution of things and the total destruction of the house of Cîteaux, on which the existence of this great Order depends' (fol. 580^V). As to the past, he was convinced that its history had been basically the story of how a great abbey had been victimized by a succession of inept or corrupt abbots, guilty of 'ambition, cupidity, inexperience, despotism, and caprice,' who were running merely after 'honors and prerogatives attached to their dignity.' Preoccupied by their selfish pursuits of pleasure and leisure, they criminally neglected 'the true interest of their monastery and the happiness of their confrères' (fol. 581^V).

Moreover, as he points out, there are no means left for the unfortunate monks of Cîteaux to remedy their desperate situation. In

other abbeys just grievances can be effectively dealt with through
the services of provincial vicars, regular visitors, 'fathers immediate,' or, as a last resort, through the intervention of the
General Chapter. But to whom should the hapless monks of Cîteaux
turn? There is no effective power above the abbot general. The
rare visitations of Cîteaux are perfunctory formalities, and since
the abbot of Cîteaux presides over the General Chapter, who would
dare to turn against him?

Neither is there any comfort in the fact that the monks can
choose their own abbots without any evidence of heavy external
pressure. As is clear from Cotheret's accounts, many elections
resulted in near-unanimity and the abbots-elect often had the deserved reputation for ability, dedication to duty, and even affa-
bility and impeccable morals. Alas, the taste of absolute power
turned the heads of nearly all of them. They underwent an amazing
change of character, becoming tyrants instead of loving fathers to
their monks (fols. 566ᵛ-569ᵛ). Thus, as a final conclusion, Cotheret clearly anticipated Lord Acton's famous dictum: 'Power tends
to corrupt, and absolute power corrupts absolutely.'

*   *   *

The abbots of Cîteaux from 1405 to 1727 according to Cotheret.

The sole reason for beginning the list with the forty-first
abbot in 1405 is that he came at the end of the critical list of
the abbots of Cîteaux by Canon Jean Marilier.[19] There are, of
course, a number of similar works both in manuscript and in print,
but until Marilier's critical review, the often faulty data of *Gallia Christiana* prevailed.

41. Jean de Martigny (1405-21 December 1428), as many of his
predecessors, was involved in a feud with the abbot of Clairvaux,
Matthieu Pillard (1405-1428), over a composition written by the
latter: *Speculum elevationis et exaltationis Ordinis Cisterciensis et etiam finalis depressionis et enervationis eiusdem,*[20] which
Cotheret obviously had in his possession. Statements in the manuscript asserting that early in the Order's history all abbots were
equal, that they were under diocesan jurisdiction, and that the
General Chapter had no legislative powers, aroused Cotheret's ire,
prompting him to go into lengthy refutations. Martigny was dele-
gated by the General Chapter to sit in the Council of Pisa (1409),
and subsequently in the Council of Constance (1414). The archives
of Cîteaux held a number of documents on both, and Cotheret noted
with pride that the abbot's name was close to the top of the signa-
tories. In 1423, he was forced to defend the tax exemption of the
Order. In fact, in 1427, Cîteaux attempted to reduce the taxes
due for the holding of Gilly (fols. 72ᵛ-78ʳ).

42. Jean Picart (1429 - 30 March 1440) was elected after the
first serious clash between the monks and the bailiff of Dijon, who,
under the pretext of guardianship, attempted to manage the abbey
during the vacancy. Picart participated in the sessions of the Council of Basel (1435-) in multiple capacities: representing his Order, the bishop of Châlon, Duke Philip the Good of Burgundy and the
University of Paris. Cotheret followed his important role from the
records of this council in his possession. The abbot created a great
impression by his opulence; he even imported great quantities of bur-
gundian wine for the pleasure of those he favored with such gifts. In
1427, faced with the dilemma of staying in Basel or moving to Ferrara,
Picart extricated himself by claiming that his duties called him back
to Cîteaux. It was the General Chapter of 1437 that abolished the
reception of communion under both species, prohibiting it even to
the celebrant's assistants. In 1438, on his way to Dijon, Picart
fell into the hands of robbers, who not only took all the valuables
he carried, but also held him and his entourage for ransom (fol. 85^v).

43. Jean Vion (1440-25 November 1458) like his predecessor, was
forced into litigation with the Dijon authorities over the right of
guardianship. The lawsuit against Saint-Germain-des-Prés over the
rent to be paid for holding Gilly continued with renewed vigor throughout his administration. Moreover, the new abbot increased the extent
of land surrounding Gilly by new purchases. Because he did not have
the cash of 4,125 livres tournois, he sold a quantity of gold and sil-
ver objects belonging to Cîteaux. Since the bailiff of Dijon extended
his guardianship over Cîteaux to the duration of the annual Chapters,
the General Chapter of 1455 decided to hold the next session in Clairvaux. The move, however, did not take place, for Duke Philip the Good
issued on 28 July 1456, a regulation which greatly curbed the ambition
of the domineering bailiff (fol. 90^v).

44. Gui d'Autun (1458 - 22 July 1462) originally a monk of Fon-
tenet and later abbot of Chaalis, received only three pages in Cotheret's narrative (fols. 90^v-91^v). He managed to thwart the ambitions of
Jean Joffroi, bishop of Autun, who obtained papal authorization for
the visitation of Cistercian abbeys. The perrennial lawsuit against
Saint-Germain-des-Prés continued, for the Benedictine monks demanded
at this time no less than 6,000 livres, accumulated by the non-payment
of rents previously due.

45. Himbert Martin (1462 - 24 March 1476), a native of Saint-
Jean-de-Losne, received much attention in the MS (fols. 91^v-100^r), not
only for his fight in Rome against the *commenda*, but also because the
narrative incorporated the career of his successor, Cotheret's favor-
ite abbot, Jean de Cirey. Abbot Martin, too, was much preoccupied
with the affairs of Gilly, but without lasting success. A peculiar
indicent forced him to intervene at La Ferté, when in 1470 the monks
decided to postulate as their new abbot a Benedictine, Jean de Toulouse. The indignant Martin deprived the monks of their right to

choose their abbot and appointed to the vacant post the abbot of
Rigny, Claude de Dinteville. The action was approved by the subse-
quent General Chapter. During the war between King Louis XI and
Duke Charles the Bold of Burgundy, both parties made gestures of
good will toward Cîteaux. The king imposed upon Saint-Germain-des-
Prés a settlement favoring Cîteaux; in 1472, Duke Charles donated
to the abbey his 'chateau' in Saint-Jean-de-Losne. In 1473, the
General Chapter authorized Abbot Martin to lead a delegation to
Rome in order to obtain from Sixtus IV guarantees against the spreading *commenda*. Jean de Cirey, then abbot of Theuley and shortly af-
terward that of Balerne, became a member of the delegation. From
this point on Cotheret used Cirey's *mémoires* for the narration of
the principal events of Cîteaux until the beginning of the sixteenth
century.[21] The delegation, in spite of great expenses and lavish
gifts, remained fruitless. Meanwhile Abbot Martin became mortally
ill. He died in Rome and was buried in the basilica of Saint Sebas-
tian, then in Cistercian possession. At this moment of frustration
and tragedy, the perfidious Cistercian procurator general in Rome,
the Spaniard Dom Falco, abbot of Saint Bernard in Valencia, took
possession of everything belonging to the deceased abbot, including
money, jewelry, and his official seal. He shared the spoils with
the dead abbot's secretary and almoner who, according to Cotheret,
worked all along with the traitorous procurator general against the
very purpose of the delegation. Because of this and the extrava-
gant expenditures in Rome, Cîteaux was financially ruined.

46. Jean de Cirey (April 1476-resigned 20 November 1501; d. 27
December 1503) the 'ideal' abbot, whose story Cotheret extended to
epic proportions (fols. 100^r-152^r). After the death of his predecessor,
Cirey was ready to return at once to his abbey of Balerne, but Sixtus
IV was so impressed by his performance as a member of the Cistercian
delegation that he decided then and there to grant Cîteaux to him by
special papal provision. Cirey humbly declined the honor and suggested that the same favor be extended to Pierre de Virey, abbot of
Clairvaux (1471-1496). The pope promptly complied and Cirey himself
carried the bull of Virey's promotion to France, unsuspecting that
his selfless generosity might turn out to be a fatal mistake. As
soon as the monks of Citeaux were notified of their abbot's death,
they unanimously elected as his successor none else than Jean de
Cirey. Upon his arrival, Cirey presented the bull to Virey and
was ready to repudiate the will of the community of Cîteaux. The
pressure on him, however, grew to be irresistible and finally the
reluctant Cirey complied with the wishes of the monks of Cîteaux.
The revocation of the papal provision for Virey and a new bull for
himself posed serious problems. Although eventually successful,
Cirey had to pay dearly for his promotion; the lifelong hatred and
scheming of his jealous competitor, the abbot of Clairvaux, cast
dark shadows over his whole administration.

It is impossible to summarize in a few words the hundred pages
of Cotheret's admiring account of Cirey's years in his high position.
It should suffice to state that in 1499 he finally settled the inter-
minable lawsuit with the Parisian Benedictines over the possession
and incorporation of Gilly. He was prepared for the fall of Charles
the Bold, and by promptly siding with Louis XI he saved his house
from serious damage and established his reputation at the royal court.
The losses of Cîteaux were, however, considerable in Beaune, Dole,
and Besançon. He participated with decisive results in the assembly
of the French clergy at Orléans in 1478 and took an active part in
the sessions of the estates of Burgundy. After the death of Louis
XI, his son and successor, Charles VIII (1483-1498), shared his father's high regard for Jean de Cirey and consulted him repeatedly in
matters of state and church.
     Cirey's greatest cross throughout his whole administration re-
mained Pierre de Virey. The latter accused him of misconduct, mis-
appropriation of money, even of heresy, using for proof forged documents. Although condemned by the General Chapter of 1482, the abbot
of Clairvaux never admitted defeat. He turned with his fabricated
charges from one court to another, and although he could never suc-
ceed, he gave up only after his abdication and retirement in 1496.
In 1488, Cirey traveled to Rome, where he remained until the spring
of 1489. Innocent VIII received him cordially and granted to him a
number of audiences as well as many privileges, among them the right
to confer the subdiaconate and diconate on his subjects. In order to
terminate the feuds between Cîteaux and Clairvaux, the pope ordered
the unification of the two abbeys, but this bull was never executed.
The chief purpose of Cirey's mission, however--papal protection
against the spreading *commenda*--remained elusive in spite of the
pope's encouraging good will.
     Cirey participated in a convention of religious leaders in
France initiated by Charles VIII, and held at Tours late in 1493.
Doing his best to implement the resolutions of this session within
his Order, he called together forty-four prominent Cistercians at
the Parisian College of Saint Bernard early in 1494. The fruits of
this assembly were the sixteen *Articuli Parisienses*, approved by the
subsequent General Chapter.[22]
     Worn out by continuous labors, Cirey resigned on 20 November
1501, and died two years later. Even if we take Cotheret's acco-
lade--'one of the greatest men and the worthiest abbots Cîteaux has
ever had'--with some reservation, we must admit he was certainly a
deeply dedicated, hard-working and talented administrator as well
as an accomplished scholar. Ultimate success was denied to him,
but he had no control either over the corrupt papal administration
or over the inevitably spreading *commenda* in France.
     47. Jacques Theulley de Pontallier (1501-resigned 25 October
1516, d. 1 November 1516) a nephew of his predecessor, was a doctor

of the Sorbonne and abbot in succession of Cherlieu, Bellevaux,
and Morimond (1494-1501). Cotheret tells us that he was both un-
grateful to and unworthy of his predecessor, but he still admits
that he built and completed in 1509 the new library of Cîteaux,
that he was the first abbot of Cîteaux who became a 'born' council-
lor of the parlement of Dijon; and that in 1512 he was invited to
sit in the Fifth Lateran Council, although he left Rome after the
first sessions. Responding to the demands of the same Council, Abbot Jacques dealt with the issues of reform at the General Chapter
of 1515. In the next year, however, after having insured himself
a rich pension, he resigned, blaming his infirmities. He enjoyed
his retirement for only five days (fol. 158^v).

    48. Blaise Larget d'Aiserey (1516-10 September 1517) was at his
election bachelor of theology and provisor of the College of Saint
Bernard in Paris, but he served as abbot of Cîteaux for less than
a year. He died in Paris in his forty-third year of age (fol. 161^v).

    49. Guillaume de Boisset (16 September 1517-25 April 1521) pre-
viously abbot of Candeil, in fear of the appointment of a commendatory abbot, was elected in such a haste that five professed monks
of Cîteaux, students at the Parisian College of Saint Bernard, were
unable to arrive by the appointed date. After much consideration,
Boisset accepted his new position, without, however, giving up his
title at Candeil. Cotheret could not relate anything notable during his short administration. He died at Brioude (Haute-Loire) on
25 April 1521 (fol. 166^r).

    50. Guillaume de Faucolnier (29 April 1521 - 26 March 1540)
was a native and monk of Mortemer, later abbot of Miroir. Cotheret
dismisses the reliability of some documents attesting to a visit of
King Francis I at Cîteaux shortly after the new abbot's election.
In 1532, under pressure from Admiral Philippe Chabot, the governor
of Burgundy, Faucolnier was forced to lease him Toutenant, an ancient grange of Cîteaux, for the paltry annual rent of 400 livres.
On the other hand, the abbot acquired a valuable vineyard near
Cîteaux. In 1533, the remains of Saint Alberic, Saint Stephen, and
other holy founders, were transferred from the cemetery and, placed
in nine cases, laid to rest under an altar of the western transept
of the church, which was called thenceforth the altar of Saint Stephen (fol. 168^r).

    51. Jean Loysier (30 March 1540-26 December 1559) a native of
Seurre (Côte-d'Or), a monk of Cîteaux and doctor of the Sorbonne,
was elected in great haste, for it was rumored that the king was
about to appoint a new abbot. But Francis I not only recognized
the new election, but offered his help against the abusive presence
of hosts of minor officials at Dijon who, under the pretext of protection, had ensconced themselves at Cîteaux for the previous two
years. The new abbot, in token of his gratitude, ordered a gigantic
bell for Cîteaux and named it Françoise. In 1555, Abbot Jean con-

structed a small château at Vougeot, center of the famous Cistercian vineyards. The monks of Cîteaux, however, did not appreciate his making expenditures, while they had to suffer privations. In fact, they turned to the royal court with their grievances against their abbot, who died shortly thereafter in his new château at Vougeot (fol. 173ʳ).

52. Louis de Baissey (6 January 1560-19 June 1564) of noble origin and already abbot of Maizières, went personally to Rome to pick up his bull of papal approval of his election. He participated in some of the sessions of the Council of Trent, and obtained a bull which prevented the Spanish Cistercians from exempting themselves from his jurisdiction. While he was abroad, the monks of Cîteaux were exposed to new vexations over the proprietorship and taxes due for Toutenant. Abbot Louis died in the Piedmontese Cistercian nunnery of Pogliola, on his way back to Cîteaux (fol. 175ᵛ).

53. Jérôme de la Souchière (1 July 1565 - 10 Nov. 1571), was elected only a year after the death of his predecessor, for the royal treasury demanded a year's income from the abbey before permission for new election was granted. Souchière was a monk of Montpeyroux (Auvergne) and later abbot of Clairvaux (1552-1571), and in this latter capacity he participated in the sessions of the Council of Trent. Early in his administration he managed to recover the grange of Toutenant. In 1569 he obtained the cardinal's hat, together with the papal permission to retain Clairvaux while he served as abbot of Cîteaux. He successfully prevented the suppression of the abbey of Vaucelles by Philip II of Spain, who wished to unite its goods with those of the archbishopric of Cambrai. Cotheret reports resentfully that the worthy prelate had never set up his residence at Cîteaux and called himself 'Cardinal of Clairvaux.' He died in Rome only six years after his election (fol. 178ᵛ).

54. Nicolas I Boucherat (12 December 1571-resigned in 1583, d. 12 March 1586), doctor of theology, prior of Reclus (Champagne), was serving as procurator general in Rome at the time of his election, and had previously participated in the Council of Trent. For the great consternation of the monks, he was subsequently recognized as abbot of Cîteaux by Pope Pius V, but not as 'elected,' but as 'appointed' by the pontiff. The pope defended his action by saying that he did so in order to prevent the king of France, Charles IX, from converting the abbey into a *commenda*. The resentful king refused to recognize Boucherat's new position and appointed an administrator over the goods of the abbey. It was only in 1572 that, upon the request of the monks, he relented and recognized Boucherat as 'elected' abbot of Cîteaux. Abbot Nicolas made great efforts to reduce the indebted condition of his monastery, but foreign invasion of Burgundy, following the 'St Bartholomew Day Massacre,' created a new and dangerous crisis. In 1576, it was only after the payment of 3,000 écus that Jean Casimir, count palatine of the Rhine and duke of

Bavaria, was willing to spare Cîteaux, Gilly, and Vougeot. In 1578
Boucherat obtained from King Henry III the privilege of serving as
'born' councilor of the parliment of Dijon, not as a personal favor, but as an honor tied in perpetuity to the abbacy of Cîteaux.
In the same year Boucherat represented the estates of Burgundy before the king at Rouen and delivered on the occasion an eloquent
speech. The abbot incurred the sharp displeasure of Cotheret for
having spent 11,400 livres for a new high altar, featuring brass
statues and columns twenty-five feet in height, and particularly
for erecting a burial place for himself, displaying his own life-
size statue, at additional expense. Cotheret's indignation is understandable, for this altar was completely demolished and the brass
carted away in the disaster of 1589. Toward the end of 1583 Boucherat resigned, after having insured for himself an annual pension of
1,200 écus and having set aside a sum for anniversary masses for the
salvation of his soul; additional reasons for bad marks from Cotheret (fol. 202^v).

     55. Edmond de la Croix (13 June 1584-21 August 1604) a native
of Troyes, monk of Clairvaux and doctor of theology, was serving at
his election as abbot of Châtillon in the diocese of Verdun, although by papal provision he also bore the title of abbot of Pontigny, which he was permitted to hold for two years after his election
at Cîteaux. The first decade of the new abbot's administration was
overshadowed by the tragic flare-up of the civil war. In 1588 the
Duc de Guise was assassinated by order of Henry III, and in turn the
king fell victim of a similar attack. Cîteaux sided with the Catholic League, but for the same reason the royalist Count of Tavannes
fell upon the monks on 17 October 1578, and systematically pillaged
the abbey for a week. What his soldiers could not take away, they
destroyed. Whatever still remained in Gilly, Miroir, and other possessions of the abbey was sacked by the army of Marshal Biron in
in 1595. Meanwhile, in 1592, the monks of Signy, previously under
commendatory rule, elected as their abbot Edmond de la Croix who,
perhaps in order to have a wider economic basis for the reconstruction of Cîteaux, accepted the new responsibility. Attempts for col-
lecting funds in behalf of Cîteaux either by the papacy or by the
officials of the League proved to be largely fruitless. A delegation sent to Henry IV by the convent of Cîteaux in order to vow fidelity to him, remained equally futile. Finally, in order to provide for funds, Abbot Edmond resorted to the sale of the goods of
Cîteaux, among them those in Beaune, for which he incurred the wrath
of Cotheret. In 1599, Henry IV authorized special collections in
behalf of Cîteaux. Since the whole country suffered under the universal devastation, however, no substantial sums were netted.

     In 1600, Abbot Edmond requested a coadjutor, whereupon the con-
vent of Cîteaux elected Nicolas Boucherat, abbot of Vaucelles, professed monk of Cîteaux, doctor of theology and former prior of

Cîteaux. In 1601, Edmond de la Croix held the only General Chapter
he was able to organize. It authorized the abbot of Cîteaux, after
a previously granted privilege by Innocent VIII, to wear pontifical
garments even when not engaged in liturgical functions, another decision severely condemned by Cotheret. In 1603, Abbot Edmond undertook a tour of visitation in Spain. It was in Barcelona that he
died in the summer of 1604. He was buried in the great Cistercian
abbey of Poblet (fol. 240r).
     56. Nicolas II Boucherat (1604 - 3 May, 1625), already coad-
jutor, took possession of Cîteaux without new election. The General
Chapter he held in 1605 made serious efforts to recover the goods
alienated during the emergencies of the previous administration. For
this project money was needed. A circular launched by the proto-
abbots in 1606 urged all French abbeys to contribute, but, as usual,
the results were meager. The same remedy was urged by the Chapter
of 1609. It was on this same occasion that there was discussed the
future of the abbey of Bellebranche, which the Jesuits tried to ac-
quire in order to broaden the financial basis of their new college
at La Flèche. As a compensation they proposed that Cîteaux incor-
porate the abbey of La Bussière. Henry IV was in favor of the proposition, but Rome and Cîteaux resisted, whereupon only the abbot's
revenue of Bellebranche was granted to the Jesuits, while, instead
of La Bussière, Cîteaux incorporated the small, poor, and depopulated
abbey of La Miroire, which in 1618 housed only five monks. Shortly
after this incident Boucherat undertook a long tour of visitation
in Germany at the expense of about 5,000 livres. The restoration of
Gilly evoked the censorious comment of Cotheret, for that house, a
former priory, was in fact converted to a summer residence for the
abbots of Cîteaux.
     Meanwhile, Abbot Denis Largentier of Clairvaux supported a
movement of disciplinary reform which had already been embraced by
several of his daughter-houses. The General Chapter of 1618 praised
Largentier's reforming efforts, but for the sake of uniformity ordered that total abstinence (the main issue of the reform) be en-
forced throughout the whole Order only from 14 September to Easter.
In 1622 the ominous appointment by Gregory XV of Cardinal de La
Rochefoucauld as visitor and reformer of monastic orders in
France opened an era of unprecedented turmoil. In 1623 the cardinal issued an *ordonnance* which called for the formation of a new
autonomous reform-congregation headed by Clairvaux. The General
Chapter of the same year sharply contested the legality of the move,
although Boucherat **privately** assured the cardinal that his wishes
would be carried out. At the same Chapter Boucherat agreed that he
would in the future visit the houses of the proto-abbots only in
the company of two of the abbots concerned. This concession turned
out to be an issue of constant feuding for a century. In the same
year of 1623 Boucherat asked his community for a coadjutor. The

unanimous choice of the monks fell on the young Nicolas le Goux de
la Berchère. Since, however, the required formalities had not been
observed, the validity of the act was not recognized by higher authorities. Abbot Boucherat died at Dijon in his sixty-third year
of age (fol. 259ʳ).

57. Pierre Nivelle (4 July 1625-resigned in November 1635; d.
11 February 1660), abbot of Saint-Sulpice and doctor of theology, was
elected by thirty-five votes against ten, after a stormy electoral
campaign in which both the coadjutor and the young nephew of Nicolas
Boucherat, Abbot Charles Boucherat of Pontigny, then only twenty-
six years old, were running for the high office. Nivelle had impressive credentials: he had already served as assistant to the
procurator general in Rome; as prior of Cîteaux; as provisor of the
College of Saint Bernard in Paris for nine years, during which he
also acted as vicar general. According to Cotheret, however, Nivelle's election was a total failure. He lacked the strength of
character to withstand the pressure exerted in behalf of the Strict
Observance ('abstinents') by La Rochefoucauld and later by Richelieu.
After a decade of inglorious blundering he was pushed aside by Richelieu, who claimed the abbey of Cîteaux for himself. Nivelle, for
stepping aside, was rewarded by the episcopal see of Luçon. The formal contract to this effect was signed on 14 February 1637 (fol.
310ᵛ).

58. Armand-Jean du Plessis, Cardinal de Richelieu (19 November
1635-4 December 1642) could only be 'postulated' by the unanimous
vote of the intimidated monks, for he was not a member of the Order.
The cardinal, however, although he always behaved as the legitimate
ruler of the Order in France, never received the required papal consent, for reasons Cotheret enumerated at great length. Invoking the
principles of the reform, Richelieu ousted the old community of Cîteaux and gave the abbey over to a handful of young 'abstinent' monks.
By similarly violent methods he 'reformed' another twenty-five houses,
so that by the end of his administration the Strict Observance had
tripled its membership. Unfortunately the internal convulsions coincided with still another sack of Cîteaux, this time by the imperial
army under Matthias Gallas, during the month of October 1636 (fol.
314ᵛ).

59. Claude Vaussin (10 May 1645-1 February 1670) could secure
his election only after two years of bitter legal fights against the
'abstinents,' who were greatly reluctant to yield to a member of the
Common Observance. Finally, out of fifty-three electoral votes Vaussin received thirty-seven, while the candidate of the Strict Observance, Abbot Jean Jouaud of Prières, was supported only by the sixteen young 'abstinents' of Cîteaux. Vaussin was originally a professed member of Clairvaux (1623), obtained the doctor's degree in
Paris (1636) and at the time of his election was prior of Froidmont
and only thirty-eight years old. He proved himself to be a talented,

skillfull, and hard-working fighter for the cause of the Common Observance. To Cotheret's great satisfaction, after twenty years of
ceaseless labors, he curbed the limitless ambitions of the Strict
Observance and forced the reform to submit to the authority of the
abbot general. The instrument of his victory was the papal constitution *In suprema*, issued by Alexander VII on 19 April 1666.[23] It
was the fruit of years of negotiations in Rome, where Vaussin's
diplomacy prevailed over the Abbé de Rancé's tempestuous defense
of the reform. But Vaussin could not long enjoy the fruits of his
victory: he died in Dijon, aged sixty-three, during the preparations of the General Chapter of 1670 (fol. 388^v).

    60. Louis Loppin (29 March 1670 - 6 May 1670) was a native of
Seurre and, although not an 'abstinent,' he retained the confidence
of Richelieu and served as his procurator general in Paris. He received forty-five votes out of a total of seventy-three. He soon
left for Paris seeking royal approval of his election. He died unexpectedly on his way back in Champagne, and was buried in the nearby Cistercian nunnery of Argensolles. He was sixty-three years old
(fol. 388^v).

    61. Jean Petit (19 June 1670 - 15 January 1692) received on
the second ballot sixty-nine votes out of the total of seventy-three.
He was then forty-four years old, a doctor of canon law, and prior
of Bonport. Since the fight with the Strict Observance seemed to
be over, the proto-abbots thought that they could afford to resume
their attacks against the abbot general, who, they charged, had accumulated a number of unwarranted privileges. The storm broke out
at the General Chapter of 1672, and continued unabated throughout
the rest of Petit's administration. The individual incidents are
told by Cotheret with a flair for drama: one involved Petit's attempted visitation at Clairvaux in 1674, when Abbot Pierre Henry
shut the gates in the general's face and denied him admission on
Christmas Eve (fols. 402^v-407^r). Eventually, with the sympathetic
help of Louis XIV and the papacy, Petit prevailed over all opposition and obtained the documents that clearly established his position as the general of his Order. This, did not, however, prevent
the unimpressed proto-abbots from using every opportunity of chal-
lenging Petit's authority, nor consequent endless litigations. That
the general had the energy and financial resources to build a new
great dormitory and an abbatial residence is only admirable. The
only irreparable setback he suffered was the total loss of Bellebranche to the Jesuit college of La Flèche in 1686. Petit, worn
out in ceaseless labors, died at Cîteaux in his sixty-third year.
For his tenacity in upholding the traditional form of government
in the Order, Petit receives high marks from Cotheret (fol. 470^v).

    62. Nicolas Larcher (27 March 1692 - 4 March 1712), a native
of Beaune, monk of Cîteaux and doctor of the Sorbonne, although he
was in his late sixties, received forty-one votes on the first

ballot out of fifty-eight votes cast. He was engaged in several
successful lawsuits against diocesan bishops who challenged his
authority over Cistercian nuns. Moreover, in the teeth of episcopal opposition, he obtained the distinction of being seated on the
occasions of the sessions of the estates of Burgundy in an armchair
similar to those that accomodated the bishops. In spite of his
overwhelming victory at his election, Larcher turned out to be un-
popular with his monks, who turned with their complaints against
him to the parlement of Dijon. The General Chapter of 1699 dis-
approved the monks' move, although it admonished Larcher to live up
to his duties and govern according to established rules and customs.
On the same occasion the right of the general to visit the proto-
abbots became again an object of hot debates. But Larcher deserved
Cotheret's praise for having defended successfully the nunnery of
Belmont against the appetite of the Jesuits, who moved that the
house be suppressed and its goods be granted to their college in
Langres. Larcher died in his eighty-second year in Gilly (fol. 514v).

63. Edmond Perrot (20 May 1712 - 1 February 1727) was elected
by receiving forty-one votes out of the total of fifty-five. He was
formerly the spiritual director of the nuns of Battant in Besançon,
and enjoyed the reputation of a model monk. Unfortunately, as Cotheret points out repeatedly, he left his heart with his nuns; in
fact, he spent more time in Besançon than in Cîteaux and built a
church for Battant from the funds of Cîteaux. As another item of
Cotheret's disapproval, he discontinued the 'abbot's table' for the
noon meals, introduced guests into the monks' refectory, where he
occasionally permitted conversation, thus creating in place of traditional silence and recollection the atmosphere of a 'restaurant.'
Although Perrot's attitude was conciliatory, he came to be involved
in a long lawsuit with the proto-abbots, who after the death of
Louis XIV hoped that they had a better chance of prevailing over
their arch-adversary, the abbot of Cîteaux. Perrot died at Cîteaux
in the night between 31 January and 1 February 1727, in his eighty-
sixth year (fol. 565r).

64. Andoche Pernot (21 April 1727 - 1748) was elected on the
first ballot by a nearly unanimous (forty-nine) vote of his fifty-
five confrères. At this point Cotheret's narrative ends. The rest
of the manuscript is spent in airing his personal opinions on the
causes of Cîteaux's decline. From his scattered remarks throughout
the work is clear that he considered Pernot the most abusive of all
the superiors of the abbey.

NOTES

1. MSS 2474 and 2475.
2. See the original receipt attached to the Tamié MS.
3. Col. 936. Canivez thought it to be the 'sole copy' of the original. He admitted its potential value but complained about its style, closer to that of a pamphleteer than that of a scholar. Referring to fol. 73, he asserted that it was written in 1738, although the date on the indicated page is clearly 1736.
4. IX (Paris, 1960) col. 825. The latest similar work, E. Brouette, A. Dimier and E. Manning, *Dictionnaire des auteurs cisterciens* (Rochefort, 1975) cols. 190-191, knows only about the Tamié MS, asserting that it has 583 pages, while the numbers indicate folios; therefore this MS contains in fact 1165 pages.
5. *The Rise of the Cistercian Strict Observance*...(Washington: The Catholic University of America Press, 1968), where the reader may find ample details going far beyond the scope of Cotheret.
6. See some of these details in Dijon MS 2475, pp. IX-XI and 677-678, and a typewritten sheet attached to Dijon MS 2474, by Alain Court, written in 1951.
   All further numbers to folios in the present study refer to the Tamié MS.
7. Municipal Archives of Dijon, B 521, année 1680, paroisse St.-Médard.
8. Joseph Jahn, 'Bericht über eine Reise zum Generalkapitel des Jahres 1699,' *Cistercienser-Chronik* 21 (1909) 178.
9. E. g., his *Observations sur le livre intitulé: éclaircissement des privilèges de l'ordre de Citeaux imprimé a Liège en 1714.* Municipal Library of Troyes, MS 699.
10. Benedikt Schindler, 'Verzeichniss der Konventsmitglieder zu Cisterz i. J. 1719,' *Cistercienser-Chronik* 9(1897) 246.
11. L. J. Lekai, 'The College of Saint Bernard of Paris in the 16th and 17th Centuries,' *Analecta Cisterciensia* 28 (1972) 210-218.
12. Tamié MS fols. 496^V-499^V. Bouhier graduated indeed as doctor of the Sorbonne in 1704. See my article (note 11) in *Analecta Cist.*, p. 216.
13. See the title under note 9, pp. 235 (23 x 34 cm), in the Municipal Libraries of Troyes, MS 699, and of Aix, MS 325.
14. This follows the previous work in the same MS 699 of Troyes, counting altogether nine folios.
15. MS 609 in the Municipal Library of Dijon, entitled: *Description historique des anciens monumens de l'abbaye de Citeaux, par monsieur Moreau de Mautour de l'Académie des Inscriptions et Belles-Lettres, avec des remarques de D. Cotheret, bibliothécaire de cette maison.* Pp. 92 (22 x 16 cm). According to a note on the inside of the binding, this MS was published in the *Mémoires de l'Académie des Inscriptions et Belles-Lettres,*

vol. F IX (Paris, 1736), Histoire, pp. 193-230.

16. This is referred to in a note following the title page of MS 699 of Troyes, by the hand of the librarian of the collection of Jean Bouhier, first president of the Parlement of Dijon, who received this MS from the author, Dom Cotheret, in 1736.

17. 'Abbatum catalogus...exit in lucem, in quo emendando in primis adjuti sumus a domino Cotheret, bibliothecae Cisterciensis erudito custode,' IV (Paris, 1876) col. 948.

18. Notes attached to Dijon MS 2475, pp. 676-677.

19. 'Catalogue des abbés de Cîteaux,' *Cistercienser-Chronik* 55 (1948) 1 - 11, and 63 (1956) 1 - 6. Two other easily accessible lists of all abbots of Cîteaux are: article 'Cîteaux' (abbaye) in *Dictionnaire d'histoire et de géographie ecclésiastique* XII (Paris, 1951) cols. 865-868, by J.-M. Canivez, who utilized Marilier's first article, but for the rest relied on the last edition of *Gallia Christiana* IV, p. 948; Archdale King, *Citeaux and her Elder Daughters* (London, 1954) pp. 1-105, presents his list almost esclusively on the basis of *Gallia Christiana*, and therefore his study cannot be considered as a work of independent scholarship.

20. According to *Dictionnaire des auteurs cisterciens*, col. 478, a copy of this MS has been preserved in the library of the Grand Séminaire of Bruges. A response to it, entitled *De prospero et adverso statu Ordinis*, has remained also in MS.

21. Cirey left behind a number of significant works. But if these *mémoires* were his autobiographical notes, they must be considered lost. Cf. *Dictionnaire des auteurs cisterciens*, cols. 400-401.

22. See these in J.-M. Canivez, *Statuta capitulorum generalium Ordinis Cisterciensis*, VI (Paris, 1938) pp. 87-97.

23. *Ibid.*, Vii, pp. 426-437.

ANGELIQUE DE SAINT-JEAN OF PORT-ROYAL: THE 'THIRD SUPERIOR' AS
'MYTHOGRAPHER' IN THE DYNAMICS OF REFORM CAUGHT IN CONTROVERSY

F. Ellen Weaver

> *Mère Angélique de Saint-Jean Arnauld...had the good fortune
> to live at Port-Royal from the age of six and to have been
> formed in piety by her illustrious aunts, Mère Marie-Angél-
> ique and Mère Agnès. Just as their natural qualities were
> united in her, so also she united their virtues, and these
> two enlightened persons saw in her such great talents and
> a grace so eminent that they judged her worthy to fill their
> place from the first years of her profession. They rejoiced
> that the good they had worked to establish would one day be
> worthily maintained by her zeal and example.*

So the *Nécrologe de l'abbaye de Notre-Dame de Port-Royal des
Champs, Ordre de Citeaux, Institut de Saint Sacrement* describes
the woman who held the office of novice mistress and sub-prioress
of Port-Royal des Champs during the critical years when the monastery was under scrutiny and then interdict for its involvement in
the Jansenist controversy, and that of abbess during the final au-
tumnal glow of glory of that ill-fated institution. The corpus of
her writings--correspondance, treatises, and works of editing the
chronicles, lives, journals and other accounts of the community--
reveals a person of influence and leadership whose life and character fit the delineation of the necrology to a degree which, taking
into account some of the characteristics of this genre, is extraordinary. Had Port-Royal not become emmeshed in the theological
controversies of the age, Angélique de Saint-Jean would provide a
striking example of the 'third superior' according to the categories developed by Jean Leclercq in his essay 'A Sociological Approach
to the History of a Religious Order.'[2] In fact, her early association with the community makes it possible to discover some of the
marks of the 'second superior' in her role in the reform of Port-
Royal. Thus she provides a fascinating 'case study' through which
to examine these categories.
As a matter of historical fact, Port-Royal did become intri-
cately involved in the controversies that broke out around the publication of the *Augustinus* of Jansenius, St-Cyran's promulgation of
it in France and his reform program, Antoine Arnauld's brilliant
presentation of St-Cyran's positions in the *Fréquente Communion,*
and the subsequent condemnation of the 'Five Propositions' on grace
said to be in the *Augustinus*. The involvement of the nuns of Port-
Royal by their refusal to sign the statement of agreement to the
condemnation--the 'formulaire'--transformed the monastery from a

center of cistercian reform to the storm center of the tempest that
was in the end to destroy them.[3]

Angélique de Saint-Jean was a young woman of twenty-five in her
first year as novice mistress, living with a group of the nuns who
had returned from Paris to the old monastery in the valley of the
Chevreuse when the first condemnation of the theology of grace in
the *Augustinus* was issued in 1649 by the Sorbonne. When she returned to Paris in 1652 to work on the *Mémoires* of Mère Angélique, the
clouds were gathering around her uncle, the *'grand Arnauld.'* During
her second sojourn at Port-Royal des Champs from 1653 to 1659, where
her duties were augmented by the additional charge of sub-prioress,
the storm broke. Arnauld was expelled from the Sorbonne in 1655,
Pascal launched his *Lettres Provinciales* in 1656, and from then on
until the end of the century the controversy raged. Angélique de
Saint-Jean returned to Paris in 1659, and in 1661 the first order
was issued by the Vicar General of Paris requiring all members of
the clergy and religious orders to sign the formulary. Immediately
Angélique de Saint-Jean assumed leadership of the nuns who opposed
the signature, and from that time forward she was a force to be
reckoned with.

Subtly her role changed. Writing the chronicles of a successful
reform is not the same as writing the defense of a group under attack. And it is this new element that makes Angélique de Saint-
Jean's work even more interesting to a historian of Christianity,
especially one whose particular interest is in the dynamics of reform in the Church. Historians for some time have been aware that
the line between chronicle and myth is sometimes blurred, especially
when the events are connected with reform movements and their charis-
matic leaders. The more I worked with the Port-Royal manuscripts
the more I realized that in Angélique de Saint-Jean Arnauld d'Andilly
I had discovered not only an interesting example of the 'third superior' with elements of the 'second superior,' but also an intriguing
case of chronicler becoming mythographer. This woman I would like to
introduce to you here. She is less generally known than Mère Angélique, the formidable reforming abbess of the early Port-Royal. I
have found Angélique de Saint-Jean to be a more complex and interesting person--and in fact it is possible to wonder how much Mère
Angélique is a creation of this gifted writer. In this brief introduction I will first sketch out the categories developed by Jean
Leclercq and show how Angélique de Saint-Jean fits them. I shall
then discuss the more interpretative issue of how the chronicler of
Port-Royal became its 'mythographer.'

One is always impressed by a work which articulates in simple
logical terms what one had intuitively grasped as the common sense
analysis of a situation. Such a presentation is even more valuable
if it provides categories, patterns, by which similar phenomena can
be analysed and understood. This is the value of the model of the

evolution of a movement which Jean Leclercq has applied to the
growth of a religious order. Of interest here is the delineation
of the significant persons in the process from reform to established institution. Fr Leclercq was analysing the establishment of the
Order of Cîteaux; in the reform of Port-Royal, *mutatis mutandis,*
the same roles can be discerned.

First is the 'founder' who is 'the one who takes the initiative
to start something new; this newness may be a rebirth, so to speak,
of the order, in which case the founder is also a reformer.'[4] In
the case of Port-Royal the reformer who is in some respects also a
founder is Mère Angélique Arnauld. The ways in which she does and
does not fit the delineation of founder is not at issue here. Let
me just say that in seventeenth century Port-Royal she clearly ful-
fils the role of founder-reformer. The community of over one hundred which she moved into Paris in 1626 was not only a reform of
the group of six she joined in 1609 but truly a new monastery of
cistercian nuns. Next in the evolution comes

> a sort of sub-leader; he usually has a less strong per-
> sonality than the founder whom he has known, to whom he
> is **personally** and deeply attached and whose work he wish-
> es to continue.[5]

The person in the community of Port-Royal who comes to mind immediately for this role is the sister of the reformer-abbess, Mère Agnès.

Finally

> then comes the 'third superior' who, chronologically
> speaking, may be the fourth or fifth; he has not known
> personally the first leader and thus is sentimentally
> free, he admires him and now feels himself to be respon-
> sibly for maintaining his foundation. Thus, he sets about
> stabilizing, organizing facts which had so far been nothing
> more than empirical and historical solutions to a given
> situation which, though it existed in the founder's time,
> is not long past. In some cases the 'third superior' may
> come to be considered as the real founder of the order un-
> der the form it took in the second generation after the
> founder's death....Frequently, also, it is in the third
> generation--always psychologically speaking--that some
> powerful mind elaborates the theology of the order, some
> gifted biographer sets down the legend of the founder,
> and a great legislator drafts the constitutions.[6]

The value of this model of roles in the evolution of a movement
is that it provides patterns for analysis and understanding. As

these patterns are applied to the reform of Port-Royal and to Angélique de Saint-Jean's role in it significant fits, and misfits,
are immediately apparent. First of all, she is not quite close
enough to Mère Angélique to be the 'sub-leader' described above;
yet she is too close to be the 'third superior' in every detail.
The model is still illuminating. Let us apply it and catch some
of this light.

First consider the role of 'sub-leader.' It would seem that
this person simply keeps the ideal of the founder alive until the
one capable of translating the charism of the leader into a lasting
form comes along. In the case of Port-Royal, since there were some
very strong associates with Mère Angélique at the time of the re-
form--notably, Mère Agnès--the 'sub-leader' was sometimes a cause
of tension rather than a simple disciple and supporter. It is the
young Angélique de Saint-Jean who admired and respected the ideals
of Mère Angélique and was determined to see that her work continued.

This would not be surprising, considering the importance that
the novice mistress plays in the formation of the young religious.
Although her famous aunts were both absent from the monastery during her early years there as a schoolgirl--Mère Angélique was at
the convent of the *Institut du Saint-Sacrement* making that ill-
fated establishment, and Mère Agnès was superior of the monastery
of Tard near Dijon--when she entered the order in 1641, at the age
of seventeen, Mère Agnès was there as superior and Mère Angélique
was novice mistress.[7] We can be certain, given these circumstances,
that Angélique de Saint-Jean was thoroughly imbued with the ideals
of the mother-reformer.

Evidence of this attachment to the spirit of Mère Angélique
can be surmised from her adamant stance against signing the 'formulaire.' Although it is quite possible that had she lived, Mère
Angélique would have been found at the opposite extreme, agreeing
with Barcos that the business of nuns is prayer not politics, something of the older woman's uncompromising adherence to a position
once taken--remember the famous *journée du Guichet*[8]--is duplicated
in her niece's refusal to sign the formulary at any cost.[9]

Clear written evidence of this attachment is found in the conferences and other works of Angélique de Saint-Jean during her own
terms as abbess of Port-Royal. For example, we read in Angélique
de Saint-Jean's commentary on the *Constitutions,* referring to the
chapter on reception of guests:

> These occasions, spoken of here in the Constitutions, by
> providing us with the occasion to inconvenience ourselves
> in many ways, are truly the ones where we are able to prac-
> tice hospitality, to discover the innermost depths of our
> heart and to know if it is really founded and rooted in
> charity. And perhaps we will discover that it is not cer-
> tainly what it should be, and that we have not entirely

preserved that spirit of charity, generosity and zeal
which, as we know, abounded in those who have governed
this monastery--above all Mère Angélique from the very
beginning of the reform as she has taught us by her example and her words.[10]

'La Mère Angélique nous a souvent dit' is a familiar phrase in
the works of her niece.

More than in her attitudes and words, however, it is in the
actions of Angélique de Saint-Jean that we read her admiration for
her famous aunt. In her standards of asceticism and intense loyalty to the ideals of the early reform she is much closer to Mère
Angélique than to Mère Agnès for whom, it is said, she had greater
emotional attachment. For example, one of the principles of the
reform was to return to faithful practice of the Rule of Saint
Benedict, and one of the customs established by Mère Angélique to
implement this was the commentary on the Rule by the abbess at the
'conference'--a formal period of recreation modeled on that described in the Constitutions of the Cistercians of the Strict Observance.[11] The collections of Conferences and Discussions of the
Rule of St Benedict by Angélique de Saint-Jean attest to her fidelity in continuing this tradition.

Another important feature of Mère Angélique's reform was the
restoration of the choice of abbess by election rather than by
nomination of the king. It fell to Angélique de Saint-Jean during
her term as abbess to carry the fight to retain this right of election to Rome.[12] We have evidence that for Angélique de Saint-Jean
this right of election was more than a gesture of independence from
royal patronage. It was following in the footsteps of Mère Angélique, an act of fidelity to benedictine-cistercian tradition. The
nuns' agent in Rome, M. de Pontchâteau, succeeded in obtaining papal support of the right of election, so that when Louis XIV asked
for restoration of his right of nomination of the abbess of Port-
Royal des Champs (he had already reestablished this right at Port-
Royal de Paris) he was refused, and on August 1681, Angélique de
Saint-Jean was reelected abbess. We find that her commentary on
Chapter 64 of the Rule of Benedict, *De l'election de l'Abbé* is sub-
titled 'Après la seconde & miraculeuse élection du huitième Août
1681.'[13]

In the reform of Port-Royal, as in similar reforms of monastic
orders, the restoration of the Divine Office to a central place in
the life of the nuns ranked alongside abstinence in importance.
Among the first changes made by Mère Angélique when she was sent
to Maubuisson to establish the reform there were to enforce the rule
of abstinence and to correct the hurried, careless manner in which
the nuns there were singing the office. In a relation by S. Madelaine Candide, found in the *Recueil* of Angélique de Saint-Jean we read:

Mère Angélique took great care to see that the Divine
Office was celebrated by the new novices [at Maubuisson]
with devotion and reverence to amend, she said, the lack
of devotion and irreverence with which it had been celebrated in that place before her time. She had brought
Madelaine de la Croix with her to teach chant to the
young nuns, and in order that [Sr Madelaine] might be
able to carry out this task better, she gave her no other
charge. Thus all day she did nothing else than to teach
them plain chant, for it was necessary that they know it
perfectly so that they could sustain it in choir over
against the older nuns, who had voices so strong and dis-
cordant that if Mère Angélique and her novices had not
sustained the chant against these nuns in a full and
strong voice the office would have continued to be per-
formed in the old style, which was more likely to distract than to edify those assisting at it.[14]

It is significant that, in spite of her stress on the performance of the Divine Office, Mère Angélique had accepted the substitu-
tion of the Paris Breviary for the monastic one. It was Angélique
de Saint-Jean who restored the monastic office. She petitioned the
Archbishop for permission to add ferial psalms to the Office on
saints' days in order to carry out St Benedict's stipulation that
the entire psalter should be recited each week. In the letter of
petition, dated 26 August 1680, she referred to the change of jurisdiction from Cîteaux, recalling that at that time Port-Royal substi-
tuted the Breviary of Paris for that of Cîteaux. Since the Paris
Breviary continued to add saints' days to the already considerable
number, the nuns were unable to complete the weekly recitation of
the psalter as bidden by their Rule. The permission to substitute
the ferial for the festal office would enable them to do this while
continuing to commemorate the feasts common to the Archdiocese of Paris.
A journal note of 19 October states that at Vespers they began to say
the ferial psalms according to the permission received.[15] The occasion made a great impression on the community--enough to be noted in
a later commentary on the life and work of Angélique de Saint-Jean:

And she could not hide her joy to have reestablished that
ancient observance of the Rule. But her joy also came
from another source, for she had a very special love for
the Psalms for which God had given her an understanding
combined with such a lively and tender piety that she
wondered how anyone could pronounce them without ardor.[16]

In these, as in many other instances, Angélique extends 'sub-
leader' to the role of 'third Superior,' for she had internalized

the ideals of Mère Angélique, and so was able to give form, theological justification, and even legislation to what in the foundress
had been 'empirical and historical solutions to a given situation.'

Jean Leclercq suggests that in the third generation there may
be several who fulfill this role: 'some powerful mind elaborates
the theology of the order, some gifted biographer sets down the
legend of the founder, and a great legislator drafts the constitutions.' Angélique de Saint-Jean had a hand in several of these
activities.

Although it seems clear that the *Constitutions* of Port-Royal
were composed, in the main, by Mère Agnès, Angélique de Saint-
Jean's manuscript copy[17] is embellished by copious marginal references to Scripture and the Fathers. And it was she who, as abbess,
attempted to gain from Rome approbation of the *Constitutions*.[18]

Among the nuns it is certainly Angélique de Saint-Jean who
qualifies as the theologian. Her variations on the theme of martyrdom[19] reveal a profound theological basis to justify the actions
of the recalcitrant nuns who refused to sign the formulary. Although she left no developed treatise of theology, it would be quite
possible to construct a small *Summa* of the theology of Port-Royal
from her letters alone.[20]

But it is above all the role of 'gifted biographer [who] sets
down the legend of the founder' that Angélique de Saint-Jean ful-
fills in eminent fashion.

In the Preface to the *Relation sur la vie de la Révérende Mère
Angélique*, Angélique de Saint-Jean relates how she came to make the
collection of accounts of the life of Mère Angélique and to write
her own account. In 1648, when Mère Angélique returned from Paris
with part of the community to the ancient monastery in the valley
of Chevreuse, the *solitaires* who had been living there since 1638
moved up the hill to a farmhouse, but remained in close contact
with the community in the valley, Port-Royal des Champs. Among
the solitaires was Mère Angélique's nephew, Antoine Le Maître, who
often visited with his aunt. Impressed by the conversations he had
with her, he felt that the 'grands trésors de grâce et de lumière'
he discovered daily in these conversations and the way in which
providence had acted in her soul to bring about great things should
not be lost to posterity. He prevailed upon his cousin, Angélique
de Saint-Jean, to collect all she could about Mère Angélique and
the reform from those who have been in the monastery with Mère Angélique from the beginning of her undertaking, asking those who were
able to write out their accounts, and herself writing down verbal
accounts. She began in 1651. From that time on, over a period of
some twenty years, Angélique de Saint-Jean worked on this collection.
There were many interruptions, periods when she was unable to find
time or tranquility for the task of ordering the accounts she had
collected and composing her own history of the life and work of the

foundress. Finally in 1672, at the death of Mère Agnès, Angélique de Saint-Jean took time to go over all the accounts, to put them in order, and to complete her own history up to the establishment of the house in Paris, using the *mémoires* she had been working on so long. At that point she left the work, leaving the continuation of the history to posterity.[21]

If that were all there were to the story, Angélique de Saint-Jean would exemplify the talented biographer. Her account is well written, and her work of organizing the other materials is done with care and taste. The story, however, is more complicated than that. The reason for the long interruptions discloses another aspect of the matter: the story of the foundress of a reform becomes the story of the foundress of a *persecuted* reform. It is a significant difference. As we indicated above, the line between chronicle and myth, even regarding a peaceful reform, is often blurred. When the reform becomes controversial, and especially when it undergoes persecution --for whatever reasons--the events easily become martyrdom and the *dramatis personae* take on heroic proportions. The *oeuvre* of Angélique de Saint-Jean, however unintended on her part, was destined to become the source of a powerful and pervasive cultural myth.

Before considering the steps of this progression, we can gain an indication of its direction by considering the writings of Angélique de Saint-Jean that separated the beginning of the Mère Angélique *mémoires* in 1651 and the completion in 1672. In 1661 the ordinance obliging all members of religious orders to sign the formulary condemning the five propositions extracted from the *Augustinus* was issued by the Archbishop of Paris, supported--indeed urged--by Louis XIV himself. One of the first writings of Angélique de Saint-Jean following this event is her account of her interrogation during the canonical examination of the members of Port-Roayl. Although there was a period of calm from 1661 to 1664, we know from her letters that Angélique de Saint-Jean was absorbed by the affair. In 1664 the pressure on the nuns to sign was augmented by the dispersal of the leaders to convents in and around Paris. Angélique de Saint-Jean's account of her sojourn at the convent of the Annunciation Sisters, the *Relation de la Captivité*, is her masterpiece. When the recalcitrant nuns refused to sign they were sent all together to Port-Royal des Champs. There were over eighty of them, crowded into a monastery designed for half that number. The story of that period from 1665 to 1669 when the non-signers were under interdict at Port-Royal des Champs is found in the Journals in which day to day events, letters, reports of the Chapter meetings and other accounts are recorded. It might be too much to say that the persecution journals were entirely authored by Angélique de Saint-Jean, but the most striking portions bear her imprint.[22] It is also certain that many of the entries in the Necrology of Port-Royal[23] are her compositions.

If these papers had been circulated within the circle of the
monastery and a few patrons and intimate friends we might speak of
them as the 'legend' of the holy foundress and the trials of the
community, but we could not think of them as myth. In fact, they
had a wide and enduring circulation, yet that alone would not quali-
fy them as myth. The term 'myth' connotes a metaphoric, a poetic,
symbolic account of events of a heroic past which relates at a deep
subconscious level to a psychological, *theological,* perception of
reality shared by a cultural group. It is repeated in many forms
and enters into the tradition of the group. At the core of the
myth is historical fact. But this historical core is less important than the perception of reality beyond fact. I invite you to
think with me, as a conclusion to this introduction to Angélique
de Saint-Jean, of the way in which her writings became the source
of the myth of Port-Royal.
     First, in what way can we say that the story of Port-Royal is
mythic? On the most general level, we can say that any story which
contains an element of suffering persecution for an ideological
cause elicits a universal human response of the mythic level. We
believe, and are glad to believe, that the human person is capable
of suffering for a cause. But Port-Royal became a symbol for something much more specific. Louis Cognet points to it when he suggests the ways in which Jansenism contributed to the emergence of
modern consciousness: the intense consciousness of the rights of
the person, and above all personal opinion, in the face of the absolutism of authority.[24] In the religious sphere the stern moral
demands of Jansenism responded to a renewed sense among French Catholics of the high seriousness of the Christian calling, which extended beyond the seventeenth century well into the beginning of
our own era. But I think another, even deeper, chord was sounded
by the nuns of Port-Royal. Seventeenth-century Paris was the center of an early feminist movement in secular society. These women
who stood up to all the masculine authorities--bishops, religious
superiors, even the king and the pope--became truly mythic heroines
of the movement in the sacred sphere. An evidence of this is the
number of nineteenth-century English women, in the period of the
feminist movement in England, who embraced them as sisters through
their translations of the writings, pilgrimages to the ruins of
Port-Royal, histories of the monastery, and so on.[25] Among the
'heroine' nuns of Port-Royal, Angélique de Saint-Jean stands out
even above Mère Angélique. The foundress, after all, escaped the
heat of persecution. She died in 1661. Mère Angélique may have
engendered her own legend as a reformer; it is Angélique de Saint-
Jean who, especially in her *Relation sur la capitivité* and the persecution journals, provides the language of martyrdom and the incidents full of pathos and courage for the enduring myth of Port-
Royal.

A myth, we have said, is retold again and again, and enters into the cultural tradition. This is the final aspect of the *oeuvre* of Angélique de Saint-Jean which fits the pattern. One of the most intriguing discoveries I made in my research into the history of the reform of Port-Royal was to find that at the source of all of the histories of the monastery and the movement is the collection of manuscripts removed from the monastery at the time of its destruction, which found its way into private collections, thence to the ancient library of St-Germain des Près and finally to the great collections at the Bibliothèque Nationale, the Mazarine, and smaller collections at private and municipal libraries in France and the Lowlands. From Besoigne and Clemencet to Sainte-Beuve, to the present day researchers, all must eventually return to the same sources. And among those sources, those which relate the story of the monastery of Port-Royal seem almost without exception to have passed under the pen of Angélique de Saint-Jean. Many of them are her compositions. Most of the others were edited and/or selected and arranged by her.

And so, rather than simply 'third superior' and chronicler, I present Angélique de Saint-Jean **Arnauld** d'Andilly as mythographer, and indeed heroine of the myth of Port-Royal she helped to create: martyr for 'the truth of God.' No one has caught the pathetic grandeur of Angélique better than Montherlant in his *Port-Royal*. Montherlant ends his drama with a speech by Angélique de Saint-Jean. As the hour of None is sounding--he reminds us that it is the hour which recalls the mystery of the death of Christ--Soeur Angélique says as she turns to go with the nuns of the Annunciation to her 'captivité':

Je **veux** dire que la nuit qui s'ouvre passera comme toutes les choses de ce monde. Et la vérité de Dieu demeurera éternallement et délivrera tous ceux qui veulent n'être sauvés que par elle.[26]

University of Notre Dame

NOTES

1. Rivet de la Grange, Dom (Amsterdam, 1723).

2. M. Basil Pennington, ed. *The Cistercian Spirit* (Cistercian Publications, 1970) pp. 134-43.

3. The best brief summary of Jansenism is found in Louis Cognet's article 'Jansenism,' *New Catholic Encyclopedia* VII:820-24.

4. Leclercq, 'A Sociological Approach,' p. 137.

5. Ibid., p. 138.

6. Ibid., p. 139.

7. F. Ellen Weaver, *The Evolution of the Reform of Port-Royal: From the Rule of Cîteaux to Jansenism* (Paris, 1978) pp. 134-35.

8. Cf. the vivid description in Sainte-Beuve, *Port-Royal*, 3 vols. (Paris, 1953-55) I:171 ff.

9. Cf. Louis Cognet, ed. *Relation de la captivité d'Angélique de Saint-Jean Arnauld d'Andilly* (Paris, 1954) for Angélique de Saint-Jean's own story of her refusal to sign and its consequences.

10. *Conférences de la Mère Angélique de Saint-Jean*, 3 vols. (n.p., n.d.) I:201-02.

11. Julius Donatus Leloczky, ed. *Constitutiones et acta capitulorum S.O.O.Cist. saeculo 17* (Rome, 1967) pp. 75-78. See my commentary in Weaver, pp. 50-51.

12. See the description of the mission of M. de Pontchâteau to Rome in Weaver, p. 117.

13. *Discours de la révérende Mère Marie Angélique de S. Jean, abbess de Port-Royal des Champs, sur la Règle de S. Benoît*, 2 vols (Paris, 1736) 2:492.

14. *Relations sur la vie de la reverende Mère Angélique de Sainte Magdelaine Arnauld, ou Receüil de la Mère Angélique de S-Jean Arnauld d'Andilly sur la vie de sa Tante la Mère Marie Angélique de Sainte Magdelaine Arnauld, & sur la reformé des Abbayes*

de Port-Royal, Maubuisson & autres (Paris, 1737) p. 114. Here-inafter referred to as Angelique de Saint-Jean, *Receuil*.

15. Paris, Bibliothéque National, MS 17,779. This manuscript in-cludes the original of Angélique de Saint-Jean's letter to the Archbishop with other Port-Royal papers.

16. *Maximes de la Mère Angélique de Saint-Jean*, Paris, Bibliothéque Mazarine, MS 2473.

17. BN, MS 13,886.

18. Weaver, p. 117.

19. See her *Relation de captivité*, and the comments on the idea of martyrdom in it in Weaver, pp. 138–45.

20. The letters are collected in a manuscript which was made ready for publication in the late nineteenth century by Mlle Rachel Gillet, found in Paris at the Bibliothéque de la société de Port-Royal, MSS Let. 358–61.

21. *Receuil*, pp. iii–vii.

22. Weaver, pp. 127–28.

23. See attribution of many articles to her by Dom Clemencet in his long introduction to Vol. III of the *Conférences* of Angél-ique de Saint-Jean.

24. *Le Jansénisme* (Paris, 1968) pp. 124–25.

25. For example: Mary Anne Schimmelpennick (friend of Hannah More), *Select Memoirs of Port-Royal* (London, 1835); Frances Martin, *Angelique Arnauld, Abbess of Port-Royal* (London, 1876); Ethel Romanes, *The Story of Port-Royal* (London, 1907); M. E. Lowndes, *The Nuns of Port-Royal as Seen in Their Own Narratives* (Oxford, 1909).

26. Henri de Montherlant, *Port-Royal* (Paris, 1954) pp. 186–87.

THE CISTERCIAN DIMENSION OF THE REFORM OF LA TRAPPE
(1662 - 1700)
PRELIMINARY NOTES AND REFLECTIONS

Chrysogonus Waddell

PRELIMINARY: TWO ORIENTATIONS

Early in the morning of Monday, 25 April, the Feast of Saint
Mark, in the year 1667, the subprior of the Swiss Cistercian Abbey
of Wettingen finished arranging his baggage, mounted his horse and,
accompanied by a servant on foot, started off on the first lap of
his long journey to Cîteaux. By rights the man in the saddle should
have been the abbot of the place, but the abbot, Dom Burgisser, was
almost sixty and of none too robust health. His subprior, Fr Joseph
Meglinger (b. 1634), had been appointed as his official delegate, and
was now on his way to the Cistercian General Chapter of 1667.
        Despite its tormented history, made up in recent centuries of
the horrors of war, pillaging, two major fires, maladministration
on the part of superiors and loose living on the part of monks,
Wettingen was once more in a flourishing condition. A community of
some forty choir-monks devoted themselves, when not in choir, to a
disciplined life of serious study: theology, philosophy, the human-
ities, and arts. The buildings of the monastic plant had recently
been modernized *au goût du jour*, and the establishment even had its
own printery. Our Reverend Father Subprior himself was very much
the product of his monastic environment: he loved his Order and its
tradition; he loved his community; he also loved his Virgil and an
occasional glass of really fine wine. All of Fr Joseph's loves are
very much in evidence in the long, detailed account he wrote of his
1667 journey to Cîteaux, the *Epistola familiaris de itinere ad Comitia Generalia*, written in the form of a letter to his friend, Johann
Jakob Mechler, a curate in the Canton of Schwyz.[1]
        In the company of the Abbot of Sankt-Urban and Vicar General of
the Congregation of Upper Germany, Dom Edmund Schnyder, Fr Joseph arrived in Dijon on a very cold May 4th. Dijon had been designated as
the gatheringplace of the assembly to be held at Cîteaux, and our two
Swiss Cistercians spent the days between Wednesday and Sunday in a
round of courtesy calls, policy-making meetings, and sight-seeing--
visits to Little Cîteaux (the Abbot General's town house and office),
to Little Clairvaux (the Abbot of Clairvaux's town house), to Fon-
taines-lès-Dijon (Saint Bernard's birthplace), to Parlement in session (where the visitors admired the impressive comportment of the
Abbot General, *ex officio* first of the *conseillers* to the First President of the Parlement of Burgundy). Evening *divertissements* included a serenade by a string quartet, a splendid supper with the

reformer Abbot of Lutzel and Pairis, Dom Bernardin Buchinger (whose published writings include a cookbook which went through several editions), another two-hour supper of special magnificence at the table of the Abbot of Clairvaux ('We don't usually dine so well,' explained Dom Pierre Bouchu, 'but you're such distinguished company'). At last, on Sunday afternoon, 8 May, the members of the General Chapter assembled, and the ceremonial calvacade to Cîteaux set off in style: the *Illustrissimus Pater Generalis* led the procession in his six-horse coach, followed by another nine coaches headed by those of the four Proto-abbots. Then came the other members of the Chapter on horse-back, two or three abreast--forty abbots, one-hundred and fifty priors (of abbeys *in commendam*) or delegates, and some hundred and thirty servants. The assembly arrived towards four o'clock amid the pealing of the great abbey-bells; the Abbot General pronounced his words of welcome, and the assembly filed into the nave of the large abbey church and knelt in meditation for a quarter-hour, while the organist regaled them with a feast for ears so lavish that our musically-minded Meglinger devotes two-thirds of a column in Migne to a rapturous description of the splendid organ.

But not everyone present was as appreciative as our Swiss delegate. Among those kneeling in the nave was a middle-aged French abbot some seven years older than the Subprior of Wettingen, but almost a decade his junior in religious profession. Indeed, the Abbot of la Trappe had been only three years a professed member of the Order; and of these three years, two had been spent in Rome as one of the two delegates of the Strict Observance. In Rome his mission had been to represent the Reform in the Battle of Cistercian Observances. The mission had been unsuccessful (at least, as he saw it). Drawn up by a specially appointed Congregation, and purporting to settle the differences between the warring parties by insuring a general standard of observance acceptable to the 'Ancients' while at the same time preserving and encouraging the spread of the 'Abstinent' movement, the papal constitution *In suprema* (1666) was now about to be promulgated at this very General Chapter attended by both Meglinger and Rancé.

The two men represent two rather different orientations. Upon becoming abbot of la Trappe, Rancé had forsworn for ever his prestigious family-name, Bouthillier, and even refused the deferential form of abbatial address 'Dom'; he styled himself simply *Frère Armand-Jean de Rancé*, and always referred to the other members of his community, not as 'sons,' but as 'brothers.' Meglinger, burger-born and given the good Swiss name Jost by his proud parents, had changed his name to the more dignified Joseph when, by entering the Abbey of Wettingen, he rose several notches above his family's social condition. Both men were well educated, but it was Rancé who had stood at the head of his class when he took his doctorate in theology at no less a university than the Sorbonne. Meglinger wrote a convoluted, pseudo-classic Latin aimed at literary effect: 'novice' becomes *ephebe*, 'church' becomes *templum;* and when he refers to the *Numen* or, still worse, to 'the gods,' this is only his precious way of referring to the one true God of revelation. As for Rancé, the rhythm of Pindar and Anacreon and Virgil was in his blood, and even when he adopted the technical vocabulary of memoranda *de rebus monasticis* and the inelegant diction of chancery style, he remained constitutionally incapable of writing a really clumsy sentence. Before leaving for the General Chapter, our prudent Meglinger took the precaution of including in his baggage two flagons of good stout wine against the rigors of the journey and the possible insufficiencies of victualing along the way. His narrative is punctuated with frequent and enthusiastic appreciations of the joys of wine and a well-spread table. But what for our honest subprior was only a sporadic plunge into the pleasures of *gourmandise* had once been for the young court *abbé*, Armand-Jean Bouthillier de Rancé, a way of life. All that, however, was long since a thing of the past; and by the time the two Cistercians met, the name Rancé was already synonomous with austerity and strict observance. During his last conversation with the *Reverendissimus Pater Generalis* at Cîteaux, Meglinger candidly voiced his conviction that the spiritual fast is more acceptable to God (and less a problem for digestion), and that the exercise of virtue can co-exist with meat on the menu: *virtutum exercitationes, et esum carnium simul haud dubie stare posse confirmarem.*[2] Rancé would agree on the order of priorities, but he baulked at any tendency to disassociate the two. Rancé's fear of an exterior observance uninformed by a vivifying spirit was at all times acute, but for him, monastic *praxis* brought interior and exterior practices into a profound harmony in which the exterior expressed, but also helped nourish, deepen and strengthen the interior.

Meglinger and Rancé. In long-lived religious institutions subject to evolution and vicissitudes, we almost always find persons representative of divergent tendencies *vis-à-vis* the past:

For a Joseph Meglinger, the distance between present observance and the unrealizable, never-to-be-repeated Golden Age of first beginnings poses no special problems. When he writes of his visit to Clairvaux, for instance, he is obviously moved, even awe-struck, by the poverty and simplicity of the oratory and other *monumenta* from days of Saint Bernard. He is sincerely overwhelmed by his visit to Bernard's humble, unpretentious hut. But he is just as sincerely lost in wonder at the tapestried and gem-encrusted splendor of the abbatial throne used on special occasions and on permanent display in the main sacristy of Cîteaux. Monastic life at Wettingen is serious, disciplined, personally rewarding; the past poses no threat for the present, and the more genial latter-day observance is not condemned by the rigors of early Cîteaux.

For an Armand-Jean de Rancé, the past (whether real or idealized) remains a permanently valid norm, an abiding invitation to return to the sources, an ever-present reproach to everything that
fails to measure up to the impossibly lofty perfection of first beginnings.

In no way, however, does Rancé's constant referral to primitive
Cîteaux pertain to the sphere of archeology. For Rancé, it is a
question of fidelity to the Gospel, fidelity to Jesus Christ. Years
later, in his *Treatise on the Sanctity and on the Duties of the
Monastic State* (1683), he was to ask the question: Were men the
founders of the monastic state? His answer was:

> No, it was Jesus Christ himself who founded it; and those
> who were raised by him to establish it in the world, at
> the different periods, which were marked out by his eternal
> knowledge, were only the ministers of his orders, and the
> executors of his holy will.[3]

Further, Rancé's whole understanding of monastic life is determined
by his understanding of Christian life in terms of *pure worship*.
In Chapter 3 of the *Treatise*, he describes the origins of 'solitary
life' with reference to

> the principal design which Almighty God proposed to him-
> self in the New Covenant which he made with men, to estab-
> lish in the world a religion worthy of his Divine Majesty,
> and to form therein true adorers, who might adore him in
> spirit and in truth, as our Lord Jesus Christ says: 'The
> hour cometh and now is, when the true adorers shall adore
> the Father in spirit and in truth'; that is to say, in
> that purity which can be the effect only of the plenitude
> of his Spirit and of the abundance of his grace.[4]

Pursuing a theme familiar to monastic historians of an earlier age,
Rancé points to the Apostles as those true adorers who had left all
things to follow the Lord Jesus in the fulness of gospel perfection.
He explains conversion in terms of a sharing in the same Spirit
transmitted by the Apostles.[5] The martyrs, too, possessed this
same Spirit in an eminent degree, and, not unexpectedly, when the
fervor of the early Church began to languish,

> God, who was pleased to maintain this perfect purity in
> his Church, preserved some of its members from the general
> relaxation, filling them with the spirit of the Apostles,
> by which being animated, they, like a new train of martyrs,
> forsook their parents, their wives and children, by a sort
> of death, which seemed not less real, less holy, nor less

miraculous, than that which the first martyrs had endured. They retired into the most distant solitudes, exposed themselves to nakedness, to cold, to hunger, and to all the injuries of the most rigorous seasons, to the fury of wild beasts, and, in a word, to the rage and envy of devils, and that IN ORDER TO PRAISE GOD, AND TO CONTEMPLATE HIS INFINITE BEAUTIES, IN THE SILENCE OF THE HEART, IN THE CALM OF ALL THE PASSIONS, AND IN THE SEPARATION FROM ALL THAT MIGHT DISTRACT THEM FROM THE MEDITATION ON THINGS ETERNAL.[6]

This concept of the monk as successor to the apostles and martyrs can rightly be challenged by the modern historian of monastic or origins, but it nonetheless represents a theme of inexhaustible fecundity for monks of an earlier age in their attempts to clarify for themselves the meaning of monastic life. And for those readers for whom the word 'penance' expresses the whole of Rancé's message to monks, an initial word of caution is in order. Essential as penance is in Rancé's practical programme for monks, it cannot be isolated from the rest of that programme without falsifying the whole picture. It is not, of course, a question of our having to *agree* with Rancé's understanding of what monastic life is all about; but it is a question of our knowing the main articulations of his thought about monastic life, so that we can situate the reform of la Trappe in its proper context. The key ideas which emerge from the preceding brief citations are to be found as the implicit or, often enough, explicit pre-suppositions behind most of the Reformer's discussions of particular points of monastic observance:

1. Monastic life is essentially a form of radical and integral Christianity.
2. Monastic life is a profoundly ecclesial life, in which the spirit of the apostles and of the martyrs lives on in the experience of their successors, the monks.
3. Monastic life is essentially ordered to a life of praise and uninterrupted contemplation.

We can, of course, rightly attribute much of Rancé's celebrated absolutism to the absolutist spirit of the century of the Great Monarch. We can just as rightly explain his 'exaggerations' and 'excesses' in terms of the rigorism characteristic of some aspects of French counter-Reformation spirituality. But my own personal impression, which grows apace with my increasing familiarity with the documentation relative to Rancé's early history and conversion-experience, is that the absoluteness of Rancé's demands on himself and on his brethren (and on others) simply reflects the urgency with which he experienced the imperatives of the Gospel. A sense of proportion--*measure*--is generally supposed to be one of the salient

characteristics of the French intellect, but not all great French
thinkers are characteristic in this respect. Georges Bernanos,
with his alternations between violence and tenderness, expressed
it wonderfully well when he wrote:

> By an extraordinary abuse of language, which would have
> stupified the ancient Greeks, the sense of proportion
> is today confused with the prudence of imbeciles--as if
> there were any other sense of proportion for a man than
> to give himself without limit to values which infinitely
> transcend the scope of his own life.[7]

Centuries earlier, another Frenchman had written much the
same thing:

> The measure for loving God is to love him without measure.[8]

Between the Cistercian humanism of a Joseph Meglinger and the
absolutism of an Armand-Jean de Rancé there could be little chance
of a real *rapprochement*. As Rancé saw it, the moderate programme
of reform advocated by the spokesmen of the Common Observance was
a monument to the prudence of imbeciles; and the genial tolerance
of the Abbot General, Dom Claude Vaussin, meant, ultimately, a failure in love, a failure to love without measure.
  So we take leave of Meglinger and Rancé at the General Chapter
of 1667. Meglinger returns to Wettingen after a round of further
pilgrimaging and pious sight-seeing; Rancé returns to la Trappe *via
recta*, confirmed in his resolve to live to the full the monastic
ideal to which he was irrevocably committed.

BEGINNINGS OF THE LA TRAPPE REFORM

  To no initial attraction of his own is it due that Rancé's own
personal destiny became identified with that of the ancient Cistercian abbey he had held *in commendam* from the age of eleven. There
is no need here to describe even briefly the early history of the
popular and mildly dissipated court *abbé*, and his conversion to a
way of life reconcilable with his ecclesiastical state as priest
and commendatory superior of a half-dozen abbeys and priories. Following a strict interpretation of the sacred canons, he resolved--
after a struggle--to renounce all but a single benefice. He dis-
embarrassed himself of these sources of revenue one by one, till
only two were left. His intention at this stage was to retire to
his Benedictine priory near Boulogne, there to pursue a leisurely
life of seclusion and penitence in congenial surroundings. But
first he had to dispose of la Trappe, on the border between Perche

and Normandy, in the diocese of Séez. Though some of the lands
worked by local peasants brought in an annual revenue, the abbey
itself was in shambles. And the dilapidated buildings merely re-
flected the moral decay of the half-dozen Cistercian derelicts who
used the place as the center of their operations--and not always
very edifying operations. The prior himself had had to disappear
in haste in order to escape criminal prosecution. If we suspect
that the first biographers of Rancé tended to exaggerate a bit, we
have only to look, for instance, at the first extant letter in which
Rancé makes mention of la Trappe, a letter written in 1649, in which
the twenty-three year old commendatory abbot informs Chancellor Pierre Séguier of the return to la Trappe of a monk who, a few years
earlier, had left the abbey after having shot down a local peasant
in cold blood. 'I tried at that time to do what I could to save
the honor of his Order,' wrote the young Rancé.[9]
     We have a reasonably accurate description of the state of the
pre-reform abbey in the before/after sketch drawn up by the Strict
Observance Visitor of the region, Dom Dominique Georges, in the report he submitted to the General Chapter of 1686.

> In those days the doors were kept open day and night,
> and women as well as men had free access to the clois-
> ter. The entrance vestibule was so black with filth
> and so dark that it resembled more some awful prison
> than a 'House of God.' On one side, a deep wine-cellar;
> and on the other, a winepress with all the equipment
> that goes with such places. There was a ladder leaning
> there against the wall--the means of getting to the upper
> storey, though the floor-boards were so broken and rotted
> through that you could walk there only at your own risk.
> Upon entering the cloister you could see that the roof was
> in ruins; it took only a slight rain to flood the cloister.
> The columns supporting the cloister roof had collapsed.
> Parlors served as stables. The refectory was a refectory
> in name only. Monks and seculars used to gather there for
> bowling as often as hot or bad weather made it difficult
> to play the game outside. The dormitory was abandoned
> and uninhabited. It served only as a retreat for night
> birds, and it was exposed to hail, snow, wind, and tempest.
> Each brother lodged howsoever he wished, and wherever he
> could find a place. The commendatory abbot's agent lived
> with his whole family right there with the monks.
>
> The account-office was empty; all you could see was dust
> and grime. Official title-deeds and documents which should
> have been kept there carefully as precious items were scat-
> tered helter-skelter under foot on the floor. For the most

part the title-deeds were scattered throughout the Province;
curés and peasants had got hold of them and this had resulted in the ruination of the temporal holdings.

The church was in no better condition than the house. All
that could be seen was broken pavements, scattered build-
ing-stones, ruins, piles of filth, cobwebs. The walls
were threatening to cave in, either because of the way
they were situated or because of the continual rains which
poured in through crack and crevice. The walls had splits
running from top to bottom. The bell-tower was ready to
topple. The beams on which it rested and the rafters and
almost everything else of wood had rotted through; and
the bells could not be rung without the whole affair shak-
ing. It was enough to make you tremble with fear.

On the high altar was a tabernacle for the Blessed Sacrament. On the right, a statue of our Lady; and on the other
a portrayal of Saint Bernard. Quite apart from poor quality of the work, piety was wounded and intelligence offended at the sight of these broken and disfigured images.

The nave of the church was so dark that, even though the
windows had no glass and gave the sun full entrance, it
was as dark as night even at high noon.

There was no monastery garden. The monastery was surrounded by soil of poor quality, in which grew thorns, bushes,
and trees.

But the height of misfortunes was the fact that, thanks
to the highway built a century earlier and which ran
close to the monastery walls, you saw there only vagabonds, criminals, assassins. Men and women gathered there
in the nearby woods; and there, as in a safe haven, they
hid to commit every sort of crime.[10]

Rancé imported large numbers of workmen, and the work of major
reconstruction began immediately. Louis XIV gave his consent for
the offending highway to be re-routed. But the main problem was
less easily dealt with. The six denizens of the unlikely community
failed to appreciate their commendator's unseasonable fit of pious
concern for their spiritual well-being. For a time, the possibility
of his sudden demise by assassination was anything but remote.[11]
Knowing that help from Monsieur de Clairvaux would hardly be forth-
coming, Rancé invoked the help of his next-door Cistercian neighbors
--the community of the Strict Observance abbey of Perseigne, of

which Dom Michel Guitton was Prior (the abbey was *in commendam*).
Dom Michel himself headed the group of six monks who arrived from
Perseigne in mid-August. A few days later, **regular conventual life**
was re-inaugurated there on the feast of Saint Bernard, 20 August
1662.

In no way was Rancé ready to cast in his lot with the nascent
community. On the 29th of the same month he was back at Boulogne,
where he writes to his confidante, Mother Louise Rogier of the Visitation at Tours,

> I finally arrived back at Boulogne, but not to spend the
> **winter** as I originally intended. I last wrote you that
> I had got the Reform started at the abbey of la Trappe;
> and truly, this undertaking seems to me so important for
> the glory of God that I cannot possibly abandon it for any
> length of time in this period of first beginnings. Though
> I'm quite convinced that neither I nor my presence there
> count for anything, the fact remains that, for the moment,
> I do feel, obliged to be there rather than elsewhere--for
> a few months, that is, till I see that things have made
> a bit more progress. But don't think that this is going
> to take me away from Boulogne. Just now I'm having work
> done here [at Boulogne]; and I haven't changed my mind or
> my arrangement **about** the place for me to settle down....[11]

The following months were to witness a gradual change in the
commendator's relationship with the tiny Cistercian community. By
way of encouraging them, he entered actively into the life of the
community, followed the regular exercises, acted as confessor and
counsellor, and even assumed for the time being the duties of novice-master. Meanwhile, the acting Superior, Dom Michel Guitton,
had returned to Perseigne, of which he had remained head even during his months at la Trappe. Writing to one of his main spiritual
counsellors, Bishop Pavillon of Alet, Rancé describes his own spiritual itinerary at this time:

> I lived there [at la Trappe] to try to consolidate the
> good which wasn't yet too solidly established; and I
> thought that if I lived with **the** religious of the Re-
> form, and like them practised abstinence from meat, this
> might serve a good purpose by way of providing an example
> of some sort to the **non**-Reform religious [three of the
> original six had stayed on at la Trappe]; and that, even
> though they might not accept the same way of life, they
> might at least begin conducting themselves in a more or-
> derly, more religious manner. After having lived in this

way for several months, the thought came to me of em-
bracing the regular life. This experience didn't last
any length of time; but it wasn't long before I felt
it again, stronger than before. It stayed with me for
more than two months, though I said nothing about it
to anyone....[12]

Aspiring at first to the role of a simple monk in the rank and file
of the community, Rancé finally capitualted to the unanimous advice
given by the several ecclesiastics he consulted. The next commendatory abbot might fail to cooperate with the aims and aspirations of
the young community. Rancé should either remain as commendator, or
else make profession and become regular abbot. By now his destiny
had become one with that of the community. On 30 May 1663, he was
at Perseigne, preliminary to the formal commencement of his novitiate. He received the Cistercian habit on 13 June. The Roman documents authorizing him to become regular abbot of la Trappe arrived
on 19 June of the following year. He made solemn profession on 26
June, and was blessed as abbot on 19 July 1664.

FORMATION AT PERSEIGNE AND A BOOK BY JULIEN PARIS

   Critics of the la Trappe reform can easily point to the brief
and not very happy novitiate of Rancé at Perseigne as a major cause
for his alleged failure to grasp the true Cistercian spirit. It was
not a normal novitiate. In October, with less than four months as
a novice behind him, Frère Armand-Jean's health collapsed. He returned to la Trappe to recuperate, and had to remain there till the
following January. Soon afterwards he was away from Perseigne for
at least two weeks on one of the strangest missions ever confided
to a novice: the nearby abbey of Champagne was in the throes of a
civil war; Ancients and Abstinents were at each others' throats, and
Novice Rancé was sent thither with the mandate to restore peace to
the troubled community. The mission was a success. But when, a
short time later, the novice baulked at carrying out yet another,
similar diplomatic mission, he once more had to leave Perseigne to
discuss his indocility and his intentions as future abbot with the
Vicar General of the Reform, Dom Jean Jouaud, at the abbey of Vaux-
de-Cernay.
   Does all this mean that Rancé at Perseigne had no chance at
all of coming into contact with authentic Cistercian sources? Hardly.
For it is almost certainly at Perseigne, if not earlier at la Trappe,
that Rancé had found the book which was to be for a long time his
major source of knowledge about Cistercian institutes and history.[13]
I refer to the bulky tome by Dom Julien Paris, Abstinent abbot of
Foucarmont (1645-1671), *Du Premier esprit de l'Ordre de Cisteaux*.
First printed in 1653, and followed by two subsequent augmented

editions in 1664 and 1670, the book was a virtual *vade-mecum* for a
reform-minded Cistercian; and the full title suggests the reason for
this: *On the Early Spirit of the Cistercian Order: With a Discussion
of a Number of Things Necessary for the Understanding and Re-estab-
lishment of the Government and Way of Life of the Founders of This
Order*. In his classic study, *The Rise of the Cistercian Strict Observance in Seventeenth Century France*, Fr Louis Lekai, O. Cist.
has called attention to the exceptional importance of Paris' tome;
I cannot help but take friendly, though firm, exception to Fr Louis'
description of the book: 'Paris' work is not a systematic treatise
on the subject but rather an oversized pamphlet, an apology for the
Strict Observance....'[14] Systematic the book is; but it is much more
than an oversized pamphlet on disputed questions.

The plan of the book corresponds perfectly with the full-length
title, and admits of four major parts.

PART ONE deals with the early Cistercian Order, and attempts to
discover the spirit of the Order by a survey of her early history,
key-legislation, and early usages. Chapter I describes the foundation of Cîteaux and its subsequent growth into an Order. Chapters
II-III analyze the Charter of Charity. Chapter IV is devoted to
the pivotal principle which is the heart of the whole book: the integral observance of the Holy Rule as the expression of the true
Cistercian spirit. Chapters V-XIII pass in review a series of concrete Cistercian usages, showing how these harmonize faithfully with
the prescriptions of the Holy Rule: norms for the foundation of
monasteries (V), the Cistercian habit (VI), vows and profession
(VII), the Divine Office (VIII), confession, Communion and Mass
(IX), fasts and abstinence (X), solitude and silence (XI), manual
labor, reading, mental prayer (XII), hospitality, and alms-giving
(XIII).

PART TWO studies the administrative machinery of the Order and
the role of Superiors: exemption from episcopal control (I), the
form of government preconised by the Charter of Charity (II), the
General Chapter (III), the system of filiations (IV), local abbots
(V), a sort of 'Mirror of Abbots' composed of texts taken from Cistercian sources and St John Climacus (VI), priors, and other officials (VII), the penitential code (VIII), and finally, a general
summary concerning the excellence of Cistercian life and observance
for the first three centuries of the Order's existence.

PART THREE makes for gloomy reading, and traces the alleged decline of the Order. Basing himself initially on bernardine texts,
Paris assigns, in Chapter I, three causes for the decline he is about
to record: 1) vanity and ambition, 2) disenchantment with austerity
and a penitential way of life, and 3) infidelity to one's particular
vocation. Subsequent chapters, based on Cistercian and papal documents, illustrate the points; and attempts on the part of papacy and
crown to correct the abuses are passed in review.

PART FOUR brings us to the per-essential question: which are the proper and necessary means to be adopted, if the Order is to recover its pristine **spirit**? Chapter I presents an ideal (perhaps idealized) picture of the Golden Age, drawn from Cistercian and non-cistercian coeval sources. Is such a renewal a matter of obligation? Chapter II replies to the question affirmatively and in no uncertain terms. But how are we to revive this spirit? The shortest, easiest way, we are told, is simply to *re-establish the integral observance (l'entier Observance) of the Rule of Saint Benedict* (Chapter III); here the author once again draws on papal pronouncements and Cistercian documents already familiar to us from earlier sections of the book. How does one go about re-establishing this integral observance of the Rule? Chapter IV spells out the answer: simply implement those early documents which expressed so well the spirit of the Order: the Charter of Charity, General Chapter decrees, the early Cistercian usages.

In brief, the message of Paris is this:

The true Cistercian spirit is to be had only by a return to the integral observance of the Holy Rule as understood and implemented by the early Cistercians.

As for Rancé, his own monastic programme was based on the principle that:

The true Cistercian spirit is to be had only by a return to the integral observance of the Holy Rule as understood and implemented by the early Cistercians.

RANCÉAN LITERALISM AND THE RULE INTERPRETED BY CÎTEAUX

The fact that we can find apparent inconsistencies in the early Cistercian programme of return-to-the-Rule is neither a sign of insincerity on their part nor a condemnation of their efforts at reform. Much the same can be said for Rancé and his attempts to revive ancient Cistercian usages at la Trappe. The occasional inconsistencies total up to nothing all that significant against the programme of renewal taken as a whole. In spite of the demonstrable rigidity of the early White Monks and of the seventeenth-century reformer of la Trappe, there was also a refreshing spirit of flexibility which we, with our mania for consistency, find puzzling. Fish, for example, was absent from the table at la Trappe, but fish was served (at least by way of indulgence) in Cistercian refectories of the Golden Age. How rigidly austere, how opposed the Rancéan norm to the authentic Cistercian breadth! But when Rancé explains the reason to a prelate worried about the meagre fare of the brethren at la Trappe, his answer does credit to this true Cistercian spirit.

Writing to an undesignated episcopal correspondent on 4 January 1682, Rancé explains why, at la Trappe, fish and eggs and wine are luxury items:

> If I were to add to our ordinary fare what you write me
> that I should, we would have to say goodbye to two-thirds
> of our brethren and close our hands to a large number of
> the poor who come to our gates every day. There are, in
> fact, seventy people living in the house, without count-
> ing guests. Our resources are too meagre to allow us to
> expand; and we thought it better to break our bread with
> the poor of Jesus Christ--whose numbers are growing be-
> yond all imagining--than to deprive them by leading a more
> comfortable life.[15]

Or again, take an even more minor dietary point such as the ex-
clusion of butter as a seasoning. Le Nain tells how the refectorian
one day forgot to put the customary butter seasoning in the community portion. He was proclaimed for it at the next chapter of faults,
at which the Prior presided in the absence of Rancé. 'If a visitor
were to be told that we don't use butter, that's all if would take
to give la Trappe the reputation for going to extremes,' remarked
the Prior. When Rancé heard of this, his response was that no visitor would disapprove of austerity in the life of solitaries; and for
himself, he preferred *not* to have butter in his own portions. A few
of the more fervent followed his horrible example, and at a later
community discussion on the occasion of one of the twice-weekly conferences, all the brethren asked to go butterless. 'Reverend Father
gave permission only for a limited period; but later on they urged
him to make it a general rule, and he thought that he ought to give
in to their insistence.'[16] I honestly do not know whether butter
was used for seasoning in early Cîteaux. Assuming it was, you may,
I suppose, conclude that the practice of eating unbuttered turnips
is indicative of a rigor little compatible with the true Cistercian
spirit. But for myself, I am less struck by the un-cistercian butterless turnip than by the very Cistercian spirit of joyful austerity and unpretentious generosity. I hasten to add that the early
la Trappe mentality was fraught with possible danger for a later
generation of successors: it is one thing for a small community of
fifteen or twenty generous monks to commit themselves to this sort
of thing; but it is another thing for them to make it normative for
future generations possibly less deeply and less enthusiastically
motivated than themselves.
      The inconsistency of la Trappe observance with the early Cis-
tercian practice goes much farther than cider replacing wine and
the elimination of butter as a seasoning, however, and it will make
this presentation easier if I simply state that, no matter how

frequently we may find the expression 'literal interpretation of
the Rule' or 'whole and entire observance of the Rule' in the writings of the Reformer of la Trappe, it is doubtful that Rancé envisaged, in the concrete, an absolutely literalistic return to the
early Cistercian interpretation of the Rule in all its details. A
useful text for our understanding of his general orientation is to
be found in his commentary on the words of the preface to the Rule
of Saint Benedict, 'As we advance in the religious life and in faith,
our hearts expand and we run the way of God's commandment with un-
speakable sweetness of love.' After providing (in keeping with his
usual practice) a Christological dimension to the whole question of
mortification and strict ascetical discipline--for monastic asceticism is, for Rancé, essentially a question of love for Christ--our
author begins borrowing material from Saint Bernard's *De precepto
et dispensatione*, where the Saint treats in divers places of the
various kinds of precepts contained in the Rule. Following Saint
Bernard, Rancé mentions a few precepts by nature immutable: loving
God, for instance, or one's neighbor. Departing a bit from Saint
Bernard, he next gives a series of examples of major precepts of
the Rule which admit of no dispensation, no matter what the contrary custom or actual practice might be: flight from worldly people, and from the spirit and affairs of the world; silence, spiritual reading. But now we come to no less than three related but
different groups of mutable prescriptions:

1. There are other [precepts] which, unimportant in themselves,
   have been able to cease and to be abolished in the course
   of time, such as the ceremonies of the Office, the distribution of hours [=horarium], the order of exercises, the
   education of children, etc.

2. There are still **others** which have been changed into contrary usages, which because of the present **state** and concrete
   situation affords greater advantage, profit, and edifica-
   tion than that which the [observance of the] law could effect if it were maintained--the washing of the feet of
   guests, for example, a separate table for the abbot [in
   the guest **refectory**], the expulsion of incorrigible religious.

3. There are still others which have been abrogated or modi-
   fied by the authority of the Church, such as abstinence
   from meat, the former austerity of night-watching, etc.[17]

All of this calls for a nice discernment of spirits, of course.
Accordingly, in spite of the fact that Rancé steeped himself in the
early Cistercian *consuetudines* and in the *cisterciensia* collected by

Julien Paris in his *Du premier esprit* and his *Nomasticon cisterciense* (1664), his own *rassourcement* had little of the literalistic about it.

Rancé seems, moreover, to have taken for granted that his own generation, be its representatives ever so zealous, were mere midgets compared to the Cistercian giants of an earlier age. Writing to the energetic but not always prudent reforming abbot, Dom Eustace Beaufort, Rancé characteristically advises him to go easy, and describes with brutal frankness the near disaster recently perpetrated in his own community:

> We took up [the fasts prescribed by the Rule] and observed them with great exactitude for two years. There were fifty religious who had asked me for this with all possible insistence; they had but one heart, one spirit, one will on this point as on all others. But there were only ten or twelve capable enough and healthy enough to keep it up....18

God does not mind, **Rancé** continues, if our fasts are not identical with those of our Fathers, so long as we do not differ from them in the really fundamental areas. And then, in an admirable formula:

> Discretion, when exempt from all laxity and carnal condescension, is a greater virtue than penitence. And you can even think of it as humility if there is a certain distance between your own exterior practices and those of our Fathers. *They* were saints, and were animated by a spirit no longer found in the same degree and the same plenitude in those who have come after them....19

CRISIS AT PERSEIGNE

Entirely too much has been made of Rancé's much interrupted novitiate as militating against his Cistercian formation. While it well may be that his novitiate training was a total loss, his contact with *Du premier esprit* was worth several novitiates. Further, the restless year he spent in and out of Perseigne doubtless helped clarify, by way of opposites, Rancé's monastic programme for his own community. If Rancé found Perseigne wanting in its Cistercian dimension—and his biographers are unanimous on this point—this can only be because Rancé could compare Perseigne in the concrete against an allegedly Cistercian authenticating norm: Cîteaux as depicted in the pages of Julien Paris.

Further, we tend too easily to overlook the critically important involvement of Rancé with the Order prior to the beginning of his novitiate. When Rancé and the unlikely denizens of unreformed la **Trappe** signed, on 17 August 1662, the concordat transferring la

Trappe to the Strict Observance, this was an official act which pre-
supposed a lengthy series of contacts, discussions, and protracted
interviews between the commendator and the representatives of the
Reform--the Vicar General, Jean Jouaud; the Vicar's Commissary, Dom
Nicolas le Guédois, abbot of Barbery; and Dom Michel Guitton, Prior
of Perseigne, who supplied the original colony of reformed monks.
For a doctor of the Sorbonne of Rancé's intellectual calibre to take
the initiative in introducing the Reform into his abbey, one may
safely assume, he had some rudimentary knowledge at least of the
aims and ideals of the group he was sponsoring. Had la Trappe been
a Premonstratensian abbey, we may be sure that Rancé would have
delved into Premonstratensian sources with a view to furthering the
current efforts at renewal. As it was, la Trappe was Cistercian.
Then, too, we must remember the extent of Rancé's participation in
community life of the nascent community at la Trappe; his involvement was total and his understanding of Cistercian life was such
that Dom Michel apparently had no qualms in designating the commendator as novice-master. And if, still later at Perseigne, the same
Dom Michel sent his novice on a mission of mediation between the
warring factions at Champagne, this is not so much a sign that Dom
Michel had momentarily lost his reason, but that Dom Michel apparently thought that, novice though he was, Rancé was already experienced enough and knowledgeable enough to carry out the mission better than any other available person.

Many years later, in a long memorandum written for his successors as abbot of la Trappe, and dealing with the salient points of
his programme of reform, Rancé himself was to say:

> When I entered the Cistercian Order, I proposed to take
> up again practices quite contrary to those I saw establish-
> ed therein; and since the Order seemed to me quite holy in
> its origin, I resolved to conform myself as much as possi-
> ble to the rules which the Founders had prescribed there
> by their examples.[20]

The truth is that in many respects the programme of even the Strict
Observance was markedly different from that of the early Cistercians. Daily recreation, weekly walks outside the enclosure, a
mere one-hour token period of manual labor for the non-priests of
the community, the virtual elimination of monks who were not priests,
with corresponding emphasis on formal studies before and after ordination...Armand-Jean Gervaise, the author of a deplorable series
of detailed but slanted and inaccurate books about the story of la
Trappe and its reformer, recounts for us a particularly dramatic
scene in which the novice, as hero, virtually on the eve of profession confronts his Superiors with his decision not to make profession unless, as abbot of la Trappe, he is allowed to adhere more

closely to early Cîteaux than is the practice in other houses of
the Reform. 'Schism!' replies Dom Michel. But both he and the
Vicar General, wanting at all costs to keep so capable a subject
in the Order, and thinking it unlikely that Rancé's castle in the
air would ever become reality, accepted the intransigent novice's
terms.[21]

Prudently discounting for Gervaise's wonted flim-flam, we find
a residue of truth which remains after the rhetorical developments
have been peeled away: Rancé did indeed receive from his Vicar General some kind of reluctant (and surely unofficial) *nihil obstat*.
It was only after Jouaud's death (1673) that serious fears were
voiced in the Reform about the particularism of a few of the houses
owing allegiance to the Reform (la Trappe and Sept-Fons were the
chief objects of concern). Further, we have from Jouaud himself a
letter sent to Rancé in the early days of the local reform; in it
the Vicar General comments freely on the particular programme followed at la Trappe, but without for a moment suggesting that it is
unauthorized. The letter, quoted in part by Rancé's biographer,
le Nain, was written at an early date when the community was still
numerically small and the problem of recruitment still deemed serious. Rancé had written the Vicar General for help in recruiting
likely candidates. Replied Jouaud:

> I can assure you that you are hardly going to find any-
> one in our Order filled with that same spirit of peni-
> tence that God is giving you, and very few who have the
> strength and courage to practice the austerity you are
> observing. For myself, I know of no one; and since this
> austerity, to the point to which you carry it, goes be-
> yond the obligation of our Rule and Constitutions--
> though it falls within [the limits of] perfection--I
> could not oblige any religious to go and embrace it
> against his will; and you yourself would not want me to
> send you anyone who is unwilling.[22]

Before reading farther in this citation, we should note several
points in this brief paragraph: 1) la Trappe observance is too de-
manding for most Cistercians; 2) the austerity goes beyond the re-
quirements of Rule and Constitutions (more about the Constitutions
in a later section of this paper). Jouaud does not however, suggest that la Trappe austerity exceeds the austerity of the early
Cistercians. Let us read on:

> I am convinced that our own laxness *(lacheté)* is drawing
> down God's wrath upon us, and that we deserve his chas-
> tisements in all justice. But if he thereby wishes to
> raise us to that high degree of penitence which you prac-
> tice, his goodness will be great enough to inspire us

with the [necessary] efficacious movement, and to give us
the strength for it. And if I do see that he is giving
this to some [individuals], I shall not fail to address
them to you. But as of now, I can say of you what was
said of our first Fathers: That you have a great many
admirers, but very few imitators.[23]

Two further points emerge: 1) Jouaud was by no means impressed
with the level of observance in the Strict Observance, but felt
this is the best that could be done apart from an exceptional out-
pouring of divine grace; 2) la Trappe's great austerity resulted
in a recruitment problem parallel to that of early Cîteaux. There
is no accusation of disobedience in departing from the standard
observance in the Reform; not even a veiled suggestion of infidelity to the Cistercian spirit or the practice of early Cîteaux. In
brief, Jouaud is saying: If you want to be singularly austere, be
singularly austere--but you shall have to accept the consequences.
    This letter is explicable only if Rancé and Jouaud had come
to a mutual understanding somewhat along the lines of what Gervaise,
ever in need of demythologizing, recounts in his *Jugement critique*.

THE ROMAN MISSION

    After his abbatial blessing in mid-July, Rancé had only six
weeks at la Trappe before disaster befell with a vengeance. Called to Paris for a meeting of Abstinent superiors, Rancé was chosen,
together with the abbot of Val-Richer, the saintly Dom Dominique
Georges, official delegate of his Observance in the matters being
controverted before a specially constituted Roman Congregation for
Cistercian Affairs.
    We are surely right to be astonished that the choice fell on
a newly blessed abbot with only two months of profession to his
credit. But Jouaud was no simpleton, and it is unlikely that the
assembled Abstinent superiors would have been so collectively ir-
responsible as to appoint at this critical juncture a delegate un-
suited to his mission. True, Rancé had access to a good number of
influential people at court, whose patronage would be helpful in
the negotiations at Rome; but this could hardly have been the over-
riding reason for his appointment. After all, the material and
spiritual recovery of la Trappe, thanks to Rancé's leadership, had
been phenomenal; and both Michel Guitton and Jean Jouaud had had
ample proof of Rancé's integrity, zeal for regular observance, and
uncompromising committment to what he rightly or wrongly took to
be the Cistercian ideal.
    It is no more than a personal opinion unsupported by apodictic
proof, but my impression is that Rancé's Roman mission did little
by way of clarifying for him the aims and intentions of the founders

of Cîteaux. He had left his abbey on 9 September 1664, and it was
May 1666, before he was able once more to be with his brethren. The
months between were, we gather from his personal correspondence at
the time, nothing if not painful. He certainly profited in a negative way in that he returned to la Trappe so fed up with party politics and the activities that go on in the corridors of power, and
so disillusioned as to the possibilities of a meaningful reform
for the Order at large in France, that his one desire was to devote himself exclusively to the service of his small, but already
burgeoning community.

    The more important extant documents touching on the Roman mis-
sion have been edited and given a careful and enormously helpful
presentation by Fr Thomas Nguyên-Dĩnh-Tuyên, O. Cist.[24] But it
seems doubtful that the half-dozen memoranda drawn up by Rancé in
collaboration with Dominique Georges can provide significant insights into the personal **monastic** ideology of the reformer of la
Trappe. The redactors of this material had brought with them to
Rome a small library of pamphlets, books, and manifestos such as
had poured forth from Abstinent pens during the preceding decades.
Of the seven **Strict** Observance memoranda edited by Fr Thomas, most
simply reply point by point to a previous memorandum or project presented by representatives of the Common Observance and dealing with
controverted questions of present structures of government, jurisdiction, points bearing on the recent history of the Strict Observance.[25] By far the most important Abstinent memorandum is the
lengthy mid-December 1664 document which purports to be a reasoned
exposé of the Cistercian ideal, of the history of the decline of
that ideal, of the recent attempt to restore that ideal, and of
the imperative need to foster and protect the Strict Observance
in which alone resides the authentic Cistercian tradition.[26] But
this impressive document, with its plethora of citations and historical references, is little more than a well done summary of
major sections of Julien Paris' *Du premier esprit,* interpolated
here and there by material taken, if I am not mistaken, from some
of the anonymous pamphlets and books authored by the prolific Abstinent leader, Jean Jouaud. Perhaps the most important lines of
the document are to be found early in the text, where the author
(surely Rancé, with the collaboration of Dom Dominique) pens the
lapidary formula:

        monastica vita poenitentia est.
Leave it to nineteenth-century and modern-day historians to confuse
and totally distort the meaning of the formula. For 'penance' read
'heroic mortifications,' and you will have the Abstinent programme
as presented by its critics: 'Monastic life (and especially life
at la Trappe) is essentially a life of heroic mortification, a life
à *la* Desert Fathers.' But this kind of simplistic understanding is
based both on an uniformed knowledge about the Desert Fathers and an

erroneous grasp of the word 'penance' or 'penitence' in the traditional monastic vocabulary still current in seventeenth-century
France. In brief, *poenitentia* is more often than not the same as
what is covered by the term 'asceticism' or 'ascetic practice.'
So when the author of our memorandum goes on to write that 'All
monks have this in common, that they devote themselves to *penance*,'
this means rather more than questionable practices of heroic mortification. Our author most certainly alludes to a life of Bernardine squalor *(vita nostra squalor est)*, groaning and tears, but
he straightway goes on to say that although the monks who follow
SS Basil, Pachomius, Anthony or Benedict all live lives of 'penance,' each of these groups has its own particular way of living
this penitential life. He notes, too, that differences in penance
as regards the chanting, the clothing, and the various other ceremonies are of minor importance. This suggests that, if these various elements can be subsumed under the term 'penance,' this term
is hardly convertible with 'heroic mortification.' The next lines
of the text make the meaning even clearer. There we read that the
main expressions of penance in the Holy Rule can be reduced to:
fasting, night-watching, silence or solitude, abstinence from
meat, manual labor, voluntary poverty. After citing chapter and
verse of the Holy Rule anent each of these practices, our author
sums up: 'In these laws the Father Saint Benedict comprised *(con-
clusit)* the penitence of his Order and ensured *(consuluit)* the
holiness of his sons.'[27]

Since the question of la Trappe penance and the Cistercian
spirit will be treated briefly in a later paragraph, no more need
be said here--except perhaps to reassure the reader who might be
concerned that anyone could sum up monastic life as essentially a
life of penance (however understood) rather than as a life of perfect love. But here the context is not the essence of Christian
life--an essence common to all expressions of life in Christ--but
simply that which is specific to monastic life and which marks off
monastic life as distinct from other forms of Christian life. All
Christians have to love; all Christians have to be obedient, chaste.
The particular means of attaining to the fulness of life in Christ
differ in kind or degree according to one's particular state of
life. You may well disagree that what marks monastic life off as
distinct from other forms of life is its ascetic programme (or,
in the terms of the present discussion, its programme of penance
or penitence); but realize that your disagreement is with a constant of tradition, East and West. When questioned recently about
the relationship between monastic life and observances, a monastic scholar of the stature of Dom Adalbert de Vogüé could reply
with tradition on his side, 'Ah, but monastic life *is* observances.'
He was saying very much the same thing as the Abstinent spokesmen
with their *Monastica vita poenitentia est.*·

At any rate, the Roman interlude came to its appointed end, and the abbot of la Trappe returned to his community.

CONSOLIDATION OF THE LA TRAPPE REFORM AND THE BIRTH OF A LEGEND

Until shortly after Rancé's return from his Roman mission, life at la Trappe had followed quite exactly the norms laid down in the Constitutions of the Strict Observance. But from there on, and for the better part of the next decade, the community--and it was always a community option--introduced gradually the main features of its particular observance: strict enclosure, three hours (at least) of daily manual work, elimination of formal clerical studies, strict silence, frugality (and more) in the refectory. From time to time details of observance underwent modification, particularly with regard to fasting. Recruits came in larger numbers, and in 1671 Rancé had to enlarge the refectory and build twenty-four new cells. Yes, cells. Very un-cistercian. But as the culprit was to explain later in Chapter Twenty-two of his *Commentary on the Holy Rule,* he had accepted individual partitioned cubicles in the dormitory at an early stage of the reform, not realizing that it offended against primitive Cistercian practice; and that later, 'having already received a large number of religious, I could not bring myself to make changes which would have disturbed the order of the monastery'-- and here he explains the practical problem of providing the brethren with sleeping-quarters during the period required for the hypothetical reconstruction of the dormitory.[28] Here I admit that Rancé was *peu cistercien.* In the Golden Age the General Chapter would have allowed two months for the reconstruction of the dormitory, after which time the abbot, prior, and cellarer would have been on bread and water every Friday till the reconstruction had been completed; obstinacy on Rancé's part would have resulted in his deposition. As it was, he could only plead ignorance, though he added that when the dormitory of the lay-brethren was built somewhat later, he was able to follow the early Cistercian ruling. Besides, as of 1675, the community had persuaded the by no means reluctant abbot to restore the early Cistercian practice of doing one's spiritual reading, not in the privacy of the cell, but in the community context of the cloister.[29]

It was not long before public attention began to focus on the reformed community; in time there was to spring up a popular form of monastic travelogue of the 'My-Visit-to-la-Trappe' genre. The first description of this kind need not detain us long, since it was set down second-hand by a Carthusian of Liget, who describes a visit to la Trappe by a native of Tours during Pentecost of 1667, only a few days after Rancé's return from the dramatic General Chapter of that year. The community is described as 'hidden to men by reason of its location, and just as unknown for its holiness.' But

because the author paints his picture in colors drawn exclusively
from a Carthusian pallette--la Trappe is a 'Mount Lebanon,' a place
of solitude for 'holy hermits,' and the life is 'filled with God
alone and empty of all that is of the mere created order'--we may
well read his glowing second-hand account with caution. 'Never has
life been lived so according to rule and in so mortified a way,'
says our Carthusian, who also suggests the reason for the unanimity
of the brethren:

> What fosters the great union of this holy house is the
> fact that the holy Abbot, through the free choice of
> his religious, is their confessor. You can imagine what
> it must be like--the wonderful example of virtue and the
> holy instructions that he gives them heart to heart *(coeur
> à coeur)*. It would take a legion of demons to sow cockle
> in so regular a community, where the union is so great
> that it resembles the union of the angels in paradise....30

More interesting, because written by an eye-witness Maurist,
is a rather long account of a visit to la Trappe a few years later,
a bit after mid-September of (I think) 1670.31 In an anthology of
pieces concerning la Trappe printed in 1683, this letter of an anonymous Benedictine to his sister, a nun, runs to some forty pages,
and can here be dealt with in only summary fashion. What was it
that a level-headed member of an exemplary reformed Benedictine
Congregation saw when he came to la Trappe?
R. P. Anonyme tells his sister quite frankly that, with the
help of Cod's grace, his visit to la Trappe could well turn out to
be more profitable than several years spent in religious life (p. 72).
He had first heard of la Trappe during a visit of his to the Benedictine abbey of Lyre, where one of the brethren had recently returned
from the Cistercian abbey, loud in his praises of the abbot and his
holy community. Our monastic pilgrim arrived towards evening, already primed to find 'a second Clairvaux, and another Saint Bernard
in the person of this worthy abbot' (pp. 72-73). So far as I know,
this is the first formulation of a theme which was to become, alas,
a commonplace among friends of la Trappe. We even find in the 1719
edition of le Nain's biography of the Holy Abbot a particularly long,
circumstantial, and somewhat fulsome comparison between Bernard and
Rancé.33 If we find the parallels grossly exaggerated and in poor
taste, Rancé would be the first to agree with us.
After a brief description of the local geography (thick forests,
meadows, marshland, and pools aplenty), of the climate (perpetual
fog and mist), and of the early history of the place, our Maurist
traveller describes his friendly reception by the 'oblate' in the
porter's lodge (the 'oblate' was one of two aristocrats who had
come to la Trappe at an early date and remained as part-time hermits).

Has he come to pay his respects to Father Abbot? Not much chance of
that, since Father Abbot sees visitors only rarely. A few minutes
later, Father Prior arrives, and the full Cistercian ritual for the
reception of a guest is followed: prostration by the Prior, a visit
to the Blessed Sacrament in church, the reading of a passage from
an edifying book, a meal--just as in Chapter 87: *De hospitibus sus-
cipiendis,* in the ancient Usages. Unexpectedly, Father Abbot himself does come to see our Benedictine after supper--suspecting the
presence of a potential postulant? No, there is no need for him to
read Père Anonyme's 'obedience'--a Maurist habit is proof in itself
that everything is in order. As for Father Abbot, he is

> well-built, rather tall [!?], and--as of the present
> writing--forty to forty-two years old [the estimate is
> off by a few years]. He speaks with such agreeableness
> and ease, that I cannot remember having ever heard any-
> one who surpassed him on this score, though he spoke
> without any affectation whatever....(p. 77).

Father Abbot is delighted to learn that our visiting Maurist has
made the journey to la Trappe on foot. 'We can do more than we
sometimes think we can,' modestly demurs Père Anonyme. Yes, replies Rancé, this has been the experience of the brethren at la
Trappe: 'What they had practised at the start out of sheer neces-
sity because of their very real poverty served to convince them of
the possibility of their subsisting in this same manner' (p. 78).

The conversation was interrupted by an emergency. Rancé had
to hurry off to assist a monk who had just had a stroke. Our visitor was to learn later that the moribund monk, Joseph Bernier, who
died on 15 September 1670, had been one of the few original denizens of the place to remain after the take-over by the colony from
Perseigne. Only gradually, we are told, had Rancé brought him gently around to the point of giving up his private possessions and of
making a general confession to another religious; for some time,
the reformed monk had been celebrating Mass daily (pp. 78-79).

Our visitor notes, too, that Rancé's homely hospitality extended to doing 'humble chores not to be expected of a simply laybrother'
(p. 79)--which, being interpreted, probably has to do with emptying
chamber-pots.

The next day, a further conversation ensued with Father Abbot
--this time in the library. Yes, there was a library at la Trappe,
and Père Anonyme admired its excellence. This was the personal library which Rancé had brought to la Trappe and, while still commendator, had willed to the community, on the condition that the valuable collection be sold for the benefit of the poor should the community ever revert to its former ways (pp. 79-80). With our pious visitor pumping Father Abbot for information concerning la Trappe obser-

vance, however, Father Abbot gently steers the conversation to other
topics when the questioner shows too much unguarded admiration. Austere though the regime is, our Maurist tells us, so often as a monk
needs any kind of alleviation, Rancé 'procures it for him with every
show of charity, and more abundantly than he desires' (p. 81). Indeed, Père Anonyme witnessed a case in point. Fr Prior informed the
Abbot that a monk well on the way to recuperation in the infirmary
prefers to have his meat-broth regime dropped; but meat-broth it's
to be, no matter how unwanted and unneeded. As a matter of fact,
Father Abbot is also acting **infirmarian** at this time, 'carrying out
his job as infirmarian with **unbelievable** care, and humbling himself
to chores which even base-born persons would often experience repug-
nance in doing' (p. 82). A long description follows on the **discipline** and regularity of the sick and ailing in the infirmary; so far
as could be helped, sickness in no way meant a levelling off of observance. One of the **infirm** brethren is described in particular.
Victim of a fever which has lasted unabated for the better part of
two years, he nevertheless insisted on chanting in choir (which he
did seated). Our visitor noted the Prior's unavailing efforts he
himself witnesses to get the sick man to take things a bit more
easy. Unable to work, the ailing monk found considerable consola-
tion in watching his confrères work! In point of fact, his health
had been somewhat better ever since Father Abbot made him swallow
some rose-water brewed from roses plucked from the thorn bushes in
which (it is said) the young Saint Benedict had rolled centuries
ago in his struggle against the lusts of the flesh. Rancé had returned from Italy with roses from Benedict's thorn-bushes. The
story has a happy ending, for the monk, hitherto unable to swallow,
at last began to eat again; and our informant later learned with
satisfaction that the ailing monk and **the** other infirm were once
more in the pink of health--*en bon point* (pp. 83-84).
There is nothing at la Trappe but what is edifying, but the
most edifying phenomenon of all is this 'excellent abbot who is,
so to speak, the key-stone of this beautiful edifice.' With a
shrewd insight into community dynamics, our narrator notes the in-
ter-action between abbot and brethren:

> What is still more marvellous is to see that, far from
> having any reservations about this rigorous manner of
> life...they are the first to urge their abbot in this
> direction *(ils sont les premiers à y porter leur Abbé)*
> --[and all this because] his good example and good direc-
> tion *(bonne conduite)* have all that it takes to win their
> hearts *(ont d'attraits pour gagner les coeurs)* (p. 86).

There are further notes on **candidates** who have left a less
strict observance in order to come and find a place 'freely and

with joy under his discipline' (p. 86); but our narrator also admits
at least one instance of Rancé's failure to bring one of the pre-
reform monks of la Trappe around to a minimally acceptable religious
observance (p. 88).

The Cantor, he felt, was particularly good, and also a good
teacher. The liturgy is carried out to perfection. 'I cannot remember ever having assisted at any Office which pleased me so much' (p.
89). The Office, too, is generally quite long, since there is in
addition to the Canonical Office the daily Marian Office and the rather frequent Office for the Dead. Reference is made to two daily periods of meditation, soon after rising (after the Office of Our Lady)
and again after Compline. But our Benedictine notes that, contrary
to the general practice of beginning meditation in common by hearing
points of meditation read out, each monk meditates according to his
personal attraction, ' since it is not right, as the abbot says, to
want to restrict God, and have him nourish each and every one with
the same kind of bread' (p. 90).

After Night Office (which began at 2 AM) and Lauds, the brethren
read in common until Prime (at 6 AM), though the summer schedule allowed for an optional hour's sleep after Lauds for those who did not
take the noon siesta. Rancé himself, however, spent the time between
Office and Prime at prayer in church (and hearing confessions, we
learn from parallel sources). The fact is, we are told by our narrator, who has this information from a recent Cistercian visitor to
la Trappe, Father Abbot allows himself only three hours sleep. The
three hours of manual work, divided equally between morning and afternoon, likewise find the abbot working harder than his brethren,
and in their midst. His preference is for the more menial chores;
and when the signal for work is given, it was quite usual for him to
break off in the middle of a conversation with a bishop or other visiting dignitary in order to get to work on time (p. 92).

Manual labor enabled the brethren to provide for their own needs
and those of the guests. By supporting themselves in this way, they
also avoided business contacts with outsiders (p. 93). The observance of strict enclosure came in for special mention, too (pp. 93-
94), as well as the utter absence of anything smacking of 'news of
the world' (p. 94). But our Maurist is careful to put this distanc-
ing from the world in its proper perspective of a coming closer to
God; and there follows an especially beautiful paragraph about the
spirit of prayer at la Trappe. Indeed, the Abbé le Camus, who was
later to become Archbishop of Grenoble and Cardinal, is quoted as
saying that the la Trappe reform is bound to perdure, given the enthusiasm of the brethren for prayer.

As we might expect, there is an awed description of the diet.
Contrary to early Cistercian practice, Father Abbot always takes his
meals with the brethren, and not even with his own blood-brother,
the Chevalier de Rancé, who had got to see his brother only very

briefly on the occasion of a recent visit. Our visiting Benedictine
(and his companion, who is mentioned only in passing) were allowed
to take dinner with the community. But Père Anonyme has to admit
the meal was tasty enough. Perhaps, he thinks, his own portion was
laced with a bit of butter. The menu is eggless and fishless; cider (dreadful stuff) replaces wine. As a guest, however, he enjoys
the luxury of a mini-omlette, a lump of butter, and a portion of
fruit more substantial than what the other monks get. The description of the refectory ends, however, on a **paradoxical** note:

> Nonetheless, if you were to see the faces of these reli-
> gious, you would say that they fed on the finest fare
> from the healthy appearance they have *(tant qu'ils sont
> en bon point)*. But what you'd find even more surprising
> is the joy which is so very much in evidence. This is
> one of the things that touched me most. They really put
> the gospel precept into practice; they don't disfigure
> their faces in order to show off their austerities (p. 100).

The narrator returns to his theme of fraternal unanimity so
apparent at la Trappe. He tells, for instance, that during the
period of Rancé's Roman mission eggs had been served in the refectory several times a week, 'but this did not last long, for the religious entered upon a holy conspiracy not to touch them' (p. 101). He
adds that if it were not for Father Abbot's insistence, the brethren
would not even take advantage of their calefactory during periods of
cold weather.
Needless to say, the silence at la Trappe spoke loudly to our
visitor. One gathers from his remarks, however, that it was less absolute than it became in later years. Speaking permission, for instance, could be asked for in writing; and when religious spoke with
each other, they did so in so low a tone that one had to listen carefully to hear (pp. 101-102). Instead of the daily talk-fests which
went by the name 'recreation' in even the more regular communities,
there was an hour-long 'conference' twice a week after dinner (at an
earlier date, thrice weekly). The community gathered in a circle in
the garden in good weather; the one presiding proposed some edifying
consideration; and each monk in turn contributed his own bit to the
admittedly formal discussion. But all this is done, we are told,
'with a great forthrightness and liberty of spirit' (p. 102). Once
a month the conference was held farther away from the abbey—sometimes even at a distance of a few miles. (Later on, the frequency
of these excursions was reduced to a few times annually, and the
brethren finally decided to have the conference only once a week.)
The **chapter** of faults comes in for little comment—possibly because it was not much different from Maurist practice. But there is
a long paragraph in praise of the learning and eloquence of Father

Abbot. The narrator quotes his unidentified Cistercian visitor
friend, already referred to, as having heard Rancé's chapter-talk
on the Feast of the Purification. Never had he heard the like, he
claimed; and if la Trappe were in his own region (Franche Comte),
the abbey would be swarming with recruits (p. 106).

Revenues by his report, were pathetically minuscule: seven to
eight-thousand *livres* for twenty-six monks, six laybrothers, and two
oblates. Three cows provide milk for cheese and butter, as well as
for the milk which is a staple item in the menu. Only one secular
is on the monastery payroll (p. 107).

All pastoral ministry with respect to outsiders was rigorously
excluded. The reason advanced is a bit unexpected: 'Christians nowadays are not sufficiently minded to conform to the teaching of the
Council of Trent' (p. 108). Possibly Rancé had in mind the celebrated uproar sparked when a priest of Saint-Sulpice felt bound in
conscience to refuse absolution to the pious but Jansenizing Duc de
Liancourt. Something just as awful could happen at la Trappe if one
weren't careful. It is interesting, too, that even though the canons
of the Council of Trent had not been officially promulgated in gallican France, Rancé was among those who accepted the decisions of the
Council as normative.

Then there was the simplicity of la Trappe!

One of the most considerable virtues that I noticed in
this holy man and in this house of God is simplicity--
whether in their conversation or in their gardens, fur-
nishings, vestments, and church appointments. The church
is solidly built, but without decoration outside or inside: the clear lightsomeness and cleanness make for its
principal beauty. The high altar is quite simple; above
it only a statue of our Lady, who holds the suspended ci-
borium with the Blessed Sacrament. The richest vestments
are simply wool or inexpensive cloth with a few silk trim-
mings....It is in this spirit of simplicity, such as Saint
Bernard had, that this good abbot has renounced all signs
of abbatial authority such as so many make such a fuss
about. He has agreed only to use the crozier when he cele-
brates Mass on the greater feasts (pp. 108-109).

Nor is his [Rancé's] simplicity any less remarkable in
his conversation; for although in times past he had gained his doctoral degree with honor and amid great applause,
and although he was at his best in public functions, possessing as he does a perfect command of the principal
languages, nowadays he devotes himself only to the reading of Cassian, Saint John Climacus, Saint Bernard, and
others of this kind, whom he counsels others to read (p. 109).

There is a final long paragraph touching on the 'lay' character of monasticism at la Trappe. None of the monks seemed desirous of ordination; nor was the abbot inclined to have a large number of priests 'as is elsewhere the practice,' against the ancient custom' (p. 110). Further, there seemed to be far fewer community officials than in most standard communities. The office of procurator was of recent introduction, in order to leave Abbot and Prior more free to devote themselves to their community ministry (pp. 110-111).

No need to pursue the subject by an analysis of longer and more systematic descriptions of life at la Trappe as recorded by other eye-witnesses. The longest and perhaps the most reliable, because written by a professional historian, is the *Description* penned by the King's historiographer, Dom Félibien des Abaux, soon after a visit to la Trappe in September 1670. The work went through many editions. But though it fleshes out (and in minor points corrects) out Maurist Anonymous, the picture is quite the same. As in the Benedictine's letter to his sister, Father Abbot is there presented in terms quite the same. 'It is a pleasure,' writes Dom Félibien, to hear Monsieur l'Abbé discourse on the happiness of the life to come:

> His words are like a devouring fire that enflames those who are listening. You remember [the author is address-ing this to the Duchesse de Liancourt]...with what elo-quence he used to express himself when he was still at court, and used to speak about the things of the world. But it's with incomparably more power that he speaks about the things of heaven....[33]

The things of heaven and a life of penitence in union with Jesus Christ are the preferred themes of the eloquent abbot, 'whose words are accompanied by an air so filled with joy that it is easy to see how deeply convinced he is of what he is saying, and the pleasure he feels when he thus expresses outwardly the true in-ward sentiments of his heart which he is trying to communicate to everyone.'[34] The brethren, meanwhile,

> are no timid, spineless slaves led by a valiant captain. These are free men, men who are generous, and who march after their head whom they obey with the utmost love....[35]

Is this all a bit exaggerated, a bit uncritical in its enthusi-asm? Perhaps. But this is an *a priori* assumption. More objective, perhaps, would be an unbiased report by someone less suspect of parti-ality. Dom Hervé du Tertre, successor to Dom Jean Jouaud at Prières, and official Visitor for the region in which la Trappe was located, could hardly be suspected of harboring a favorable bias towards the

independent abbot of la Trappe. He arrived at la Trappe for the
regular visitation in 1676, and left a *carte de visite* which has
been many times reprinted along with a second *carte de visite*
from a second visitation by the same Visitor in 1678. The first
visitation card begins with a description of the composition of
the community: its forty-six members came from every walk of life
and from many different provinces. Some had been

> students from various colleges, others calvary men, others
> soldiers, others clerics, still others priests of the dio-
> cesan clergy or of religious congregations; there were doc-
> tors of theology, religious of various Orders, such as Can-
> ons Regular, Hermits of Saint Augustine, Benedictines--even
> from the Maurist Congregation--Celestines, Franciscans, re-
> ligious from the Congregation of Val des Choux, and even
> Cistercians from both Observances, the Common and the Strict;
> as well as monks from divers conditions and professions,
> and of every different age-group.

> Nevertheless, and despite this great diversity, difference,
> and disparity, we found them so closely united by the bond
> of charity, so much at one in everything, so devoted one
> and all to their duties, and so universally zealous for
> regular observance, and enjoying together so profound a
> peace, that during the three entire days spent in carry-
> ing out the regular scrutinies, we received no complaint,
> neither the Superiors against the inferiors, nor the in-
> feriors against the Superiors, nor the inferiors against
> each other. Not only did we not perceive or note any dis-
> content, murmuring, division, dissension, alienation, par-
> tiality, aversion, or mutual dislike, but there was not
> even the slightest appearance or even the mere shadow of
> any of these things....[36]

The Visitor then admits that he found it neither necessary nor
suitable to leave the community with any particular prescription
or regulation. The rest of the *carte de visite* is simply a long
ferverino about love of solitude, the practice of silence, and the
avoidance of idleness--all expressed in terms of perfect conformity
with the la Trappe regime. The second visitation card is shorter
than the first, and far from expressing any reserve whatsoever a-
bout the nature of the particular la Trappe observance, the Visitor praises it without qualification, and insists on the obligation of the brethren to remain faithful to it.[37]
    For our own purposes, such a report is important by reason of
its official and objective nature; but it is also much less informative than the unofficial narratives which deal with concrete points

of observance. Here, however, we may raise the question: Are the
la Trappe particularisms contrary to the **true Cistercian spirit?**
If so, the official spokesman of the Strict Observance was not a-
ware of it; and all he could do, when face to face with the phenomenon of la Trappe, was to praise God and urge the brethren to
continue faithful to their way of life.

We do not have the *carte de visite* of Dom Dominique Georges,
who visited la Trappe on 16 November 1685, but we do have a lengthy
report he presented to the General Chapter of 1686.[38] Like Dom
Hervé de Tertre, he was struck by the diversity of origin, profession, and character of the members of the community:

> but charity so perfectly unites them that they all bear
> together the yoke of the Lord with one and the same spirit
> and will, as the Prophet says, for they have but one heart
> and one soul: they desire only to die to the world and to
> themselves and to live for God alone. They love their ab-
> bot in a holy harmony and understanding accompanied by sin-
> cerity and humility. They find all their joy in remaining
> attached to him and in opening their conscience to him,
> and in obeying him in everything--which results in their
> always enjoying a profound peace, a sovereign repose, and
> a tranquility such as naught can **trouble.** You never see
> the brethren arguing; no senior rises up against a junior,
> and the junior never complains about his senior; for, just
> as the Rule prescribes, they render one another as whole-
> hearted an obedience and respect as can be desired, with-
> out ever giving any outward sign of the slightest contra-
> diction by means of word, sign, or gesture.[39]

There is a brief paragraph on the communal nature of all their
practices, which leads to the summary statement: 'One can see but
one soul animating many bodies.' And what is the reason for this
'extraordinary happiness, and so perfect a mutual charity?' We
might be a bit puzzled to be told that the source of all this is
'the holy practice of perpetual silence,' but this is precisely
what Dom Dominique says:

> This law is so inviolable that they never speak except
> to their Superiors [abbot, prior, perhaps a few others];
> but this law is so voluntarily observed that even were
> one to allow them to speak, they would never agree to
> do so, as they have protested more than once. For they
> know perfectly the excellence of the precious and ines-
> timable fruits of this tree of life (that is to say, si-
> lence), and they daily taste its pleasures.[40]

Dom Dominique then proceeds to a detailed description of the
horarium, which is essentially the same as the earlier description
by our Maurist. Particular attention is given to the weekly or bi-
weekly conference. I like, too, the paragraph on the chanting of
the Office:

> Their singing is grave and devout; it edifies, it touches.
> They never spare themselves, and they praise their Creator
> with as much strength as zeal. Their voices blend in per-
> fect harmony, so much so that one would say that, just as
> they have but one heart and one soul, so also they have
> but one voice. They commence, continue, make the mediant
> pause, and end the psalm-verse together. Those assisting
> [i.e., visiting guests] cannot help but admire their mo-
> desty and their recollection.[41]

This description sounds almost as though it were a paraphrase of
the little work popularly attributed to Saint Bernard, *Institutio
Sancti Bernardi quomodo cantare et psallere debeamus.*[42]
    Dom Dominique also perceptively notes that, during the time
not otherwise spent in community exercises, the brethren are totally free to spend their time as their own piety directs--*par le
pur mouvement de [leur] piété*--because, we read, 'there is absolutely no law for that.'[43]
    There is a long paragraph on manual labor, a detailed descrip-
tion of the refectory regime, and a description of spiritual reading done in common in the cloister.[44]

> As regards their Father Abbot, he is totally devoted to
> directing, consoling, and instructing them. His vigi-
> lance is uninterrupted, as is the infinite care he takes
> of all their physical and spiritual needs, temptations,
> and infirmities. He works without respite to teach them
> their duties by his own word and deeds and to support
> them by his continual prayer before God, remembering as
> he does that he has the care of souls. He sacrifices
> himself wholly in his direction of them, and he sacri-
> fices his very life for their sake, by doing more than
> his infirmities allow him to do. For this he leaves all
> other affairs, as well as the guests, with whom he speaks
> but very rarely. What wonder then that he is so tenderly
> loved? Although he has appointed confessors in the monas-
> tery, to whom the brethren can address themselves, not a
> one thinks of doing so, and he hears the confessions of
> everyone.[45]

As for the laybrethren,

They live in as profound a silence as do the monks, and
though it seems impossible that they perform their crafts
without speaking, not a single word ever escapes them,
even by surprise; and they content themselves with ordinary signs [this refers to the Trappist sign-language restored at la Trappe, and in use till recent times]. You
never see them idle or doing something useless; they are
always busy with the hardest tasks, and yet they keep
their piety nourished by means of holy meditations. One
sees in them a great simplicity, an extreme modesty, a
surprising seriousness and humility. They render each
other as exact an obedience as they would give their abbot,
obeying at the slightest sign. They never undertake anything or take any initiative except according to the will
of the one in charge. They respect the Father Abbot and
love him with their whole heart and with a perfect love.
They regard him as holding the place of God in their respect; and they listen to his least word as to a sacred
oracle, storing it away in the depth of their heart. They
are united with one another by the bonds of a pure and
sincere charity....Before leaving, I had the laybrethren
assembled and I told them to pray to God insistently for
the preservation of their Father Abbot's health. When I
asked whether they would do so with a good heart, they
prostrated, moved by a single spirit, broke out weeping,
and raised cries to heaven, asking God to take them from
this **world** before taking their Father Abbot from it.[46]

All this emotionalism may dismay us a bit, but it is, after,
all, the rather theatrical *grand siècle*.
Dom Dominique continues with a detailed and extremely interesting description of the monastic plant which we must pass over
here.[47] Given the long-term friendship which united the Visitor
and the abbot visited, we can presume that Dom Dominique was dis-
posed to be edified when he came to la Trappe. But he was also
official Visitor of the region carrying out an official function
and responsible to the assembled General Chapter. The essential
integrity of the man and the basic accuracy of his *rapportage* cannot be called into serious question.

INCONSISTENCIES IN TWO DIRECTIONS

In the preceding pages many texts have been quoted or summar-
ized concerning life at la Trappe and particular points of observance. The picture which emerges is, I suggest, inconsistent in

two directions: 1) with respect to early Cîteaux, 2) with respect
to current ideas about the nature of la Trappe observance under
Rancé.

La Trappe and Early Cîteaux

I have suggested that Rancé was anything but literal in his
return to Cistercian sources. What most strikes me, however, is
that, whatever may have been differences in points of particular
practices, the harmonization of all the various elements making up
the day to day life results in a balance no less admirable at la
Trappe than at Cîteaux. Prayer in common, spiritual reading and
solitary prayer, and manual labor are generally accepted as the
chief components of the Cistercian's daily life; they have to enter into a harmonious inter-relationship in such a way that one
element re-enforces the others. Emphasis on one at the expense of
the others has always resulted in a far-reaching metamorphosis; and
it would be extremely interesting were someone to do a detailed
study of the evolution of the Cistercian Order through the centuries in terms of the emphasis accorded these three essential areas
of monastic living.

The major difficulty in studying the balance between these
practices in early Cîteaux is the fact that the balance was cons-
tantly shifting. Time was measured, not on an equal-hour basis,
but by a system dividing the time between sunrise to sunset into
twelve equal hours, and sunset to sunrise in as many equal hours.
If the sun rises at 4 AM at the summer solstice, and at 8 AM at
the winter solstice, the actual length of an 'hour' will necessar-
ily vary from day to day. When, for instance, the amateur of Cistercian origins, Dom Dorothée Jalloutz, decided in 1765 to follow the
early Cistercian horarium based on the ancient system of unequal hours,
he had to post a new horarium for the brethren of Sept-Fons every two
weeks.[48]

The following Tables are useful points of reference for an
understanding of the *problématique*, and are copied with very little
adaptation from the history *fiches* edited so wonderfully well by Fr
Jean de la Croix Bouton.[49] My own occasional reservations about
points of detail change nothing of the general picture which emerges.

	Summer Solstice End of June	2 Mths. Later 20–25 August	Notes
Rise	1:45 AM	2:40 AM	1 hr. 30 mins. before dawn
Vigils	2	2:50	a bit after rising
End of Vigils	3	4	Vigils takes an hour in summer
Interval	a few minutes	a few minutes	*parvissimo intervallo*
Lauds	3:10	4:10	*incipiente luce*—includes Lds. of Dead
Interval	3:45	4:50	till sunrise
Prime	4	5	at sunrise (1st hour)
Chapter			right after Prime—lasts c. 15 minutes
Work	4:40	5:40	right after Chapter
End of work	7:15	7:45	first bell for Terce (30 minutes before)
Interval			half-hour interval
Terce	7:45	8:15	before end of third hour
Mass	8	8:30	after Terce—fourth hour
End of Mass	8:50	9:15	
Lectio	8:50	9:15	*usque ad horam quasi sextam*
Sext	10:40	10:50	at the sixth hour
Dinner	10:50	11	right after Sext
End of dinner, Méridienne	11:30	11:40	
End of Méridienne	1:45 PM	1:30 PM	a bit before middle of 8th hour
None	2	1:45	*mediante octava hora*
'Biberes'	2:15	2	right after None
Work	2:30	2:15	right after *Biberes*
End of Work	5:30	4:30	towards end of tenth hour
Interval	5:30		half-hour interval
Vespers	6	5	during eleventh hour—includes Office
End of Vespers, Supper	6:45	5:45	of Dead
End of Supper, Interval	7:15	6:15	
Reading before Compline	7:30	6:30	
Compline	7:50	6:50	
Retire	8	7	first hour of night

HORARIUM FOR WORK DAYS—TWELFTH CENTURY CITEAUX—SUMMER SEASON

	Winter Solstice End of Dec.	2 Mths. Later 20–25 Feb.	Notes
Rise	1:20 AM	1:25 AM	8th hour of night
Vigils	1:30	1:35	
End of Vigils	2:50	2:50	
Lectio			*accenso lumine ante armarium et in capitulo*
Lauds	7:15	6:20	*incipiente luce*
Interval			till sunrise
Prime—Mass	8	7	at sunrise (first hour)
End of Mass	9:10	8:10	
Interval	a few mins.	a few mins.	
Terce	9:20	8:20	end of second hour
Chapter	9:35	8:35	
End of Chap.–Work	9:55	8:55	
End of Work	11:10	11:10	
Sext	11:20	11:25	at sixth hour
Return to Work	11:35	11:40	
End of Work	12:50 PM	1:20 PM	1st bell for None (30 mins. before)
Interval			half-hour interval
None	1:20 PM	2	at ninth hour
Dinner	1:35	2:15	right after None
End of Dinner	2:15	2:55	
Lectio			till Vespers
Vespers	2:50	4:10	during 11th hour—includes Office of Dead
End of Vespers	3:30	4:50	
Interval			very brief
'Biberes'	3:40	4:55	
Reading before Comp.	3:45	5	'by daylight'
Compline	3:55	5:20	
Retire	4:05	5:30	beginning of night

HORARIUM FOR WORK DAYS—TWELFTH CENTURY CITEAUX—WINTER SEASON

These tables are, of course, only for ordinary work days and
take no account of the special variations on fast days outside
Lent or during Lent itself. The summer season affords only a mini-
mal time for *lectio* in private. Lauds follows upon Vigils almost
right away; and the interval between Lauds and Prime is too brief
to allow for anything by way of reading--which is moreover excluded
at this time by the ancient Usages (summer season, Ch. 69; winter
season, Ch. 74).[50] The half-hour between the end of morning work
and Terce, the hour and fifty minutes between the end of Mass and
Sext, and the half-hour between end of afternoon work and Vespers
comes to rather less than three hours available for reading and
prayer in private. Further, the several weeks devoted to field
work during the mowing season and the harvest season reduced this
available time to almost zero. The winter season brought with it
the luxury of the long period between Vigils and Lauds--a period
which could vary between four and a half hours (this is a bit generous) to three and a half within a two-month period, with a further
shortening of interval time as the winter wore on. But the rest
of the day allowed for only a half-hour between end of work and
None, and a further period between dinner and Vespers which was as
little as thirty-five minutes towards the end of December, but increased to an hour and a quarter two months later. With so many
variations, I would hesitate to suggest a precise time available
for private prayer and reading during this winter season, but perhaps something between four and five hours would not be much off.
     Depending on the solemnity of the liturgical day, the brethren
of la Trappe rose at 1 AM, 1:30, or 2 AM, and the various Offices
and meditation were arranged so that Lauds ended around 4:30. An
hour-long interval separated Lauds from Prime, and there were two
half-hour intervals between Sext and None and between dinner and
afternoon work. There was time for another hour and a half of
lectio before Vespers; after supper or collation there was generally another half-hour available before Compline reading. The
brethren went to bed at 8 PM in the summer season, at 7 PM in the
winter, but the schedule was adjusted so that basically the same
amount of time was available for prayer and reading. On most work
days this would have remained a fairly constant four hours. Manual
labor accounted for three hours (though the time for it could be
lengthened on occasion)--less than the average at Cîteaux, but much
more than in standard Reform abbeys or Common Observance abbeys,
where study replaced work or was reduced to a token hour of putter-
ing around the garden or doing household chores.
     The time devoted to chanting the Office in early Cîteaux is
more than problematical, since the tempo of the Office was subject
to variation according to the season and the sleepiness of the brethren. Though the Office of the Dead was not a primitive practice,
it was introduced at so early a date that it too should be worked

into the normal early Cistercian Office-schedule estimate. All in
all, I think that Fr Jean de la Croix's estimates about the length
of the Office are a bit ungenerous, and that five to six hours in
church would correspond reasonably well to the average monastery
practice.

At la Trappe, there was not only the Canonical Office and the
frequent Office of the Dead (though much less frequent than at early
Cîteaux), but also the daily Office of Our Lady. Though even Julien
Paris was aware that evidence of its intrusion as a regular part of
the community *pensum servitutis* was late, he nevertheless argued in
favor of its official character from an early date in the Order's
liturgy.[51] Certainly Rancé himself would not have been inclined to
eliminate this accretion as a non-cistercian intrusion. One might
think that this multiplication of Offices made for a radical difference in length between Cistercian practice and Trappist practice,
but this was not the case, for Vigils and Lauds were sung in full
only on the greater feasts. I personally regret the adoption of
this *recto tono* rendition (in universal usage in the Order) but
the result was that the Office at la Trappe was probably not more
than an hour longer than the Office at Cîteaux--if even that--
since the la Trappe Office horarium includes two periods of meditation which might more correctly be lumped with the time available
for prayer in solitude. (On days when the Office was longer, these
meditation periods were abbreviated; and in order to provide more
interval time, Rancé often had the matutinal Mass celebrated privately on days of two Masses, while the brethren went to chapter.)

Although I wish to stress the extreme approximative nature of
all these estimates, I rather doubt that a readjustment of these
estimates would affect the overall picture in any significant way.

Office--*lectio* and solitary prayer--work. Is the balance at
la Trappe in keeping with the early Cistercian balance? I think
so. What is missing at la Trappe, though, is the coordination of
the rhythm of monastic life with the rhythm of the changing seasons
--a point on which the seventeenth century was less than sensitive.

Mention has several times been made of set periods reserved
for mental prayer. These corresponded to prescriptions harking
back to General Chapters of 1601 and 1605, as well as to n. 18 of
the papal constitution *In suprema* (1666). Hardly a practice of
the first Cistercians! Still, there was a solid weight of scholarly opinion behind an interpretation of the phrase found at the end
of Chapter Twenty of the Holy Rule ('In community, let prayer be
very short'), which held that the practice referred to was indeed
the practice of meditation in common. Incorrect though we now realize this exegesis to be, it was held by many--among them Rancé,
as can be seen by his own commentary on the relevant passage in
Chapter Twenty of his *Explication de la Règle de Saint-Benoît*.

But what about those weekly or bi-weekly conferences? How

'Cistercian' are they? Not very, we realize nowadays, with our
more sophisticated tools of historical inquiry. We can here find
our cistercianologist, Julien Prais, a bit inconsistent with himself, for in his list of modern monastic practices which are not
to be found in early Cîteaux, but are yet to be tolerated, the
tenth and last is precisely the daily conference.[53] Earlier in
his *Du premier esprit,* however, he had presented a quite different
picture. He began by showing how the daily commentary on the Holy
Rule was made in chapter either by the abbot or by a monk designated by the abbot. But such a commentary at this time of day must
have proved awkward, he argued, since it left so little time for
private Masses and for spiritual reading. Thus, around 1256, the
monks would simply have changed the hour for this commentary and
turned it into a discussion, and he quotes chapter and verse of
the *Institutiones Capituli Generalis Cisterciensis.*[54] I am sorry
to relate, however, that as early as 1232 the General Chapter had
approved this kind of colloquy as a positive substitute for the
'illicit colloquies' which, alas, were all too common at the time.[55]
Rancé, therefore, cannot be faulted too severely for his once-a-
week or twice-a-week conferences. If it was not a twelfth-century
usage, it missed out on being so by only three decades.

     What about the abbot as ordinary confessor? I rather doubt
that anyone nowadays could demonstrate to what extent abbots in
the early days of the Order habitually heard the confessions of
their religious with any degree of regularity. It is certain, however, that till the sixteenth century, each religious was obliged
to make to his Abbot at least an annual confession, covering the
period since his last annual confession. To ensure liberty of conscience, this practice was prohibited by general Church legislation
in the sixteenth century,[56] but religious wishing to approach their
abbot for confession were entirely free to do so. This is, indeed,
counselled even in the *Rituale* of 1724 proper to Cîteaux, where the
abbot is referred to as Ordinary, priest and proper confessor to
all the religious (Book IV, Ch. xi, 6). I rather suspect that at
Cîteaux, however, the Abbot General functioned as Father Confessor
less regularly than at la Trappe.

     And so it goes. The general impression is one of a sincere
fidelity to early Cistercian practice, but a fidelity which admits
of the possibility of adaptation. I am disappointed in my working
out of this entire section, for originally I had intended to present a careful analysis of some of the documents dealing in more
detail with precise aspects of la Trappe observances. The documents were three in number.

     1. The popular, frequently printed and frequently revised
Constitutions de l'Abbaye de la Trappe, printed under this ambitious title in 1671 (and often thereafter), but without the authorization of Monsieur de la Trappe. 'Only a few minor house-rules,'

Rancé called them, and rightly so, but they are interesting for all
that.

2. Much less well known, but well worth careful analysis, is
the memorandum Rancé drew up as an old man, spelling out details of
his administration which struck him as noteworthy or as calling for
some word of explanation. So far as I know, the text is to be found
only in the 1719 edition of le Nain's *La vie de Dom Armand-Jean le
Bouthillier de Rancé* II, pp. 674-684, where the thirty-three pastoral practices enumerated are headed by the editor's rubric, 'Direction Proposed by Father Abbot When He Became a Religious and Accepted the Government of His Monastery.'

3. By far the most important and the lengthiest is the unedited
*Declarationes in Regulam Beati Benedicti ad usum Domus Dei Beatae
Mariae de Trappa*, which is followed in the unique manuscript (Paris,
Bibliothèque nationale, ms. lat. 17134) by a French translation of
the same. This text represents a radical re-working and amplifica-
tion of the *Constitutiones Strictioris Observantiae Ordinis Cisterciensis in Regulam Sanctissimi Patris nostri Benedicti*. These Cons-
titutions--which apply the major chapters of the Holy Rule to Cistercian life as interpreted concretely by the Strict Observance--
have been edited (and brilliantly edited) by Fr Julius Leloczky,
O. Cist.[57] Even before this edition was available, readers of Fr
Aurèle Mensàros' dissertation, *L'abbé de Rancé et la Règle Bénédictine*,[58] had been informed of the existence of the parallel la Trappe
Declarationes, and of the general nature of the contents of this
work ('exhortations and prescriptions in the manner of brief explanations on the chapters of the Rule').[59] It was Fr Leloczky who
recognized the Rancéan work as an adaptation of the Strict Observance *Constitutiones*,[60] and though he stopped short of a full edition of the text, he reproduced in his notes to his edition of the
Strict Observance *Constitutiones* numerous la Trappe parallel texts
and gave summaries of others. It is thanks to the kindness of Fr
Leloczky and of his confrère Fr Louis Lekai that I now have at hand
Fr Leloczky's transcription of the la Trappe *Declarationes*, and I
hope in the future to work up an analysis of this first of all of
Rancé's extant monastic writings. At that time I will give in detail my reasons for assigning the year 1670 as the date of composition. I shall also discuss the nature of these *Declarationes-Cons-
titutiones* (in Strict Observance houses, they were read at the morning chapter after Prime--a section of the Holy Rule with its accom-
panying explication given by the *Constitutions*). In his presentation of the Rancéan adaptation, Fr Leloczky rightly points out that
the author's intention is to render even more austere the official
norms of the Strict Observance.[61] But Sr M. Pierre de Grox, in
what is surely one of the finest studies of the monastic thinking
of the la Trappe reformer, notes that at the level of observances,
Rancé's reform 'seems indeed markedly closer to early Cîteaux than

the customs current in other monasteries of the Order in the seventeenth century.' [62] Sr de Grox had come to this conclusion on the
basis of the la Trappe variants given in the notes to Fr Leloczky's
edition of the *Constitutiones*. Had she had the integral text of the
la Trappe adaptation, she would surely have repeated her affirmation
with renewed emphasis. But even here, I think the comparison of the
la Trappe *Declarationes* with the Strict Observance *Constitutiones*
results in a somewhat nuanced conclusion:

1. In general, but only in general, the texts proper to la
   Trappe are not only more 'austere' (Leloczky), but closer
   to early Cîteaux (de Grox).
2. A good number of these 'more austere' elements have indeed
   a *fundamentum in re* in early Cistercian practice, but often
   find a more absolute application at la Trappe (silence, enclosure, for example).
3. In spite of the evident tendency towards absolutism, the
   Rancéan norms avoid any extreme of literalism in those observances not directly bound up with some evident spiritual
   value (arrangement of exercises, horarium, rubrical prescriptions).

Perhaps, too, passing mention should be made of the 'omissions'
in the Rancéan *Declarationes* with respect to the Strict Observance
Constitutiones--omissions signalled by Fr Leloczky.[63] There is nothing about a ten-day annual retreat, but one can only surmise that
la Trappe regime was in its intensity an uninterrupted retreat; and
surely, this popular counter-reformation exercise could hardly be
said to have a precedent in early Cistercian practice. Again, Rancé omits mention of taking the discipline during Lent. But at la
Trappe, as at early Cîteaux, the discipline was used simply as an
occasional punishment, and not as a community exercise. Rancé had
a horror for any kind of mortification or penitential exercise which
could call showy attention to the individual monk. Singularity in
penance was eschewed as rigorously as mortal sin. Then, too, the
Declarationes are silent as to the frequency of confession and Communion. In point of fact, the house-rules referred to a few paragraphs earlier under the pretentious title *Constitutions de l'Abbaye de la Trappe* (re-printed afterwards as *Règlements*) speak of
weekly Communion and feast-day Communion. But the reticence of
the *Declarationes* is indicative of Rancé's almost pathological concern for individual freedom in these areas of one's spiritual life.
At a time when, even in religious houses, Communion was normally
preceded by confession, Rancé's position was that a monk should be
ready to receive Communion at any moment; and the frequency of confession is something to be worked out between penitent and abbot.
In her excellent study, 'L'Abbé de Rancé et l'esprit de la pratique
eucharistique,' Denise Pezzoli suggests that Rancé's pastoral practice was closer to that of Saint Pius X than to that of a restrictive

interpretation of the norms laid down by the Council of Trent; and
the many monks who received Communion three or four times a week
did so with a frequency which would have been astonishing in even
the most regular communities of that rigorist age.[64] On one point
Rancé did show himself a bit less flexible: priests were expected
to celebrate Mass every day unless Father Abbot gave permission to
the contrary.[65] This surprises me a bit, since at least some of
the priests at la Trappe were of the orthodox Jansenist persuasion
and would have found the idea of daily celebration of Mass contrary
to their Eucharistic piety. (Theological pluralism was no problem
at la Trappe, since all theological discussions were banned; everyone had to conform to the decisions of the Church in disciplinary
and theological matters, but otherwise one was quite free.) We
have already seen an instance of Rancé's unwillingness to impose
particular points of meditation on the brethren. And it might be
useful here to quote a passage from the *Mémoires* of Monsieur le
Honreux de Saint-Louis, semi-hermit at la Trappe, who never ceased
to be astonished at Father Abbot's ability to adapt himself to
each individual person:

> I remember seeing one day three persons of outstanding
> virtue. 'Look,' [the holy Abbot] said to me, 'there
> are three gentlemen, each going to God by a quite differ-
> ent path.'...But seeing that I was surprised at what he
> had said, he added: 'That shouldn't surprise you, Mon-
> sieur. Eternal Wisdom leads men by an infinitely di-
> verse number of ways, none of which resembles the others.
> You'd have a hard time finding four [monks] in this com-
> munity who are being sanctified in the same way: for the
> science of a Director consists particularly in examining
> with a great deal of application the temperament, the
> inclinations, and the degree of grace of each individual,
> so as to conform to it as much as possible. Without this,
> [the spiritual director's] ministry will be useless for
> the souls who are in his hands.'[66]

In brief, my own impression is that, on the question of an
annual retreat and the discipline, Rancé is quite 'Cistercian';
and that his pastoral practice with respect to confession and Communion would have done credit to Saint Bernard or any other abbot
of the Golden Age.

La Trappe and Present-day Cîteaux

Though Rancé had fervent admirers among his spiritual pro-
geny during the first two centuries following his death, it must
be admitted that even in the nineteenth century the praise voiced

in official Trappist quarters was tempered (usually in private) by
a more reserved attitude. And though the brilliant scholars and
historians among the brethren of the Common **Observance** have never
been particularly remarkable for their admiration of Rancé and the
la Trappe phenomenon, it can be said in all truth that if you wish
to find a really extreme anti-rancé position, chances are that
you'll find it among the Trappists.

The hostility triggered by the mere mention of the name Rancé
is understandable when one takes into account the historical situation after the French Revolution. In France the problem of the two
Observances received a radical solution: all houses of both Observances were simply wiped out. But before the final dissolution, a
band of less than twenty-four monks of la Trappe managed to escape
to Switzerland, where Trappist life continued near Fribourg, in
the former Carthusian monastery of la Val-Sainte. It was, however,
a 'Trappist' life far different from what Monsieur de la Trappe had
envisaged for his own community--a life reduced to a sub-subsistence
level due in part to the necessitous circumstances, but also due in
part to the heroic demands imposed, with their full backing, on the
brethren by the leader of the enterprise, Dom Augustine de Lestrange.
When Cistercian life returned to France, the new or restored monasteries were populated by colonies of monks under the general direction of Dom Augustin. Even before his death Trappists were divided
into two camps: those who felt obliged to continue faithful to the
extraordinary regime of Dom Augustin, and those who insisted on a
return to the relatively moderate regime of Monsieur l'Abbé de Rancé. Already in the eighteenth century, moreover, la Trappe had e-
volved considerably, and the distance between the seventeenth-century phenomenon and its counterpart a century and a-half later was
considerable. Impossible to recount here the effects of the feuding between 'Augustinians' and 'Rancéans', or their eventual recon-
ciliation when three Trappist Congregations finally entered into a
union in 1892, the present-day Order of Cistercians of the Strict
Observance. Some of the monastic personalities of that troubled
century are as remarkable as those of any other century in Cistercian history, and I certainly have no intention of being judgmental
about a period of monasticism in evolution marked by much that was
noble and authentic. But neither can I see a particularly profound
continuity between the Order at that time and early Cîteaux--or early
la Trappe. Yet even in the eighteenth century there were individuals
who, wearied by the questions disputed between 'Rancéans' and 'Augustinians,' began wondering whether one ought not think of a return to
early Cîteaux rather than a return to la Trappe or Val-Sainte. It is
understandable that in time, all that was morbid, narrow, or unbal-
anced in the Strict **Observance** came to be considered 'Trappist' as
opposed to the authentically 'Cistercian,' and this impatience with
la Trappe has grown apace as the riches of early Cîteaux have become

more and more accessible to us through the work of historians and
editors of early texts. In the words of a celebrated couplet:

> *Oh, monastic life was happy*
> *Till Rancé came to la Trappy.*

And this, indeed, is the quite correct interpretation given to the
life and teaching of the several Trappist spiritual teachers whose
lives have been written in recent years: Dom Vital Lehodey, Dom An-
dre Malet, Dom Gabriel Sortais. Thus one reviewer of Dom Chenevi-
ère's biography of Dom Malet, *Toi seul me suffis*, rightly notes Dom
Malet's sustained effort to return to the spirit of Saint Benedict
by 'turning away from an insistence--too exclusive since Rancé--on
austerity.'[67] And the same reviewer, in a paragraph devoted to Dom
Guy-Marie Oury's *Dom Gabriel Sortais (1902-1962)*, no less rightly
refers to Dom Gabriel as an 'abbot much concerned to return to "pre-
rancéan" traditions'[68]--though I mention in passing that Dom Gabriel
never allowed anyone to speak critically in his presence of either
Rancé or Augustin de Lestrange. Perhaps it is the much respected
and beloved Dom Vincent Hermans, for so long Definitor at the Strict
Observance Generalate, and so deeply versed in every aspect of Trappist life, who best expresses the conviction which seems to be all
but universally accepted in the Order:

> He [Rancé] took up again, in point of fact, almost all
> the observances of early Cîteaux, *but not its real spirit*.[69]

I am myself deeply convinced that the Rancéan la Trappe we are
all reacting against is a much transmogrified Rancéan la Trappe.
This is not particularly important, however, so long as we are sincere and reasonably successful in our attempts to be faithful, in
the changed conditions of our present world, to the tradition we
recognize as God's special gift to us Cistercians. Rancé himself
would be the first to object to any focus on la Trappe at the expense of Cîteaux. If I focus upon him, it is mostly a matter of
personal attraction, admiration, and love--an attraction, admiration, and love which I don't expect many will share. At the same
time, I cannot help but feel badly that so many of the brethren
who speak with enthusiasm about Athonite monasticism or the *Apoph-
thegmata* or Russian mysticism or twelfth-century Cistercian spirituality blank out when it comes to la Trappe. Our reading of Saint
Bernard's *De gradibus humilitatis et superbiae* requires, on our
part, a certain appreciation of the literary genre, the technical
vocabulary, the *Sitz im Leben*, the current of tradition in which
this treatise takes its rise. It also helps if we can recognize
Bernard's sources and know a bit about his teaching as a whole.
I suggest that we bring to our reading of Rancé (should we ever

have occasion to read him) the same approach we have to reading
Cassian or Bl. Guerric or the Rule of Saint Benedict--or the Up-
anishads or *Paradise Lost*.

Take, for instance, Rancé's notorious preoccupation with penitence and austerity and humiliations. What does he mean by *péni-
tence?* Are we so sure that it corresponds exactly with our own
current ideas about penance? When we read that Jesus' Good News
was a proclamation *poenitere!* we know very well that his 'do penance' is a great deal richer than what we usually mean by 'doing
penance'; and we prefer the translation 'repent'. But even this
is inadequate, and we try to invest it with the profound meaning
of *metanoia*, a change of heart, with all the deepest ramifications
of the biblical understanding of heart. Rancé's own understanding
of *penitence* is even richer, in point of fact, because not only is
it rooted in the biblical proclamation of *poenitentia*, but it has
picked up other nuances as well--we have already seen how it can
often serve more or less as the term for the ascetic life in general. But perhaps most essential for our understanding of Rancéan *penitence* is its christological dimension. He writes, for instance, that

> As the penitence of a monk owes its birth, strength, and
> merit to the penitence of Jesus Christ, so ought it to be
> a continual retracing, a faithful imitation of *his* peni-
> tence.[70]

Jesus a penitent? The idea strikes us as odd. But Rancé is
formal: 'To know what the penitence of solitaries ought to be, we
must consider what the penitence of Jesus Christ was.'[71] And as
our professional penitent begins speaking about Christ's life of
penitence, we begin realizing that this is Jesus' life of self-
sacrificing love, and that monastic penitence as Rancé understood
it is a direct and immediate sharing in the saving work of Jesus
Christ. So, too, when Rancé returns again and again to the theme
of humility, or when he quotes almost *ad nauseam* Saint Bernard's
axiom that the way to humility is through humiliations, the context
is never far from being a christological one--a life of humility
and humble service as a means of sharing in the *kenosis* (our preferred term nowadays) of the Lord. For *kenosis*, however, Rancé,
like most writers of his period, would use the term *anéantisse-
ment;* and 'annihilation' is definitely not a congenial term. It
should be used by us only with circumspection, but this changes
nothing of the real content of the term as understood by Rancé.

Perhaps one of the most striking practical applications of
Trappist penance is to be found in the long series of *Relations*
concerning the deaths of holy Trappists, written by Rancé princi-
pally, and continued by others till by the mid-eighteenth century

the series filled five volumes.[71] The scenario is almost always
the same: 1. the life of the subject before entering la Trappe
(a] pretty awful, or b] exemplary); 2) exemplary life at la Trappe;
3) serious illness, almost always with insistence by the moribund
monk on maintaining monastic regularity; 4) edifying death. I am
enormously fond of these accounts, even though it is impossible to
read more than two at a time without experiencing literary indi-
gestion. The *Exordium Magnum* includes many such stories, but wise-
ly intersperses them with miracle-tales or vision-accounts or dia-
bolical apparition/temptation narratives. At any rate, the high
point of most of the *Relations* is reached when the dying monk is
asked whether he wishes to die 'in penitence.' This is a technical
term which goes back to Sulpicius Severus' account of the death of
Saint Martin; it means dying on sackcloth and ashes. Morbid? Not
at all. Ashes are strewn in the form of a cross (often by Father
Abbot himself), and the monk's life is consummated by his dying
wholly united with the Lord Jesus on the cross of salvation. There
could be no better symbolic expression of the final words of the
Prologue to the Rule of Saint Benedict about sharing by patience
in the sufferings of Christ that we may deserve to be partakers also
of his kingdom. As for its 'Cistercian' character, this practice
of dying on sack-cloth and ashes is prescribed in Chapter 94 of the
early Usages.
     Those who hold that, no matter how sincerely Rancé wished to
revive early Cîteaux, he missed out when it came to the spirit of
Cîteaux because of his exaggerated emphasis on penance and austerity might have a point. But the point is weakened considerably
the more one looks more closely at the actual theory and practice
at la Trappe, as the preceding paragraphs suggest. We have to be
honest in our reading of Cistercian texts from the Golden Age. Furthermore, if you find asceticism-penance a bit unsettling, avoid
the collections of *Statuta;* keep away from the hagiographical literature; and skim past about half the narratives in the otherwise
charming *Exordium Magnum*. When we read, for instance, about Bl.
Raynald 'putting himself to death all day long through his labors,
vigils, fasts, and other exercises of holy discipline,'[72] or about
Peter of Toulouse, 'who raged against himself vehemently, and afflicted his flesh beyond belief by his labor and pain, nightwatch-
ing, fasts, and other crucifying penances,'[73] or about William of
Saint-Aubin, who 'assiduously crucified his flesh with its vices
and concupiscences, and daily dragged out a long martyrdom'[74]--
well, it's just a bit unsettling to find the alleged Trappist spirit infiltrating Cîteaux.
     Part of the contrast between Rancé and early Cîteaux lies less
at the level of ideas than at the level of literary expression. Read,
for example, Saint Bernard's marvellous Third Sermon for Easter,
where the Saint structures his Easter message on the command given

Naaman the Leper to wash seven times in the Jordan. Jesus is introduced as the Good Physician; and our healing is to be effected
through a regime of seven purgatives (tied in with the Passion-
theme) and seven restoratives (tied in with the seven Resurrection
appearances). 'Jordan' obviously means 'descent,' so our seven-
fold leprosy is cleansed by our descending in imitation of Jesus
in his lowliness; and our seven leprosies are proprietorship of
earthly goods, pomp and vanity of the present life, bodily gratifi-
cation, murmuring, boastfulness, self-will, attachment to our own
judgment. Several of these 'leprosies' are dealt with at dispro-
portionate length, and one has the impression that perhaps Saint
Bernard began running out of time, for when he comes to the 'restoratives'--the seven Resurrection appearances--each of which is
connected with a particular gift of the Holy Spirit--he does no
more than outline the material. The result is that, in a sermon
of six sections and 132 lines in the Rochais-Leclercq critical edition of the sermons, five sections (111 lines) are devoted to our
getting rid of our leprosy, and only one section (21 lines) deals
with the Resurrection and the gifts of the Holy Spirit. There are
more or less seventy-two biblical citations or adaptations or allusions. Then turn to Rancé's Conference 39 'Pour le jour de Pâque,'
which has as its text Col 3:1-2, 'If then, you have been raised
with Christ, seek the things that are above, where Christ is seated
at the right hand of God. Set your minds on things that are above,
not on things that are on earth.' Rancé begins by proposing the
effect which the Resurrection ought to produce in us: a) detachment
from things of earth, b) affection for things of heaven. As children
of the Resurrection, our principal goal should be detachment and love
of God. Easter is a day full of mercy, with enough holiness to sanc-
tify the whole world. But why is the whole world not transformed by
holiness? And now Rancé the pessimist begins speaking: because most
people fail to prepare for Easter so that Jesus can communicate this
new life. How does one prepare, then, for the Resurrection? The
same way Jesus did. Jesus is the model, Jesus is the example. Then,
with the help of Luke 24:26 and Philippians 2:7, Rancé shows that,
in order to share in the glory of Jesus, we should want 1) to die
like Jesus died, 2) to pardon our enemies, 3) to abase ourselves by
a voluntary humility, and 4) to embrace an obedience unto death.
Each of these points is developed in turn.
>   1) Jesus, by dying, gave up his natural (and sinless) life,
>   while we have to give up a life of sinfulness: disordered
>   lusts, passions, self-love, till Christ lives in us wholly.
>   This destruction of everything negative in us, then, is a
>   faithful likeness of the death of Jesus Christ. (Once a-
>   gain, Rancé's moralizing is almost always directly related
>   to our participation in the Mystery of Christ.)

    2) We have to pardon our enemies, even as Jesus did. This
       section is a bit odd, since it's not explicit in the Phil-
       ippians text on which nn. 1, 3 and 4 are based. One sus-
       pects that Rancé might himself be working hard to think for-
       giving things about the critics of la Trappe.
    3) Abasement. This is a lovely treatise on the simplicity of
       holy infancy as opposed to worldly wisdom and power, with
       Jesus once more as the model.
    4) Obedience, finally, is presented as an exigency of disciple-
       ship; and this obedience is, of course, a sharing in the
       obedience of Jesus.
The summary represents one of Rancé's typical christological formu-
lations: nature (fallen nature, that is) is replaced as the principle of life and action by Jesus Christ, who is our life, and who
inspires, leads, guides, and works. This last point ought not to
be overlooked: Jesus is not only exemplar, but efficient cause, the
principle of action. God died for us, and we should die for him,
says Rancé. But this death is really a fullness of life, and John
14:23 is quoted to good effect: 'If a man loves me, he will keep my
word, and my Father will love him, and we will come to him and make
our home with him.' Make good use of the privileged opportunities
you have as cloistered religious to live all this to the full, we
are exhorted. But the last word is a word of joy, the eschatologi-
cal invitation to joy: 'Enter into the joy of your Lord.' Only
Rancé, with a twist characteristic of his translations/paraphrases of
biblical texts, writes, 'enter into the *enjoyment* of the glory of
your Lord.' The structure of this sermon is characteristically perfect. No digressions or disproportionately long developments as in
Saint Bernard. Point by point, everything falls into perfect order,
and in a French of great and unaffected beauty and dignity. There
are perhaps seventeen biblical citations, all of them literal.
    The essential structure of the two sermons is much the same,
as is the basic content. Rancé, however, is more markedly christological in that direct reference to the Lord Jesus is explicit in
line after line. His use of Scripture is totally different from
Saint Bernard's use of the sacred text, in that Rancé is depress-
ingly faithful to what he had learned as a young cleric in his
course of sacred eloquence; and though he is wholly at home with
the Fathers, he himself would never think of treating one of the
sacred texts in the free and easy way in which a Saint Bernard does
so (much to our delight, though much to the anguish of the professional exegete). Bernard teems with color, figures, allusions, 'a-
busive' applications of sacred texts; Rancé cleaves to the seventeenth-century rules of sacred eloquence. If we were to re-cast
Saint Bernard's sermon by taking the thought-content and removing
most of the artificial and poetic conceits (such as Naaman's seven
plunges into Jordan), we might end up with something not far removed

from the sermonizing of the abbot of la Trappe--though Rancé's
christological substance is here richer than Saint Bernard's in
that Jesus is not only the model for, but the end of our striving
(discipleship means following Jesus for love of him) and the principle of our action.

     Although I still much prefer reading Saint Bernard to reading
Rancé, I'll be a bit more cautious when I generalize about Rancé's
'moralizing' conferences and similar writings. Moralizing it is,
but with doctrinal foundations as solid as anything in Saint Bernard. I personally regret very much Rancé's excellent schooling in
homiletics; it ruined him as a continuator of the early Cistercian
style. As a matter of fact, there are still extant a few writings
in which our author was more free to pour himself out in a personal
way, and these make me regret all the more what we have missed. The
utterly perfect meditation which goes by the name of *Désir de la
solitude*75 is in the great tradition of Saint Augustine, Saint An-
selm, Saint Bernard; and though the content begins with the strong-
est possible *fuga mundi* affirmations, it soon becomes a *fuga in Deum*.
Translate it into Latin, insert it among William of Saint-Thierry's
Meditativae Orationes, and the unsuspecting scholar would doubtless use
it to demonstrate that in William, the theme of desire so dear to Saint
Gregory the Great attains its purest and most lyrical expression. Let
me at least quote (in French) the closing lines--

> *Soyez mon occupation, ma consolation et ma joye dans le tems
> comme j'espère que vous le serez dans l'éternité;
> et afin que ie ne sois point trompé dans mes ésperances
> dés à present, Seigneur,
> rendez-vous tellement le Maistre et le Roy de mon coeur,
> qu'il n'ait d'inclination de pensées et de mouvemens,
> que vous n'y ayez formé par l'opération de vostre Esprit,
> de sorte que je puisse dire et me vanter avec vostre Saint Apostre
> que ie ne vis plus,
> mais que vous estes véritablement ma vie,
> et que vous vivez en moy beaucoup plus que moi même.
> Vivo autem, iam non ego:
> Vivit vero in me Christus.*

As a matter of fact, however, this kind of writing is to be found
scattered throughout Rancé's literary production. He was the world's
least original thinker, so far as I can see; and when he wished to
demonstrate a point, he almost inevitably resorted only to the pil-
ing up of authoritative proof-texts connected by his own running
commentary. But even then, he would from time to time give in to
his wonted lyrical outbursts. Indeed, the excellence of Rancé's
literary diction became even a matter of reproach, if we are to
believe some of his critics. I think of the lines from the satir-
ical *Portrait en vers de M. l'abbé de la Trappe*--

Déclamer contre la science,
et secrètement dans les bois
s'étudier à l'éloquence
en des termes purs et choisis.[77]

Bernard wrote a glorious twelfth-century Latin; Rancé wrote a noble seventeenth-century French. Tastes in literary style change; I'm told that nowsdays Bossuet is more popular in Italian translation than in the original French. But what I here wish to suggest is simply the observation that though Bernard and Rancé differ in literary expression, the substance is much the same more often than one might think. Further, no matter what the differences of literary style, the excellence of Rancé's French is in the spirit of the great twelfth-century Cistercian school. Perhaps, too, I can here interject a parenthetical note to the effect that Rancé, like more than one early Cistercian, never lost his attraction for classical literature. In 1691, his old friend, Canon Nicaise of Dijon, sent him, just off the press, a rather affected study about the classical sirens--*Dissertation sur les Sirènes, ou Discours sur leur forme et figure*. Rancé replied:

> I only glanced at your work on the sirens; but I confess
> that I didn't dare do more than glance. All the fabled
> forms and figures of the past awoke, and I realized that
> I wasn't really as dead as I ought to be. What a realiza-
> tion! It made me reflect a great deal. You see how much
> I've profited from it all....[78]

In an exchange of letters concerning this paper, my friend Fr Louis Lekai has suggested that a basic factor in gauging the Cistercian character of la Trappe would be the place of prayer in their lives: were they simply penitents all out for heroic mortification? or were they contemplatives? The question is right to the point, yet it is not an either/or question. The ideal monk of la Trappe was certainly a penitent in the sense explained above. But his life of penitence was rooted in and directed towards the deepest possible kind of prayer. Obviously, no one will suggest what percentage of monks at la Trappe reached the point of transforming union as compared to the percentage of monks to do so at Clairvaux under Saint Bernard. But not only prayer, but an uninterrupted prayer was supposed to be the climate in which the brethren of la Trappe lived. Nowadays even the most contemplatively oriented monk or nun would smile at the extreme lengths taken at la Trappe to avoid the slightest possible *dissipation*--another technical word which means, not frivolousness, but anything distracting from the one thing necessary. A monk with a slight case of sniffles was forthwith dispatched to the chapter-room (with door closed) during community

meditation, for fear he might distract a brother. Letters from
home were communicated to the monk only in important matters, for
fear that the letter could occasion distractions. Custody of the
eyes was in function of continual prayer. And the training the
brethren had in *lectio divina* meant training in the craft of prayer,
so essentially bound up was reading with prayer. Indeed, the central argument of Rancé against formal or scientific studies for monks
was the incompatability of such intellectual effort with an experience of continual prayer. Much has been made of Rancé's exuberant
devotion for Cassian and Saint John Climacus--often by persons who
are familiar with neither author and who tend to write off the entire Desert Father tradition as an affair of pyrotechnical feats of
mortification. They wrote mostly about prayer, mostly about realizing here and now the most perfect possible presence of the coming
Kingdom of God within the heart of the individual; and they also
wrote about everything that will lead to and perfect this kind of
prayer which is also perfect love. Saint Bernard's mystical theology is practically pure Cassian.

       Penitence/asceticism in this tradition (and by *this* tradition
I mean the tradition of la Trappe, of Cîteaux, of the Holy Rule,
and of the monastic East in general) is directly ordered to contemplation. The classical doctrine is simple enough and forms the basic structure of Saint Benedict's teaching about monastic life: the
monk-to-be comes to the monastery, where he a) rids himself of his
vices (negative, b) acquires the virtues (positive). This is the
'active life', to use the term consecrated by early usage, the ascetic life, the penitential life. As vice is eradicated and as virtue grows deeper and becomes more connatural, the Holy Spirit more
and more becomes the principle of all activity; imperfect motivations
(fear of hell, desire of reward) give way to pure love of God, perfect liberty of spirit; and love casts out all fear. This is the
contemplative life, the *vita speculativa*. Within this general framework there is room for countless variations by different writers or
even in the same writer, but the basic structure remains. In the
great classical tradition, attention focussed a great deal on the
ascetic programme, not only because it normally comes first in order
of chronological priority, but because one does not generally map
things out too precisely for an individual who has been raised to
the heights of the *vita speculativa*. How well this was understood
by Rancé, who refused to have a meditation-text read aloud for fear
it might constrain God's mode of action on the individual monks!

       Granted that all the texts describing the profoundly prayerful
life of the brethren of la Trappe have to be demythologized somewhat, and that their literary genres have to be taken into account,
the impression is overwhelmingly that of a prayer-life of deep and
sustained intensity.

       Having said this, I should add that there must have been a good

number of the brethren who, for one reason or another, were not
raised to a particularly lofty degree of wordless prayer. Rancé
himself would be a good example of what I mean. As an old man in
the infirmary, he remained devoted to his recitation of the Office,
quite literally till the moment of his death. Over and above his
Office, he used to pray an entire psalter daily. Further, after he
had prayed his Night Office (and Lauds, I think), he used to pray
for a full hour for the Church and for the clergy--le Nain tells us
how his lips would move and how he would smile as he mentioned particular prelates whom he knew and loved, one by one. I find this
immensely moving. But this is not the prayer of the mystic whose
prayer-life has been simplified to a point where words are unneces-
sary and even hurtful.

But perhaps my best answer to the question, 'Were the monks of
la Trappe contemplatives?' would be simply to quote the splendid
summing-up in the study by Sr M. Pierre de Grox:

> Praying for him [Rancé] was before all else being atten-
> tive to God, remaining in communion with God, acting with
> a view to God in a perfect purity and *disponibitité* of
> heart. In brief, his prayer reflected his temperament,
> which was more active than contemplative. He used to
> quote with predilection the 'sentiment of the saints' ac-
> cording to which:
>
>> a religious can satisfy this duty to pray without
>> ceasing when the will of God governs his whole life;
>> when his heart is filled with God's love; when he
>> abides in God's order in all things; when he has one
>> only desire, which is to please God; when, in all his
>> actions, he regards God as his end, and when he under-
>> takes no action without first asking God, with insis-
>> tent prayer, in keeping with Saint Benedict's teach-
>> ing, to grant his blessing to the work, and to be
>> pleased to bring it to perfection...When a solitary
>> observes this exactitude, and when he lives in this
>> piety, we can say that all his ways are holy, that
>> his life is nothing but a sacrifice of praise, that
>> he is praying at all times, and that even though, in
>> his various exercises, God sometimes escapes his at-
>> tention, he keeps him nonetheless in the fidelity and
>> in the disposition of his heart.
>
> This prayer, which is nothing other than the 'language,
> the word, and the expression of the heart,' this prayer
> which is at times implicit and is always affective, this
> attitude of a soul attentive to its Lord in all its actions

--this the abbot of la Trappe never ceased recalling to
his monks, reckoning it to be 'all the strength and power of solitaries.' Still more, as it was not just a simple 'conversation (with God) about pious subjects, but
the very movement of the heart, the expression of its
sentiments and its desires,' it followed that the Trappist should 'regard it as their treasure and their riches, that they should prefer it to all else, esteeming
it neither less holy, nor less essential...nor less recommended than the celebration of the Office.' For did
not this prayer, like that of the Office, have God as its
one sole object?'...These Rancéan texts--and a good many
analogous texts--speak sufficiently of themselves to dis-
pense us from the need of a long commentary to exculpate
their author from the accusation of having forgotten 'prayer' in his description of monasticism. Whether it be the
prayer of the simple presence of God, of conformity to his
will, or intercessory prayer, or the affective rumination
of sacred Scripture, the prayer of the monk of la Trappe
indeed belongs to the most **authentic** monastic tradition,
and has contributed to the monk's sanctification no less
than has his 'unbelievable perseverance in austerities,'
more celebrated though this latter be.[79]

Enough. Despite the poor organization of these remarks, I
have wanted chiefly to suggest that, at the level of particular
observances, Rancé effected a Cîteaux-wards movement that stopped
short of being overly literal. I've wanted also to suggest that
there are grounds for being cautious about sweeping generalizations
to the effect that **the** spirit of la Trappe is alien to the spirit
of early Cîteaux.
    Perhaps I should honestly note, however, my impression that
Cîteaux was second in Rancé's order of priorities--always presuming,
of course, the Gospel was his primary point of reference. Rancé had
a passion for Cîteaux because he was convinced that it was in Cîteaux
that Saint Benedict had found the most faithful, wisest interpreter.
Recently I have had the great joy of reading Dom Adalbert de Vogüé's
doctrinal and spiritual commentary on the Rule of Saint Benedict.[80]
How Rancé would have rejoiced over such a work! It is astonishing
how, at the conclusion of each of. the twenty-two chapters, Dom Adalbert's summing-up accords with Rancé's basic stance. When, for instance, in his remarks on the oratory and prayer in private, Dom Adalbert concludes:

        Not laughter, but tears; not recreations, but recollec-
        tion; not amusements, but compunction. The spiritual
        ideal of Benedict is that of *penthos* of antiquity, of

the joy which the Spirit pours forth in the soul in the
depths of penitence and of waiting.[81]

he is describing not only the monk after the heart of Benedict, but
the monk after the heart of the reformer of la Trappe.

There is no doubt about it: Rancé terrifies. The response to
the Gospel which he asks from us is a response total and unqualified.
When he asks, 'What is a true religious?,' he answers: 'He is a man
who, having renounced the world, and all visible and perishable
things by a solemn vow, lives only for God, and is occupied only in
such things as are eternal.'[82] And we feel uncomfortable as we begin to realize that he really means it.

I began with a visit to la Trappe, and I wish to end with another which is virtually unknown. When the English essayist and poli-
tician Joseph Addison had cashed in on his Latin poem *Pax Gulielmi*--
the government had awarded him a pension of 300 pounds--he set off
for Blois, France 'to get the language.' Writing to Bishop Hough,
the deposed president of Magdalen College, where Addison had taken
his degree, the itinerant Englishman said in part:

> And truly by what I have seen of the French they are the
> happiest Nation in the world. 'Tis not in the power of
> want or slavery to make 'em miserable. There is nothing
> to be met in the country but mirth and poverty. Every
> one sings, laughs and starves....One would wonder in such
> a merry nation to find so melancholy a people as are in
> many of their convents, one of which I shall take the li-
> berty to describe to your Lordship, because it makes a
> great noise in the world, and is much the severest in
> France. It is called the Abbey de la Trap, situate in a
> desert on the borders of Normandy. There are in it about
> 150 Religious, most of 'em persons of Quality, and many
> that were considerable officers in the Army. They feed
> on nothing but herbs and roots, dressed up with oil in-
> stead of butter, and a very coarse kind of bread. Their
> drink is small cider. They work in their fields and gar-
> dens each of 'em at least three hours a day. One sees in
> their faces all the marks of mortification and humility.
> They treat passengers out of the fruits of their own rais-
> ing, and lodge 'em within the Convent for three or four
> nights together. The strangers are desired to talk but
> little with 'em, and in particular to tell 'em no news.
> When my friend and I went thither a Father received us
> upon his knees, after that read a chapter of Thomas à
> Kempis to us, and upon our desire led us to the Abbot de
> la Trap, who was the first author of this reform. He has
> lived notwithstanding all the austerities of his order to

four score years of age, and has still his senses entire,
though they are forced to carry him on his straw bed to
the Masse which he still frequents at the most unseasonable hours. He has written books in a very polite style
which are highly esteemed; he is looked upon as a Saint
and will probably have a place in the Calendar. The Father
who accompanied us gave us an account of their first reception of the late King James, who often visits 'em as
your Lordship may see in the French Gazettes. The present
Abbot led him into the great Hall where he sent for the
whole Fraternity, told 'em they might look upon the stran-
ger that was before 'em (for otherwise they are never to
lift their eyes from the ground) and that 'twas the King
of England that gave 'em the honour of a visite. Upon
which the King told 'em he had heard a great character
of their piety, and that he was come to desire their pray-
ers, for himself and his subjects, many of whom he had
rendered miserable. In his whole harangue, to conform it
to the Genius of the place, he represented himself rather
as the one that had injured his people, than one that had
received any Injustice from 'em. So the Fathers wept and
retired severally to their devotions. I am afraid your
Lordship will wish me again at Blois if I take the freedom of troubling you with many such tedious letters....[83]

Poor Joseph Addison! Repelled, yet somehow puzzled and drawn...
Our own reaction is very much the same. Montaigne had a saying that
features large in a modern classic, William Armstrong's *Sounder:*
'Only the unwise think that what has changed is dead.'

The boy had asked the teacher what it meant, and the teacher had said that if a flower blooms once, it goes on blooming somewhere forever. It blooms on for whoever has seen
it blooming.[84]

Some of us have seen the springtime of la Trappe, and the flowers
are the flowers of fair Cîteaux and Clairvaux and la Ferté and Pontigny and Monte Cassino and Nitria and the desert of Judea.
     And will the flower blooms of our own **springtime** live on in the
memory of those who come after us?

Gethsemani Abbey

NOTES

1. First printed under the title *Descriptio Itineris cisterciensis quod ad comitia generalia ejusdem sacri Ordinis, faventibus Superis, feliciter expedivit F. Joseph Meglinger, religiosus sacerdos monasterii B. Mariae de Maris Stella, vulgo Wettingen, mense Maio anni 1667* (Lucernae: Typis Godefredi Hautt, s.d.); but more generally accessible in the re-print in PL 185:1569-1622. Translation and paraphrases of sections with additional notes and commentaries by H. Chabeuf, *Voyage d'un Délégué au Chapitre Générale de Cîteaux en MDCLXVII. Étude sur l'Iter cisterciense de Joseph Meglinger*, in *Memoires de l'Academie de Dijon*, 3ᵉ Serie, Tome 8 (1883) pp. 169-405.

2. PL 185:1615 BC.

3. *De la sainteté et des devoirs de la vie monastique*, Ch. 2, Question 1. The first edition was in 1683, with another edition the same year, another undated, and further editions in 1684, 1701, and 1846, all printed in Paris. Quotations from *Sainteté* here are taken from the delightful but often inaccurate translation by 'A Religious of the Abbey of Melleray, la Trappe,' *Treatise on the Sanctity and on the Duties of the Monastic State...*2 Vols. (Dublin: Richard Grace, 1830).

4. *Sainteté*, Chapter 3, Question 1.

5. Ibid.

6. Ibid. Translation corrected in the final lines.

7. As quoted by Robert Speaight, *George Bernanos. A Study of the Man and the Writer* (New York: Liveright, 1974) p. 16. The original source is Bernanos' *Lettre aux Anglais* (Atlantica Editora, 1942) p. 82.

8. Saint Bernard, *Liber de diligendo Deo* I, 1:'Causa diligendi Deum, Deus est; modus, sine modo diligere.' The expression can be traced back to Origen.

9. Paris, Bibliothèque nationale, ms français 17391: Correspondence de Pierre Séguier, Tome 25, f.216r. Transcribed in part in L. Dubois, *Histoire de l'abbé de Rancé et de sa réforme* (Paris: Ambroise Bray, 1866) I: p. 212, note 3.

10. Frequently printed in various collections of **writings** concerning

la Trappe. Here translated from the *Procés Verbal* printed at
the end of Livre VI, pp. 251-274, of P. Maupeou, *La vie du
T.R.P. dom Armand Jean Le Bouthillier de Rancé, abbé et réformateur du monastère de la Trappe* (Paris, 2nd ed. 1703) II.
Book VI begins a new pagination series.

11. Translation based on the ms. copy of the letter, Paris, Bibliothèque Mazarine, ms. 1214, f.27v-28r. Quoted with minor variants in Dubois I: 219.

12. Utrecht, Rijkarchief, Fonds Port-Royal (without classification
number)--the second in a series of three letters to Pavillon.

13. Already by mid-December of 1664 Rancé was quoting copiously from
the book and summarizing major sections of it in a memorandum
submitted to Fagnani, one of the chief members of the special
Congregation formed to study Cistercian affairs. Rancé's famili-
arity with the tome presupposes an exposure to it virtually im-
possible in the immediately preceding months. He had left la
Trappe in early September and had arrived in Rome on November 12.
After his abbatial blessing, he was at la Trappe barely six weeks.
His acquaintance with *Du premier esprit* must have taken place at
Perseigne during his novitiate, if not before, in the context of
the negotiations concerning the transfer of la Trappe to the
Strict Observance.

14. L. J. Lekai, *The Rise of the Cistercian Strict Observance in
Seventeenth Century France* (Washington, D.C.: Catholic University Press, 1968) p. 184.

15. Quoted *in extenso* in Marsollier, *La vie de dom Armand Jean Le
Bouthillier de Rancé, abbé régulier et réformateur du monastère
de la Trappe, de l'Étroite Observance de Cîteaux* (Paris, 1703)
II, Livre IV, ch. 9, p. 95. Sections also quoted in Dubois I,
pp. 626-627.

16. Le Nain, *La vie du Révérend Père Dom Armand Boutillier de Rancé,
Abbé et Réformateur de la Maison-Dieu Notre-Dame de la Trappe,
de l'étroite Observance de l'Ordre de Cîteaux* (Rouen, 1715) I:
pp. 190-191.

17. *La Règle de Saint Benoist, nouvellement traduite et expliqueé
selon son véritable esprit, par l'auteur de la vie monastique*
(Paris, 1689 [2nd ed.]) I: pp. 95-96.

18. *Lettres de piété choisies et écrites a différentes personnes*
(Paris, 1702) II: p. 90.

19. *Lettres de piété* II: 93-4.

20. Le Nain, *Vie*, Livre VII, ch. 15, (Paris, 1719) II: p. 674; in referring to le Nain's editions, I have distinguished between the edition of 1715 (Rouen) and that of 1719 (Paris), two rather different versions.

21. Account given in full in Gervaise, *Jugement critique mais équitable des vies de feu M. l'Abbé de Rancé* (London [= Troyes], 1742); cited *in extenso* in [H. Séjalon], *Annales de l'Abbaye d'Aiguebelle* (Valence: Jules Céas et Fils, 1863) II: pp. 562-564; also in A. Mensàros, L'abbé de Rancé et la Règle bénédictine, in *Analecta Cisterciensia* 22 (1966) 168-169, note 39.

22. Le Nain, *Vie*, (1715) I: pp. 191-192.

23. Ibid.

24. 'Histoire des controverses à Rome entre la Commune et l'Etroite Observance de 1662 à 1666,' in *Analecta Cisterciensia* 26 (1970) 3-247.

25. Document 14, p. 102 of the edition described in the preceding note. This is a memorandum submitted in mid-December to Fagnani; the delegates of the Strict Observance summarize the aims and ideals of the reform, propose reasons for the general decadence of the Order in France, and also propose practical means for a general reform.

26. Document 14, p. 103.

27. *La Règle* (note 17) p. 76.

28. See for further details the not yet published paper by P. Lucien Aubry, 'Personne et Communauté: Rancé et la Trappe,' p. 8 (232).

29. As translated from the text quotation in Aubry (note 28) pp. 7-8 (231-232).

30. Opinions concerning the date of this letter differ. The version here used is taken from the collection of Trappist material (no editor's name given), *Description de l'Abbaye de la Trappe avec les Constitutions, les Reflexions sur icelles; La Mort de Quelques Religieux de ce Monastère, Plusieurs Lettres du R. P. Abbé; et une briève Rélation de l'Abbaye de Septfons* (Lyon, 1683) pp. 71-111. The letter bears the title, *Lettre d'un Religieux*

Bénédictin de la Congrégation de saint Maur, à sa soeur Religeuse. Sur l'excellent manière de vivre des Religieux de la Trappe.

31. When Rancé died, Bossuet would write: 'What aan I say...except that he was another Saint Bernard in doctrine, in piety, in mortification, in humility, in zeal and in penitence, and that posterity will number him among the restorers of monastic life: and may God multiply his children on the earth...' A much-quoted passage, here translated from the excerpt found in Dubois II, p. 692.

32. Dubois, II, pp. 692-701.

33. Translations based on the French of the 1671 edition, *Description de l'Abbaye de la Trappe* (Paris) pp. 105.

34. *Description*, pp. 108-109.

35. *Description*, p. 81.

36. Le Nain, *Vie* (1719) II: pp. 719-720.

37. Ibid., pp. 723-725.

38. In Maupeou, *Vie*, pp. 251-274.

39. Ibid., pp. 251-252.

40. Ibid., p. 253.

41. Ibid., p. 257.

42. Edited with translation and introduction by C. Waddell, 'A Plea for the *Institutio Sancti Bernardi Quomodo Cantare et Psallere Debeamus*' in M. B. Pennington (ed.), *Saint Bernard of Clairvaux. Studies Commemorating the Eighth Centenary of His Canonization*, CS 28 (Kalamazoo: Cistercian Publications, 1977) pp. 180-207.

43. *Proces Verbal*, p. 258.

44. Ibid., pp. 258-261.

45. Ibid., p. 261.

46. Ibid., pp. 261-262.

47. Ibid., pp. 264-274.

48. As reported by Fr Jean de la Croix Bouton p. 141 of the work referred to in note 49.

49. *Histoire de l'Ordre de Cîteaux.* Tirage à-part des Fiches 'Cisterciennes,' (Westmalle, 1959) I: pp. 142-143.

50. See P. Guignard, *Les monuments primitifs de la Règle cistercienne* (Dijon, 1878) p. 167: 'sedeant in claustro...sed non legant;' p. 177, same prescription.

51. Paris, *Du premier esprit,* Première Partie, Ch. VIII, iii, pp. 118-121 (ed. of 1670).

52. Canivez, *Statuta capitulorum generalium Ordinis Cisterciensis ab anno 1116 ad annum 1786* T.7: p. 210: Cap. X of a proposed schema of regular observance; p. 251: Statute 12 for the year 1605.

53. Paris, *Du premier esprit,* Quatrième Partie, Ch. IV, iv, p. 202.

54. Ibid., Première Partie, Ch. XI, ii, pp. 166-169.

55. Canivez, *Statuta* T.2: p. 101, Statute 5 for 1232.

56. Dossier of documentation and discussion of Cistercian practice in Paris, *Du premier esprit,* Seconde Partie, Ch. V, Section II, vi, pp. 291-294.

57. *Constitutiones et Acta Capitulorum Strictioris Observantiae Ordinis Cisterciensis (1624-1687)* Bibliotheca Cisterciensis 4 (Rome: Editiones Cistercienses, 1967) pp. 67-142, with Introductory Notes, pp. 47-66.

58. *Analecta Cisterciensia* 22 (1966) 161-217.

59. Ibid., pp. 188-189.

60. Leloczky, *Constitutiones,* pp. 61-64.

61. Ibid., p. 62.

62. 'Un monachisme volontaire' in *Cîteaux. Commentarii Cistercienses* 20 (1969) 276-354.

63. Ibid., p. 281.

64. Leloczky, *Constitutiones*, p. 63.

65. In *Collectanea O.C.R.* 23 (1961) 138-147.

66. *Les réglemens de l'Abbaye de Nostre-Dame de la Trappe en forme de Constitutions* (Paris, 1698) p. 78.

67. Unedited *Mémoires* of Le Honreux de Saint-Louis, Paris, Archives du Ministère des Affaires Étrangères, Ms France 1442, pp. 167-168.

68. C. Savart, in *Revue d'histoire de la spiritualité* 53 (1977) 362.

69. Ibid.

70. *Spiritualité monastique* (Rome, 1854--mimeographed) p. 325.

71. *Sainteté*, Ch. 12, Introduction, p. 214.

72. Collections of these edifying account were printed as early as 1677. The 1755 edition in five volumes included some sixty separate accounts.

73. Before appearing in the *Exordium Magnum*, much of this material was included in Heribert's *De miraculis Libri Tres*, and the present citation may be identified in PL 185:1273.

74. PL 185:1278.

75. PL 185:1280-1281.

76. Only a fragment is reproduced in Dubois II, p. 424. The excerpt reproduced farther on is taken from *Recueil de plusieurs Lettres du R. P. Abbé de la Trappe, avec la Relation de la Mort de quelques autres Religieux de cette maison. La Description de l'Abbaye de Sept-Fonds. Et un discours du R. P. Abbé touchant la reforme outrée qu'on dit estre dans son Monastère* (s.l., s.d.) pp. 103-108.

77. *Recueil* (n. 75) p. 108.

78. Transcribed from Paris, Bibliothèque d'Arsénal, ms. 6541, f. 312--a 'Recueil' compiled by Jean-Nicolas de Tralage. The verse is here dated 1692.

79. Letter 120, dated October 4, 1691; B. Gonod (ed.), *Lettres de Armand-Jean le Bouthillier de Rancé, Abbé et Réformateur de la Trappe* (Paris: Amyot 1846) pp. 204-205.

80. De Grox, *Un monachisme*, pp. 320-321.

81. A. de Vogüé, *La Règle de Saint Benoît*, Tome 7: *Commentaire doctrinal et spirituel* (Paris: Cerf, 1977).

82. Vogüé, pp. 358-359.

83. *Sainteté*, Ch. 1. Question 1, p. 1.

84. I have a copy of this rare and splendid text, originally printed in October 1913 in *The Flying Leaf* (the bulletin of a devotional society called the Society of the Annunciation), thanks to the kindness of Fr Martin Smith SSJE. The text is here excerpted from pp. 14-15 of Bulletin 53.

85. W. H. Armstrong, *Sounder* (New York, Evanston, San Francisco, London: Harrow Books, paperback edition 1972) p. 116.

CISTERCIAN PUBLICATIONS INC.

Titles Listing

THE CISTERCIAN FATHERS SERIES

THE WORKS OF BERNARD OF CLAIRVAUX

Treatises I: Apologia to Abbot William, On Precept and Dispensation — CF 1
On the Song of Songs I — CF 4
On the Song of Songs II — CF 7
The Life and Death of Saint Malachy the Irishman — CF 10
Treatises II: The Steps of Humility, On Loving God — CF 13
Magnificat: Homilies in Praise of the Blessed Virgin Mary — CF 18
Treatises III: On Grace and Free Choice, In Praise of the New Knighthood — CF 19
On the Song of Songs III — CF 31
Five Books on Consideration — CF 37
On the Song of Songs IV — CF 40

THE WORKS OF WILLIAM OF SAINT THIERRY

On Contemplating God, Prayer, and Meditations — CF 3
Exposition on the Song of Songs — CF 6
The Enigma of Faith — CF 9
The Golden Epistle — CF 12
The Mirror of Faith — CF 15
Exposition on the Epistle to the Romans — CF 27
The Nature and Dignity of Love — CF 30

THE WORKS OF AELRED OF RIEVAULX

Treatises I: On Jesus at the Age of Twelve, Rule for a Recluse, The Pastoral Prayer — CF 2*
Spiritual Friendship — CF 5*
The Soul — CF 22

THE WORKS OF GILBERT OF HOYLAND

Sermons on the Song of Songs I — CF 14
Sermons on the Song of Songs II — CF 20
Sermons on the Song of Songs III — CF 26
Treatises and Epistles — CF 34

OTHER EARLY CISTERCIAN WRITERS

The Letters of Adam of Perseigne I — CF 21
John of Ford—Sermons on the Final Verses of the Song of Songs, I — CF 29
Idung of Prüfening—Cistercians and Cluniacs: The Case for Cîteaux — CF 33
The Way of Love — CF 16
Works of Guerric of Igny—
Liturgical Sermons I — CF 8
Liturgical Sermons II — CF 32
Three Treatises on Man: A Cistercian Anthropology — CF 24
Isaac of Stella—Sermons on the Christian Year — CF 11

THE CISTERCIAN STUDIES SERIES

EARLY MONASTIC TEXTS

CHRISTIAN SPIRITUALITY

MONASTIC STUDIES

CISTERCIAN STUDIES

STUDIES BY DOM JEAN LECLERCQ

THOMAS MERTON

FAIRACRES PRESS, OXFORD

*   out of print